STABLE
CORE TRAINING

A New Approach to Rider Alignment, Centering, Grounding, and Positive Tension for Elite Performance in the Saddle

JOYCE KRAMER
Certified Personal Trainer

Photographs by Jayson Benoit | Illustrations by Satu R. Young

Trafalgar Square
North Pomfret, Vermont

First published in 2025 by
Trafalgar Square Books
North Pomfret, Vermont 05053

Copyright © 2025 Joyce Kramer

All rights reserved. No part of this book may be reproduced, by any means, without written permission of the publisher, except by a reviewer quoting brief excerpts for a review in a magazine, newspaper, or website.

Disclaimer of Liability
The author and publisher shall have neither liability nor responsibility to any person or entity with respect to any loss or damage caused or alleged to be caused directly or indirectly by the information contained in this book. While the book is as accurate as the author can make it, there may be errors, omissions, and inaccuracies.

Trafalgar Square Books encourages the use of approved safety helmets in all equestrian sports and activities.

Trafalgar Square Books certifies that the content in this book was generated by a human expert on the subject, and the content was edited, fact-checked, and proofread by human publishing specialists with a lifetime of equestrian knowledge. TSB does not publish books generated by artificial intelligence (AI).

Library of Congress Cataloging-in-Publication Data
Names: Kramer, Joyce (Equine personal trainer), author.
Title: Stable core training : a new approach to rider alignment, centering, grounding, and positive tension for
    elite performance in the saddle / Joyce Kramer, Certified Personal Trainer.
Description: North Pomfret, Vermont : Trafalgar Square Books, [2024] | Includes bibliographical references and index.
Identifiers: LCCN 2024028331 (print) | LCCN 2024028332 (ebook) | ISBN 9781646012008 (paperback) |
    ISBN 9781646012015 (epub)
Subjects: LCSH: Horsemanship.
Classification: LCC SF309 .K896 2024 (print) | LCC SF309 (ebook) | DDC 798.2--dc23/eng/20240809
LC record available at https://lccn.loc.gov/2024028331
LC ebook record available at https://lccn.loc.gov/2024028332

Franklin Method® and some Franklin Method® balls are registered and trademarked names, respectively. This notice serves to acknowledge this applies to all references used throughout this text after the marked first reference.

Photographs by Jayson Benoit
Illustrations by Satu R. Young
Book design by Lauryl Eddlemon
Cover design by RM Didier
Index by Michelle Guiliano (linebylineindexing.com)

Printed in China

10 9 8 7 6 5 4 3 2 1

This book is dedicated to the well-being of horses everywhere.

CONTENTS

Note from the Publisher — x
Foreword by Heidi Hauri-Gill — xi
Note to the Reader — xvi

Introduction — 1

PART 1: THE FOUNDATION OF RIDING WELL — 5

Chapter 1: Alignment Is Dynamic — 7
It's All About Centering — 7
Centering Exercise 1: Axis Turn — 9
Centering Exercise 2: Move from Your COG — 10
Centering Exercise 3: Half-Ball Head Balance — 10
Centering Exercise 4: Balance Board Ball — 11
Alignment Explored — 12
Riding on the Vertical — 16

Chapter 2: A Grounded Rider — 19
Grounding Explored — 19
Grounding in the Saddle — 20
Grounding Exercise 1: Shaking Out Unwanted Energy — 21
Grounding Exercise 2: Sacrum Sink — 21
Grounding Exercise 3: Barefoot Grounding — 22
Grounding Exercise 4: Crawling — 22
Grounding Exercise 5: Growing Roots — 22

Chapter 3: Positive Tension Is the Key — 23
Muscle Tone and Positive Tension — 23
Positive Tension Exercise 1: Sandpaper Boards — 26
Positive Tension Exercise 2: Goldilocks Zone — 27
Positive Tension Exercise 3: Diagonal Connections — 29

Chapter 4: Breathing as a Fuel Pump — 32
Whole Body Breathing — 32
The Rider's Fuel Pump — 33
Breathing Exercise 1: Checking for Verticality — 35
Breathing Exercise 2: Assistance of the Tongue — 36
Breathing Exercise 3: Do Re Me — 36
Breathing Exercise 4: Standing Diaphragm Stretch — 37
Breathing Exercise 5: Lying Diaphragm Stretches — 38
Breathing Exercise 6: Hands-Free Balloon Breathing — 39
Breathing Exercise 7: Backpack Breathing — 39
Breathing Exercise 8: Playing Instruments — 41

Chapter 5: Proprioception and Feel — 42
Proprioceptive Props — 42
The Art of Feeling — 43
Developing Proprioception and Feel Exercise 1: Photo Imagery — 45

Developing Proprioception and Feel
    Exercise 2: Eyes Shut Touching — 46
Developing Proprioception and Feel
    Exercise 3: Hot Water Bottle Balancing — 46
Developing Proprioception and Feel
    Exercise 4: Feel Your Seat Bones — 47
Developing Proprioception and Feel
    Exercise 5: Mounted Hand Proprioception — 48
Developing Proprioception and Feel
    Exercise 6: Distance Proprioception — 49
Developing Proprioception and Feel
    Exercise 7: Ring Geometry Proprioception — 50
Developing Proprioception and Feel
    Exercise 8: Flag Walk — 51

Chapter 6: Vision and Visualizing — 53
A Rider's Vision — 53
Exploring Imagery — 55
Vision and Visualizing — 56
    Vision Exercise 1: Eye Crossovers — 58
    Vision Exercise 2: Palming the Eyes — 58
    Vision Exercise 3: Shifting Eyes Balance Poses — 58
    Vision Exercise 4: Near-to-Far Focus Flutters — 59
    Vision Exercise 5: Bouncy Ball Glow — 60
    Vision Exercise 6: Sharp Eyes — 60
    Vision Exercise 7: Soft Eyes — 62

Chapter 7: Movement Patterns and Mobility — 64
Movement Explored — 64
Neuromuscular Functioning — 65
Fluidity of Movement — 66
Mobility — 66
    Mobility Exercise 1: Target Practice — 67
    Mobility Exercise 2: Standard Hip Hinge — 67
    Mobility Exercise 3: Single Leg Hip Hinge — 68
    Mobility Exercise 4: Nose Plant Squats — 70
    Mobility Exercise 5: Bow to Squat — 71
    Mobility Exercise 6: Football Shoulder Drops — 72

Chapter 8: Postural Patterns and Self-Carriage — 74
Characteristics of Good Posture — 74
Riding Posture Tips — 76
Self-Carriage — 81
    Self-Carriage Exercise 1: The Pokes — 81
    Self-Carriage Exercise 2: Posture Breathing — 82
    Self-Carriage Exercise 3: Human Lead Rope — 82
    Self-Carriage Exercise 4: Overhead Wall Press — 83
    Self-Carriage Exercise 5: Single Leg Wall Push — 84
    Self-Carriage Exercise 6: Back to Blades — 85
    Self-Carriage Exercise 7: Side Superhero — 86

PART 2: FINDING YOUR POSITION — 87

Chapter 9: The Secrets of Fluidity — 88
Our Fluid Nature — 88
Fluidity of the Rider — 89
- Fluidity Exercise 1: Bounce Away — 91
- Fluidity Exercise 2: Basketball Bounces — 91
- Fluidity Exercise 3: Slither and Shake — 91
- Fluidity Exercise 4: Bubbling Spring Acupressure — 92
- Fluidity Exercise 5: Elegant Mansion Acupressure — 92
- Fluidity Exercise 6: Roll 'Em — 93

Chapter 10: Fascial Connections — 94
Fascial Connections Explored — 94
Fascia and the Rider — 98
- Myofascial Exercise 1: Pandiculars — 102
- Myofascial Exercise 2: Standing Straddle Bend (Pandicular Type) — 103
- Myofascial Exercise 3: Side-Tap Walk (Bouncy Type) — 104
- Myofascial Exercise 4: Wall Springs (Bouncy Type) — 105
- Myofascial Exercise 5: Rolling Out — 106

Chapter 11: Muscle Activation and Recovery — 107
Muscle Myths and Facts — 107
Muscle Activation Explored — 110
- Muscle Activation Exercise 1: Adductor Lifts — 111
- Muscle Activation Exercise 2: Left Side Activation — 112
- Muscle Activation Exercise 3: Glute Poke and Punch — 113
- Muscle Activation Exercise 4: Triceps Shake and Wiggle — 113
- Muscle Activation Exercise 5: Independent Body Parts — 114
- Muscle Activation Exercise 6: Glute Activation Walk — 114
- Muscle Activation Exercise 7: Activated Riding — 117

Rest and Recovery — 117

Chapter 12: Letting Tension Go — 119
The Body and Stress — 119
Techniques of Letting Go — 120
Letting Tension Go — 122
- Tension Release Exercise 1: Playful Movement — 122
- Tension Release Exercise 2: Thin Straw — 124
- Tension Release Exercise 3: Meditation Walk the Course — 124
- Tension Release Exercise 4: Tighten and Shake — 124
- Tension Release Exercise 5: Barrel Roll — 125
- Tension Release Exercise 6: Base of Skull Point — 125

Chapter 13: The Rider's Pelvis — 126
The Pelvic Arch — 126
- Neutral Pelvic Exercise 1: Hoof Picks — 127

Pelvic Balance — 127
Pelvic Floor Muscles — 131
- Pelvic Floor Muscle Exercise 1: Power Buttwalking — 134
- Pelvic Floor Muscle Exercise 2: Crawling on Forearms — 134
- Pelvic Floor Muscle Exercise 3: Lizard Crawl — 135
- Pelvic Floor Muscle Exercise 4: Baby Bounce Squats — 136

Pelvic Floor Muscle Exercise 5: Pop-Up Stance	136
Pelvic Floor Muscle Exercise 6: Sounds for the Pelvis	137
Pelvic Floor Muscle Exercise 7: Pelvic Connections	138

Chapter 14: The Rider's Rib Cage — 139

Rib Anchor Explored — 139
The Lift of the Sternum — 142

Rib Cage Exercise 1: Rib Cage Trainers	143
Rib Cage Exercise 2: Chicken Wing	143
Rib Cage Exercise 3: Rib Cage Pulls	144
Rib Cage Exercise 4: Mounted "C"-Curve Iron Out	144
Rib Cage Exercise 5: Mounted Arm Sliders	145
Rib Cage Exercise 6: Mounted Rib Cage 360s	145

Chapter 15: The Rider's Neck and Head — 147

The Neck Connects — 147
The Head Aligns with the Spine — 149

Neck/Head Exercise 1: Bobbleheads	151
Neck/Head Exercise 2: Duct Tape Roll Up	151
Neck/Head Exercise 3: Turning Head Hovers	152
Neck/Head Exercise 4: Head Planks	152
Neck/Head Exercise 5: Barbell Head Balances	153
Neck/Head Exercise 6: Marble Heads	154
Neck/Head Exercise 7: Head Hangers	155

Chapter 16: Shoulders, Arms, and Hands — 157

The Shoulder Complex — 157
Jobs for Arms and Hands — 158

Shoulder/Arm/Hand Exercise 1: Overhead Rope Pull	161
Shoulder/Arm/Hand Exercise 2 Kitchen Counter Stretch	162
Shoulder/Arm/Hand Exercise 3: Scap Pushes	162
Shoulder/Arm/Hand Exercise 4: Trace a Horseshoe	164
Shoulder/Arm/Hand Exercise 5: Yo-Yo 'n Hoop	164

Chapter 17: Feet, Ankles, and Legs — 166

Treat Your Feet Well — 166
The Rider's Legs — 170

Foot/Ankle/Leg Exercise 1: Heel Walk	172
Foot/Ankle/Leg Exercise 2: Toe Spreading	172
Foot/Ankle/Leg Exercise 3: Foot Twists	172
Foot/Ankle/Leg Exercise 4: Side Slides	173
Foot/Ankle/Leg Exercise 5: Slomos	174
Foot/Ankle/Leg Exercise 6: Calf Lengthening	174

Chapter 18: Fluid Hips, Stable Spine — 175

Fluidity of the Hips — 175
Stability of the Spine — 177

Fluid Hips/Stable Spine Exercise 1: Ride Your Noodle	180
Fluid Hips/Stable Spine Exercise 2: Scorpion Seat	181
Fluid Hips/Stable Spine Exercise 3: Hip Extension Release	182
Fluid Hips/Stable Spine Exercise 4: Heel Skating	183
Fluid Hips/Stable Spine Exercise 5: One Stirrup Work	183
Fluid Hips/Stable Spine Exercise 6: "T" Arm Cavalletti/Jumping	184
Fluid Hips/Stable Spine Exercise 7: Stability Hug	185

Chapter 19: Nourishment: Outer and Inner Fitness — 186
Outer Fitness — 186
Inner Fitness — 188

Chapter 20: Teaching Humans and Horses — 190
Sense, Feel, Discover — 190
The Art of Self-Correction — 191
The Rider's Team — 194

PART 3: STABILIZING YOUR DEEP CORE — 199

Chapter 21: Ride From Your Guts! (A Visceral Approach) — 200
Muscles, Bones, or Organs? — 200
Ride with Passion — 202

Chapter 22: Beneficial Sounds — 206
The Body's Vibrational Energy — 206

Chapter 23: Warm-Up and Cool-Down for Riders — 210
Why Warm Up and Cool Down? — 210
Warm-Up/Cool-Down Exercise 1: Arena Skipping — 211
Warm-Up/Cool-Down Exercise 2: Belly Button Vertical Breathing — 212
Warm-Up/Cool-Down Exercise 3: Full Body Shakes — 212
Warm-Up/Cool-Down Exercise 4: Bouncy Ball Warm-Up — 213
Warm-Up/Cool-Down Exercise 5: Throat Warm-Ups — 213
Warm-Up/Cool-Down Exercise 6: Heart Breathing — 213
Warm-Up/Cool-Down Exercise 7: Grounding Stance and Walk — 214
Warm-Up/Cool-Down Exercise 8: Head Band Squat — 214
Warm-Up/Cool-Down Exercise 9: Head Wiggles — 215
Warm-Up/Cool-Down Exercise 10: Trunk Circles — 216
Warm-Up/Cool-Down Exercise 11: Figure Eight Hip Circles — 216
Warm-Up/Cool-Down Exercise 12: Side Wall Circles — 217
Warm-Up/Cool-Down Exercise 13: Pop-Up Walks — 218
Warm-Up/Cool-Down Exercise 14: Overhead Wall Bird Dogs — 219
Warm-Up/Cool-Down Exercise 15: Positive Affirmations — 220

Chapter 24: Your Deep Core — 221
Exploring the Deep Core — 221
Core Activation Exercise 1: Play an Instrument — 225
Core Activation Exercise 2: Scoop the Goop — 225
Core Activation Exercise 3: Core Walk — 225
Core Activation Exercise 4: Deep Core Sounds — 226
Core Activation Exercise 5: Wall Push — 226
Core Activation Exercise 6: Boot Flicks and Pulls — 226
Core Activation Exercise 7: Whole Body Scramble — 227

Chapter 25: Stability Exercises for the Deep Core — 228

The Stable Rider — 228

- Core Stability Exercise 1: Warm-Up Logs — 231
- Core Stability Exercise 2: Dress-Ups — 231
- Core Stability Exercise 3: One-Arm Shopping — 232
- Core Stability Exercise 4: Unilateral Step-Ups — 232
- Core Stability Exercise 5: Stability Breath Practice — 232
- Core Stability Exercise 6: Ball Balancing Walk — 234
- Core Stability Exercise 7: Medicine Ball Tosses — 234
- Core Stability Exercise 8: Hanging Froggy Lifts — 235
- Core Stability Exercise 9: Stir the Pot — 236
- Core Stability Exercise 10: Harnessed Obstacle Walk — 237
- Core Stability Exercise 11: Long-Lining for People — 237
- Core Stability Exercise 12: Wiper Hoops — 238
- Core Stability Exercise 13: Perturbances — 239
- Core Stability Exercise 14: Unilateral Leg Raises — 239
- Core Stability Exercise 15: Mounted Imbalances — 240
- Core Stability Exercise 16: Stirrup Stand — 241
- Core Stability Exercise 17: Swinging Gates — 242

Chapter 26: SLAM Lessons (Seat Lessons And More) — 243

Why SLAM? — 243

- SLAM Exercise 1: You Are a Tree — 244
- SLAM Exercise 2: Swinging Bridge Imagery — 245
- SLAM Exercise 3: Belly Button Singing — 245
- SLAM Exercise 4: Metronome Movements — 245
- SLAM Exercise 5: Sandpaper Seat — 245
- SLAM Exercise 6: Creative Whips — 246
- SLAM Exercise 7: Hot Water Waist Pack — 246
- SLAM Exercise 8: Mounted Neck Lengthening — 247
- SLAM Exercise 9: Hand Ball Helper — 247
- SLAM Exercise 10: Plumb Line Mounted — 248
- SLAM Exercise 11: Flying Hugs — 249
- SLAM Exercise 12: Fixing the Drifts — 249

Chapter 27: Invest Further — 251

Standard Equipment — 251

- Invest Exercise 1: Ball Jacks — 253
- Invest Exercise 2: Pull-Ups — 253
- Invest Exercise 3: Pendulum Swings — 254
- Invest Exercise 4: Sawhorse Ball Tosses — 254
- Invest Exercise 5: Balance Board — 255
- Invest Exercise 6: Long Line Stop and Go — 256
- Invest Exercise 7: Overhead Battle Ropes — 256
- Invest Exercise 8: Large Half-Ball Balance — 257
- Invest Exercise 9: Tilt Board Hoops — 258
- Invest Exercise 10: People Jumping — 258
- Invest Exercise 11: Unilateral Barbells — 259
- Invest Exercise 12: Jumping Jills — 260
- Invest Exercise 13: Water Wheel Bounces — 260
- Invest Exercise 14: Figures on Stilts — 261
- Invest Exercise 15: Pogo Core Bounces — 262

Appendix: Equestrian Training Pyramid — 263
Bibliography and Recommended Reading — 265
Acknowledgments — 269
About the Artist — 271
Index — 272

NOTE FROM THE PUBLISHER

I was remarkably lucky to grow up in a time and in a place where horses and riding could be part of my daily life—something not so easy to come by today, as farms and open spaces disappear and the sport grows more expensive. And then, when it came to riding later in life—after a publishing career in London and New York, and travel, and marriage—I found myself in the middle of what would be a seismic change in how people approached riding horses. That change was initiated at the time by the unique ideas of a woman named Sally Swift, who gave me—and my husband, too—riding lessons. Sally wanted me to take the concepts she was teaching and the notes she was taking on scraps of paper and napkins, and turn them into a book. Given my publishing background, I agreed to help her do that.

And so what would become the book *Centered Riding,* and then an organization by the same name, was born.

What was also born was the publishing arm of the book distribution business I ran with my husband Ted on our Vermont farm. *Centered Riding* would be the first of the hundreds of books we have published "for the good of the horse."

It is hard for me to believe 2025 marks the 40th anniversary of *Centered Riding's* publication. Sally has been gone now many years (she died in 2009 at age 95), although the organization her book inspired lives on. So do what were once considered her unusual ways of using visualization and body awareness to create harmony with an equine partner—many younger riders have grown up in the saddle knowing no other way to ride than "Sally's way," although it is likely they do not know it. It is ubiquitous.

It is because I could be part of the spread of Sally's work that I am excited about what you will find in these pages. Joyce Kramer is another local Vermont horsewoman, just like Sally was, who has come to us with a desire to share her ideas for teaching better body awareness in the saddle. Many of her concepts intrinsically relate to Centered Riding, and Joyce acknowledges Sally's influence on her work, as well as that of others like Mary Wanless and Moshe Feldenkrais, but her imagination has springboarded from there into whole new realms. It really is wonderful to see how we can continue to evolve as self-aware horse people and conscientious athletes. It is an honor to witness the successes that can be the result of continued growth and education in the sport we all love.

Like Sally, Joyce has ideas that can help us be better partners for our horses. And *that* is worth sharing.

Caroline Robbins
Publisher, Trafalgar Square Books

FOREWORD BY HEIDI HAURI-GILL

My first conversation with Joyce Kramer was on the phone, and I knew immediately I had to get to know her. She had all the right answers and ideas as a riding instructor, and she was calling about an ad I had placed for exactly that. Fairly early in the conversation she told me she didn't want to be an instructor, but that she had called on a "hunch." I was disappointed that she didn't want to teach, mostly because I was tired and really needed help, but also because there was "something more" I could sense with her that I wanted to tap into. She noted she really enjoyed kids and riding camps, so we scheduled an appointment to talk about the possibility of her running my summer camps.

Our first meeting was both wonderful and concerning. Wonderful because what a glowing soul Joyce is! Concerning because she had just agreed to help me run my summer camps and yet she was clearly not in her best health (I had no idea at the time that she been dependent on a walker to walk and just trying to graduate to a cane!). But she had the best ideas for camp and they ended up a huge success. Joyce promised me four more years of pouring her heart and soul into what I now thought of as our camps.

While the campers were eating lunch one day, I noticed Joyce watching me ride. I figured she would be complimentary like most other people had been. I knew she had riding experience and plenty of it—mostly in the jumpers. I continued riding and hoped that she was enjoying it, although something told me she was looking deeper than the average person.

About a week later, Joyce approached me and said some nice things about my riding, but I could see a look in her eyes that made me want to know what she really thought—the part she wasn't giving me. We'd had a super relationship from the moment I'd said "Hello" to her on the phone, so I went ahead and asked what she'd really seen the week before. She hemmed only for a moment, then said, "Well, actually, I saw some places where I could help you get stronger."

I have to admit that my first response was, "Really?" in a sort of doubtful manner. But when she started to tell me what she meant I was pleasantly surprised by her remarks, thinking that she'd nailed some of the things I was working on, and had even suggested some new ideas that resonated deeply with me.

When Joyce next came to discuss our final preps for summer camp, she was a whole new person! Not only had she lost weight, but she was far more nimble and active. Many times I came across her in the arena on her hands and knees in the sand with the kids, doing exercises and pretending to be horses. I had instant envy. I wanted to do what the kids were doing! I was Mom to two young boys and had lost that fitness you typically have "before kids." It had become a bit harder for me to exercise because I spent all my time working and making sure my kids were moving and fed, and doing all the things that moms do. I was starting to "feel my age."

These two events led to the moment I set up an appointment with Joyce—for myself. During that first appointment she gave me an assessment test. It was hard, and I was disappointed in my performance. It became apparent to me that I had lost sight of how to be "my best riding self." Joyce's workouts started pretty simple, but she quickly had me progressing along and really clearly seeing why I needed what she had to offer.

I remember one day we were doing a workout in my farmyard, and Joyce put a contraption on one of the hitching posts we used for the camps. She told me to put my feet in it and do mountain climbers. I tried and looked up at her…and she had "that look." (I became used to "that look," which was a cross between knitted eyebrows and confusion.) I asked what was wrong, and she said something along the lines of, "You need to do that much faster and much more under your chest." My response was something along the lines of, "Really? Who can do that?" She then promptly put her feet in the straps and showed me a set of mountain climbers that was fast and furious! To make matters worse, when she was done, she wasn't even winded.

At another session we were sitting in the dirt in my farmyard (our favorite place to train, apparently), and Joyce asked me to put my legs as far apart as possible in a "V" position—"You know," she said, "like as close to a split as you can get." I got my legs as far apart as I felt I could, and there was that darn look!

"Can't you go farther?" she asked.

"I mean, who can except a gymnast," was my response, "and how will that really help me ride better?"

"You need to be soft and stretched in your hips to follow your horse," was Joyce's response. Then she did the unthinkable as an older lady who doesn't exactly have the shape of a 16-year-old gymnast—she did a full-on split!

All I could think was, *Really?*

Joyce was always learning, studying, and finding new ideas of ways to get me to use myself better. She started using different terms as she developed her method, and I started to feel real results. I asked her to work with my riding students.

What happened next was amazing.

Joyce had me do an "official assessment," which consisted of three parts: strength, suppleness, and riding. During that time, she also determined what sort of learner I was. (This was one of the benefits of her very customized fitness plans.) What I couldn't believe were the details she took away from those assessment factors. At first some of the things she focused on seemed a bit random, like neuromuscular training, and proper breathing. I was there to get strong to ride, and at first I did not see the relationship of those things to my ability on a horse. She had me do things that at times felt silly or childlike, such as rolling down a hill and then back up it, or dragging weights behind me as I rode a bicycle. Others were the strangest assignments! She had me stand on one leg while teaching for gradually lengthening periods of time and re-stack hay in the hay room. She had me sit on sawhorses and do things she called "compacting the hips" or lie on the ground playing with my scapula to learn to "pack" my shoulders. She took me for a drive in her car and asked me to do a fencer's lunge around every turn to feel how I could "activate my core" or "lead with my rib cage." She had me walk around blowing up balloons, then do it on my horse! She had me ride with an eye patch on. The best was when she told me to sit on the floor and move across it with my seat bones. (In the barn she overheard me telling someone about what she had me do, and I said, "I was butt walking!" Ever since, that is her name for this particular exercise!)

How do you explain to someone that you can learn to use your seat bones better on a horse by "butt walking" on a 10-foot carpet? What I can say is it really made me ride so much better, and quickly.

At the time I had a Dutch Warmblood who was quite tricky. He was hot in all the right ways for an FEI horse, but I hadn't yet really mastered how to make that benefit me. Instead I had become frightened by him and had started to ride him with tension in my body. I was afraid of my beautiful and talented horse. That was a horrible spot to be in, especially as a professional rider. But as Joyce and I worked more and more together, I became stronger, and my fear started to dissipate. When my horse made a wrong move, I no longer felt unsafe. Instead I felt deeply glued to him.

Two things started happening. The first one was that things got so much easier to do while I was on a horse. My goal for this horse was to take him to Grand Prix, and I actually began to feel on track to doing so. I wasn't sure how the strange things Joyce had me do were helping, but they sure were helping! The second thing was that my students were all working out with Joyce, and we were all working more and more together with the same vocabulary. I could say "Pack your shoulders," and the riders knew exactly what I meant. I could say, "Anchor your ribs," and boom, my students had the right shape in their body with the right activation. Joyce and I were on a roll, not only with my own training but with combining our knowledge to help others. It was so fun to have this true partnership. We tried many new ideas together. Often she would walk down the barn aisle, and I would say, "Uh oh—looks like you have a new great idea!"

By the time we had been working together for maybe four or five years, Joyce started bringing in more and more tools, or "toys," that helped me learn how to generate movement with my core, rather than with momentum or my arms flailing or legs kicking. I learned about scooters on the floor and the words "pike to plank." I learned how to use a TRX®. I learned how to be "a horse in a harness" attached to my midsection while Joyce did all she could to try to take me off balance. I relearned how to use a pogo stick and stilts. We even started to use a pool where we rode pool noodles, played pool polo, and worked on synchronized swimming movements. I wanted to ride Grand Prix dressage, not become a synchronized swimmer! But the control of the body and core necessary for that sort of swimming is incredible. It wasn't long after we started incorporating it in my training that I realized new ways to activate my horse and help "lift him" off the ground.

We hit hard parts. One especially hard part was learning to ride two-tempi changes. For me, a slow-by-nature person, getting the rhythm was so hard. I could teach lateral work all day long, I could teach a horse how to do a flying change, but when it came to teaching him to do them so rapidly that they had to come every other stride, I struggled. Joyce had me go out to the arena and "ride on my feet." I had to walk and think about what should happen when. The first place I put together the Intermediaire 1 test was in the pool, riding a noodle, pedaling my legs for propulsion, visualizing doing all the movements. It was crazy! But it was completely normal to Joyce. Whatever was hard for me to do in the show ring we did in personal training sessions. If her first idea didn't work to get the feeling through to me, she tried endless new ways to make it happen. (People always comment that I smile when I am on my horse—now you know that it is because I am probably thinking of whatever crazy thing Joyce had me do to improve the movement I am riding.)

Then I took a misstep off of a curb and broke my femur. It was a terrible fracture and needed a plate and nine pins in a leg that I already had issues with, mostly due to another old fracture in my foot. Joyce and I were both devastated. She called and said there were a few things we could do during the time that I had to spend off my leg completely. I asked what she had in mind, and in her usual chipper way, she said, "I am not entirely sure yet, but I will be prepared on Friday."

When she arrived to find me in a clump on a recliner, she noted something about how things didn't look so good and that we had better get started. I had my doubts. The great thing was, any time I had doubts, Joyce always proved me wrong. The first thing we did was move to a dining room chair, put my legs on the coffee table, and open and close them by sliding them along the surface. Then we did some seriously modified planks and other movements. When we were done, I told her that it felt so normal and so great to move my body. What she didn't see was that when she left, I cried because I now had some hope that I would be able to ride again within a reasonable amount of time with her help.

After four weeks (still no weight-bearing allowed) she had me on the vaulting barrel, working my core and balance. At eight weeks the doctor was so impressed with my strength overall that when he sent me to physical therapy they put an orange sticker on the folder that said "High Achiever—Caution!"

Joyce knew I did better in a group setting for my fitness training, so she called in other riders who were also ambitious and ready to try anything. I got to work out with my students and found new appreciation for all of them in different ways. You could catch us doing planks together with our hands or feet touching, using each other's energy and balance instead of relying on our feet or hands on the ground. We did resistance stretching in pairs where we would help each other and push each other. It was so fun.

Finally, the time came to reach my goal with my horse and ride the Grand Prix test. Joyce was there, along with everyone else who had helped us get there. When I came out of the ring after my test, she was the one who looked the proudest! She came over to me and said, "You have it! I see it in you! You have the connections we have been working on!" It was the most glorious feeling—we had done it.

I eventually moved to Florida, and I miss my New Hampshire farm, all the students, and most of all, the creative ways that Joyce and I worked together. Never has anyone besides my parents believed in me like Joyce. I feel like she believes in all her students like this. She has such a gift of putting body awareness, strength, intent, and ability together and pulling the best out of her riders. With the addition of her exceptionally valuable book, she is able to share what was at first our own private games and experiments, then a small and humble business, and now a thriving masterpiece of so many concepts, all in one place and for all riders. I know you will find incredibly helpful and unique techniques to get yourself more stable in the saddle in these pages. I also know you will find that the hard stuff can be fun!

Heidi Hauri-Gill

USDF Certified Instructor/Trainer, L-Grad with distinction Bronze and Silver Medalist Owner of First Choice Riding Academy (Enfield, NH) for 35 Years

NOTE TO THE READER

"Nothing ventured, nothing gained."
—John Heywood

The seeds that grew into this book were planted in October of 2008. I had just spent 10 years relying on a walker or cane to get around. My disability was due to an inherited spinal condition and undiagnosed Lyme disease, topped by neurological complications that were caused by a toxic exposure on a job site. (My numerous falls from training horses did not help.) Medical support had not helped my condition, nor had alternative therapies.

So why did I call in response to an ad for a riding instructor? Here I was, disabled. But I had a desperate longing to get horses back in my life and took the risk of trying to find out if there was a way to make that happen. When I got to Heidi and Bob Gill's First Choice Riding Academy in Enfield, New Hampshire, and got out of my car, I impulsively threw my cane into the back seat. The delightful smell of horses lured me into the barn and dissolved my worries, and for the first time in 10 years, I walked unaided down the barn aisle and into the viewing room for my interview. Heidi hired me on the spot to be her summer camp director. I will always be deeply grateful to the Gills for giving me that chance (and for the gifts of healing and getting my life back).

During the hot afternoons at the camp I taught a class called "Centaur Training." I crawled around the sand arena with the kids as they absorbed the different ways a horse moves at walk, trot, and canter. I was unaware of it at the time, but these movement patterns are quite similar to some of the Feldenkrais neuromuscular retraining exercises. They healed and strengthened me to such a degree I could give my walker and canes to Goodwill!

I began to study movement and holding patterns, ultimately becoming a certified personal trainer. And as I began integrating this knowledge in my riding instruction, it struck me that the "gym rats" were not my strongest riders. I had one client who had done a one-minute plank every day for 25 years, yet she did not use her core when she rode. Further, she rode mechanically, and not passionately.

What was going on? I had to find out! I abandoned what many might consider the "standard protocol" for developing strength, endurance, and stability. With much experimentation, I developed a system that brought out the "inner elite rider" in my clients. Their function and performance improved dramatically. It is these discoveries that I share in the pages of this book. Consider it an invitation to step outside of the box and invest in yourself.

From my experience, working with hundreds of riders, I have discovered that the human body adapts its best and most permanent postures through embodied imagery, and not through the study of anatomy and biomechanics. Certainly, these disciplines are worthy of study and understanding. But in the process of trying to mold oneself to the anatomical or biomechanical "ideal," extra bodily tension, as well as overthinking, are typically generated, and both water down the potential benefits. I find that often, trying to adhere to an anatomical or biomechanical ideal negatively affects the rider's suppleness, timing, and coordination. Of course, that weakens the horse's ability to understand the rider's intent as well as her aids. Therefore, I advise my clients to become familiar with the basics of anatomy and biomechanics, but not to overdo their studies.

The approach I encourage my riders to use is one that promotes their *embodied experience*. Embodiment encompasses integrating your body's sensations and experiences into your postures, movements, behavior, and even your identity. You honor the emotions that may be discovered to have been "stuffed and stored" in the body's tissues. For example, perhaps you store your stress in your hips! There is great individual variation in this area when we consider it from person to person.

The embodied approach helps you discover the stresses as well as the pleasant feelings that your body carries with you all day, both on and off horseback. One reason it is important for the rider to discover these sensations is because they are etched in the body's tissues in the form of energy. Horses are creatures of energy, and they read with great accuracy the messages our body's tissues send forth. For example, when you are feeling fearful but go out of your way to hide that fear, you are not fooling your horse. You are only perhaps fooling yourself. And it's not just our fears that horses read accurately, it's all our emotions and sensations, including pain.

A rider's embodiment work is boosted by the addition of imagery. Through the use of visualizations and internal "imagined video," the rider can sense and feel herself riding with great confidence, elegance, and accuracy. When this is accompanied by relaxed and rhythmic breathing, the trickle-down effect is that your body experiences the sensations and is quite successful at automatically rearranging itself to achieve the image in your mind. The brain prompts the body to create the desirable amount of positive tension and the best alignment for itself. Stability and suppleness become byproducts rather than direct goals. This gives a greater and more natural feeling to both the rider and her horse. Athleticism is rather magically enhanced for both parties.

Because embodied imagery is central to my approach, I have adapted workout guidelines with a result that is much different from "traditional" fitness workouts. I have found when I give my clients a specific number of reps, sets, amount of weight, or time to hold a pose, they focus on the number and not on the experience. Their form suffers and they don't derive the superior benefits of the embodied imagery they are generating. It is much more effective when I allow students to learn how to be in touch with the messages their bodies are trying to give them. This is why you will find I typically use the guidelines of working "to fatigue," then resting briefly before repeating the exercise. It is not uncommon for a new client to look quizzically at me and declare, "How do I know when I reach fatigue? I can't tell!" That is when I know our real work together will be centered on helping her discover her body's "messages," and the exercises become incidental. Please remember that it is the mind that poses the questions, but it is the body that gives the answers.

These are the reasons you will find very few specific guidelines about how many or how long to do the exercises in this book. But by following along, these pages will guide you on how to understand and get in better touch with your riding body. This approach will help you to become more independent about tailoring a custom-made exercise program for yourself. You are the best expert in your own life. Allow your body and your mind to guide you. I am not comfortable with establishing a student's dependency on me for the answers. I offer my impressions. But I want each rider I work with to become empowered and independent. If I cannot help you to foster this independence, I give you nothing of lasting value.

Enjoy the process of self-discovery that awaits. It will lead you to the inner elite rider that dwells within you.

Joyce Kramer
Wilder, Vermont

INTRODUCTION

When I started Stable Core Training®, LLC (a personal training business targeted for equestrians), I was driven by the mission to find answers to three questions:

1. What helps a rider find and feel her center?

2. Which exercises promote the spinal stability and joint fluidity that elite riders enjoy?

3. How can I make my riders strong and independent of me?

As I struggled to find the answers to these basic questions, I kept bumping into a wall of discrepancy between what riders *assumed* they needed and what they *actually* needed to improve their riding. For instance, there are many great books and videos on how to ride well that serve as a wonderful foundation to an equestrian's education. But riders often cling to these methods exclusively as a way to learn or to supplement their trainer's instructions. I consider this a form of tunnel vision that embraces the "think then do" mode. The gains achieved this way take many years and much hard work. And in my experience, those gains are quite limited. I was seeking an approach that would build upon the foundation of book-video-lesson learning, and give the rider a leg up to significantly better and more intrinsically driven performance. In three sections of this book, I share with you the approach I've discovered. It answered all three of my initial questions. Every trainer has her own spin on how to ride well, even within the same discipline. Therefore, this book does not present a system; it offers an approach that supports you in whatever way your trainer prescribes. Enjoy!

PART 1: THE FOUNDATION OF RIDING WELL

The centered, stable, supple rider can ride in total harmony with her horse because she is well balanced and can communicate with clear aids. This section of the book focuses on aspects that need to be in place in order for a rider to achieve that. Aspects such as alignment, centering, grounding, and positive tension are explored through imagery and photos. The use of these counteracts the tendency to overstudy and over think, as it encourages and nurtures a sense of feel. Finally, I address healthy unmounted (ground-based) movement and postural patterns that support a rider's ability to selectively follow or change her horse's movements.

PART 2: FINDING YOUR POSITION

For riders who are establishing their riding posture or for those who have lost their position due to injuries, habits, or simply time away from the saddle, this section provides a direct route to establishing, or returning to and even exceeding, your former level of riding. I explore the relationship of a rider's body parts and the way they are connected by myofascial chains (bands of muscles with connective tissue). I also use imagery to explore the unique characteristics and proper positioning of the body's sections, such as pelvis, rib cage, head, hips, and feet. And I teach you how to connect those parts by feel into a whole, strong, supple position that allows your horse to carry himself and balance well underneath you.

PART 3: STABILIZING YOUR DEEP CORE

Stabilizing your deep core is important because doing so reduces extraneous movements a rider might unintentionally make; it brings your body into a position that is centered and balanced; and it enhances communication with your horse via an energetic exchange.

In this section I present specific, unique, holistic ways for a rider to get in touch with her deepest parts, such as her bones, her spinal stabilizers, and her internal organs. Photos of exercises to develop core stability are included, along with step-by-step instructions on how to execute them safely. Please note it is good to feel some exertion with these exercises, but not pain. If there is any pain with an exercise, stop immediately. Before starting this or any exercise program, visit your health care provider and abide by any limitations, contraindications, or suggestions given.

The chapter on SLAM (Seat Lessons And More) lessons gives suggestions to trainers on specific proprioceptive props to help riders feel when they are centered and aligned, with good core engagement. I find this to be a critical step to improve riding, and it is the missing link in many ground-based programs. SLAM lessons teach riders how to integrate the benefits of ground-based exercises into the saddle. With proprioceptive props, riding well becomes a reality instead of a theory.

The chapter on beneficial sounds offers solutions to both trainer and rider on how to stimulate the rider's deep core engagement and bring stability to her posture. Coupled with imagery and proprioceptive props, this is a unique and highly effective way to improve both sense of feel and performance.

There are many good books available on how to ride, and also on how to support your riding with unmounted exercises. Typically these books include illustrations of the rider's bones, muscles, and even fascial chains. In this book you will find few of these, because in my experience, this approach feeds the left hemisphere of the rider's brain, the one that likes to analyze in a logical, sequential ways with as much detail as possible. This is not bad, but consider that you need both left and right brain to ride well. The right side of the rider's brain supports her ability to be creative and to *feel* her alignment and position, as well as to *feel* the quality of her horse's movements. Riding by feel becomes more and more important as you move up to more advanced riding levels. The ability to feel is a key factor in self-correction.

A rider who utilizes more of her right hemisphere brain through imagery, sounds, and special exercises can be in close sync with her horse. There is no muddy water associated with her aids. She understands her horse and her horse understands her. They both speak the same language. And that is the language of rhythm!

This book teaches you how to do "crossover exercises," in which both left and right brain hemispheres work together. I emphasize a visceral, holistic, and integrative approach, developed with the help of hundreds of horses and thousands of riders who were open enough to try something novel. The gains in their performance have been astounding. Please join me in this journey. Your horse will thank you!

PART 1

THE FOUNDATION OF RIDING WELL

A well-aligned rider does not hold fast to a position. Riding effectively and fluidly on a moving horse involves many micro adjustments to keep the rider aligned with the axis of gravity. For this to occur, it is necessary to be both grounded and centered in order to ride well.

PART 1

CHAPTER ONE
ALIGNMENT IS DYNAMIC

IT'S ALL ABOUT CENTERING

Water-skiing position happens when the rider is not in touch with, or loses track of, her body's center (fig. 1.1). When the rider is standing still, the center of her body is just below the navel and in front of her sacrum (which forms the back of the pelvis). The rider's center is a point where the aspects of her body are divided into equivalent halves: top/bottom, left/right, and front/back. Practicing the exercises in this chapter will help the rider get a feel for where her center is.

It is important for a rider to be in touch with her center so she can effectively balance, carry herself, and direct her weight while in the saddle. On a moving horse, there are physical forces coming at the rider that she needs to account for and negotiate, including gravity, momentum, inertia, ground reaction forces, centrifugal forces, and centripetal forces. But the rider's performance depends on her ability to keep her center balanced over her horse as they move together in a dynamic manner: they may change directions, speeds, and bend quickly and frequently, and the

1.1 A nightmare for equestrians of all disciplines! It's the dreaded "water-skiing position," the result of using your horse's mouth to support your body weight and pinching his sides to maintain your equilibrium. How does this happen, and what can you do to avoid it?

rider needs to remain centered throughout. The most successful riders are in constant touch with their centers. They feel and look balanced, alert, poised, and receptive, yet ready for action. Due to the movement of the horse and the physical forces of the environment at work, centering is dynamic (moving) and requires the rider to make frequent minor, smooth positional corrections in order to stay in balance and move to the exact extent that her horse is moving. This is why a rider who strives hard to achieve an imagined "ideal" position sometimes looks stiff and locked up. She is unable to stay centered and balanced over her horse, and her movements will appear forced and jerky.

Centering also embraces a flow of energy throughout the rider's body, as well as to and from her horse. The effective rider receives energy from her horse and directs it to her center. Her center then redirects the energy flow throughout her body, which absorbs the motions of her horse (for example, marching, swinging, bobbing, bounding, or jumping).

1.2 The rider's center is highlighted. Notice it is somewhat below the belly button, but deeper inside the body. Due to differences in our individual body shape and muscular profile, the center will be in a slightly different place for all of us. When you get in touch with your center, you connect to your horse in a way he clearly understands. This will improve your performance.

To find your center, put one hand in front of your belly just below your navel, and the other hand behind you just below the top of your pelvis (fig. 1.2). Now start slapping yourself vigorously enough to feel vibrations between your two hands (deep inside your body). If you feel tingling, you've got it! Sense the spot where the energetic vibrations meet—this is your center. Do this just before, or even during, a ride.

Let's explore some other ways to get a sense of your center so you can avoid the pitfalls of being towed along like a water-skier. To do this, we will use touch, movement, voice, visualization, imagination, and awareness.

CENTERING EXERCISE 1:
Axis Turn

STEP 1: Hold a dowel over the crown of your head to get a sense of where your central axis is (fig. 1.3).

STEP 2: Turn (rotate) around that axis, first clockwise, and then counterclockwise.

STEP 3: Close your eyes and repeat. Your goal is to go one full time around with your eyes closed, and stop exactly at—or close to—your starting spot.

STEP 4: You can add to your sense of feel by doing the above steps barefoot. This exercise will help you feel the strength and stability that emanates from your center.

1.3 Axis Turn

ONE: ALIGNMENT IS DYNAMIC | 9

CENTERING EXERCISE 2:
Move from Your COG

Step One: Place a yoga strap below your waist at about center-of-gravity level (fig. 1.4).

Step Two: Learn to move from your center by pulling yourself around in all directions.

Step Three: Have a partner hold the strap and lead you around with your eyes closed, which helps prevent you from anticipating the movement.

This is a valuable exercise because it instills correct unmounted movement patterns—and that gives rise to better posture and a higher frequency of self-correction when mounted.

1.4 Move from Your COG

CENTERING EXERCISE 3:
Half-Ball Head Balance

This is a fabulous exercise for learning to center yourself under an object, much as our horses have to balance under us. First, a word of caution: do not do this exercise if you have any head or neck conditions, or if it is painful when you first attempt it.

Step One: Hold a large half-ball on your head while making sure your head is directly over your spine

1.5 Half-Ball Head Balance

(fig. 1.5). The ball is filled with air, and the air tends to move around without warning. Hold the ball in place and only reposition it in the event it is about to fall off! (I've also had great results using a large hot water bottle instead of the half-ball—see p. 46.)

Step Three: To center an object on your head, you must center your whole body. This is a feeling that easily transfers to mounted work, and the ability to center yourself in this way results in better balance and less gripping or unwanted tension while mounted. Visualization complements the gains of this exercise by imagining you are the horse, and the object on your head is the rider. Watch what your automatic response is when the object tips forward, leans back, leans left, and leans right. You will begin to have new-found respect for your horse!

CENTERING EXERCISE 4:
Balance Board Ball

Step One: Sit on a smooth board (2 inches by 4 inches or 2 inches by 6 inches will do) suspended between two sawhorses (fig. 1.6).

Step Two: Toss a medicine ball directly upward in front of your centerline.

Step Three: Toss it high in the air so that it lands left of center.

Step Four: Toss it again so it lands right of center.

One must be centered to avoid a fall when sitting on a narrow surface; therefore, I strongly suggest wearing a riding helmet for this exercise. The addition of a helmet also changes the location of your center of gravity slightly. It's good to get in touch with that displacement while unmounted. Oh, and as you do this exercise, try growling deeply like a bear! Make it loud and proud and your center will reverberate the sensation.

1.6 Balance Board Ball

ALIGNMENT EXPLORED

Many books on riding show illustrations or photographs that insert a vertical line through a rider's ear, shoulder, hip, and ankle. A rider who is eager to improve typically tries to force her body into this imaginary stick-like position (similar to a post found on a merry-go-round horse). And as her horse moves, she avidly tries to adhere to that image and position. This is unfortunate, as it not only promotes tension in both horse and rider, it also results in the rider continually falling out of alignment due to the lack of suppleness in her joints. The outcome is this rider instinctively and reflexively clenches or braces her muscles to try to stay in balance. Riders are often unaware they are doing this.

The problem starts with the visualization that portrays the body as a series of interconnected solid shapes, such as stacked boxes. But our bodies are largely fluid, and they behave more like water balloons (fig. 1.7).

You can imagine how difficult it is to stack three large water balloons—now imagine trying to do it on top of a moving horse! In this case, the three water balloons are your head, rib cage, and pelvis. It's a good thing we have a backbone to stabilize us. It is difficult, but not impossible, to orient ourselves to verticality, where our center of gravity is in a vertical plumb line over

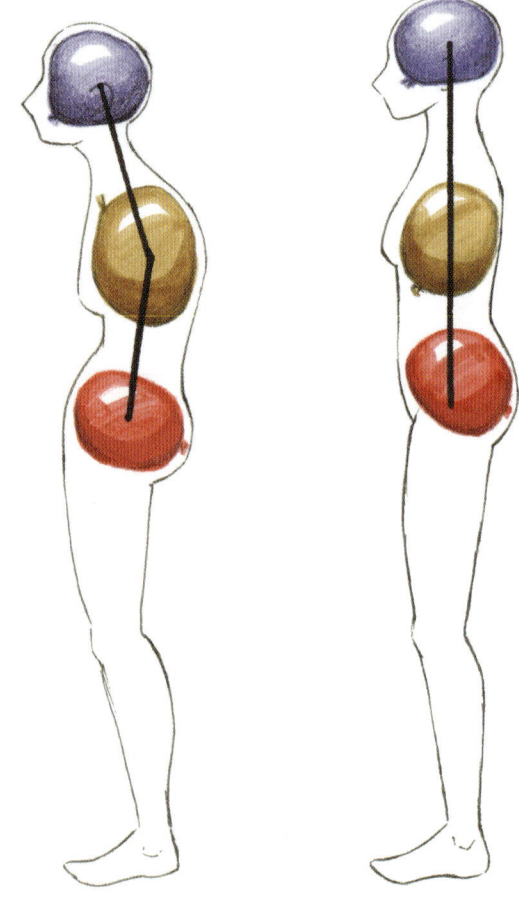

1.7 The human body is substantially fluid in composition (60 to 70 percent, typically), and this illustration portrays the difficulty of trying to get water balloons to stack in a fixed position.

our base of support (fig. 1.8). To be in alignment and deal with gravitational forces, the rider's center of gravity needs to be in a vertical line directly over her base of support, which in turn needs to be directly over the horse's center of gravity. A rider should strive for this vertical arrangement of her body in all movements and at all gaits (fig. 1.9). Maintaining

1.8 Jennie halts her mare Indian Eternal Bliss and taps the area that contains her *center of gravity* to get in touch with it. For most of us, it's a little below the navel/top of pelvis. She will also get in touch with her *base of support*. Your base of support is the area or areas that hold up your body weight and transmit the weight-bearing forces elsewhere. In a dressage saddle, Jennie's base of support is going to be the floor of her seat (the triangular area between both seat bones and the pubic bone). I stand ready with some proprioceptive props such as Franklin Method® Balls to pass to Jennie if needed. (These balls are further discussed in chapter 5, beginning on p. 42. Franklin Method Balls are a significant help in developing feel of parts of the body and how they work together to produce good alignment. Using them deepens the connection to your horse and improves performance.)

1.9 Jennie demonstrates an exercise that will improve her ability to know when she is aligned well. While keeping either or both her eyes closed, she deliberately leans forward, backward, to the left, and to the right. (At first, you might be more comfortable trying this exercise with first one eye closed, then the other.) This exercise will enhance her sense of feel and develop her awareness of when she is truly balanced. She is now in touch with her center of gravity and her base of support (here, the floor of her seat).

this vertical arrangement of the rider's body helps your horse to move and balance underneath you. A horse's center of gravity is located in the girth area, under where the rider sits. Its exact location is influenced by his body build, musculature, and training experience. When the rider's center of gravity is aligned as explained, she can carry her own weight, while keeping her joints supple to absorb the movements of the horse. This allows for clear seat and weight aids, rather than abrupt or nagging aids. Your horse will better understand you.

Compared to many other mammals, humans have a small base of support, a high center of gravity, and a heavy head. All of that combined gives us a stability challenge. Wearing a riding helmet is essential for safety, but it slightly alters the location of your center of gravity. I ask riders working on balance or core stability to wear a helmet when working out on the ground, because doing so will prepare them for establishing stability when they are mounted with their helmet.

A rider who holds her head in a forward position when mounted is almost certainly doing the same thing when she is on the ground

1.10 Here Jennie demonstrates a forward head position. Due to modern lifestyles and habit, many people hold their heads and necks in front of their spines. But the spine extends up into the neck right to the base of the skull—so when your head and neck are in front of your spine, you have essentially destabilized your spine.

(fig. 1.10). A head hanging in front of the spine, knees locked out in hyperextension, and a pelvis tucked under are all examples of adapting to the forces of gravity. Undoubtedly, gravity will be the winner here. Some of your muscles will become locked rigid and short, while others are painfully stretched and locked in a long, tortuous type of traction. You simply cannot bring your best riding to your horse when you are not in proper alignment (fig. 1.11). Nor are you safe. When you are misaligned, energy does not flow from rider to horse or horse to rider. There's a blockage. It's like your cell phone being in a dead zone.

1.11 Now Jennie is in a jumping position, and her lower legs are her base of support. As she bends from her hips, notice that she has kept her head and neck over her central axis. This will give her a strong position over fences. Her eyes should stay soft and focused beyond each jump to the horizon. A soft, focused gaze will help her keep her horse in good balance, which will help her negotiate her fences.

RIDING ON THE VERTICAL

Alignment includes the relationship between body parts as well as the relationship between those parts and the horse (or ground). As a practiced personal trainer, I have ways to assess if someone is well-aligned. However, it is rare for a stable to have a trained ground professional at their disposal, so the rider herself needs to develop a feel for when she is in alignment and "on the vertical" (fig. 1.12). Here is a checklist to make that process easier:

- Is your body weight supported by the triangle of the floor of your seat? (A reminder that the floor of your seat is formed by the triangle connecting your two seat bones to your pubic bone. You should feel all three of those points solidly on the saddle.)

- Are your left and right seat bones weighted the same amount?

- Is your spine pain-free, with a feeling of strength and stability?

- Do your muscles feel somewhat "activated," but not to the degree of "clinging" or clenching?

- Do you feel like you are carrying your own body weight to stay upright rather than allowing your horse to mainly support your body weight?

- Are your feet under your seat? To check, stand in your stirrups and put your arms out in a "T." If your feet are under your seat, you will be able to balance.

- Are your shoulder blades "double packed"? When your shoulder blades are "double packed," you are aiming each shoulder blade toward the opposite back pocket. At the same time, you are also aiming each back pocket (pelvic half) toward the opposite shoulder blade.

1.12 Jennie's body is seeking a vertical line that runs through her ears, shoulder, hip, and ankle. In this verticality, Jennie's seat bones will plug into receptors in her horse's back that allow for the subtle communication needed. As we explored in this chapter, verticality is not static, but involves a continual interaction between the horse's movements and the rider's subtle actions. This generates feelings of deep connection, calmness, receptivity, and expressiveness.

- Is your front line free of tension, with a soft quality?

- Check your *pelvic tilt*. Imagine your pelvis is a bowl of water. The bowl should be angled forward just enough to create a steady *drip, drip, drip* out the front. If there is a steady *flow* of the water out the front, your pelvis is tilted too far forward. If there is no imaginary dripping out the front edge, your pelvis is tucked too far under. The *drip, drip, drip* signifies a *neutral pelvis*. I often advise riders to make a slight "ducky tail" to do this (fig. 1.13).

- Put your hands on your sides at the bottom of your rib cage. These are your lowest ribs. Are they tucked rearward a little bit, toward your spine? I call this "anchoring" the rib cage (see p. 68). The slight tuck of the bottom ribs supports the lumbar area and gives the rider a solid "dressage back." It also lifts the top portion of the sternum upward and outward.

- Is the back of your neck lengthened upward and rearward, such that your head is directly over your spine?

1.13 To establish a neutral pelvis with your seat bones pointing straight down, you need a very slight forward tilt of the pelvis. So imagine you have a bit of a "ducky tail" to get a slight "drip" from that pelvis bowl.

If you answered "yes" to all these questions, you are probably in good alignment. Part 2 of this book will explore body parts and their relationship with each other further (see p. 87).

> **chapter takeaway** ✓
>
> **Proper alignment is contingent upon your ability to be in touch with your body's center. For most people, the center point will be just in front of the top part of the sacrum (which forms the back of the pelvis). A rider who is in touch with her center can balance, carry herself, and direct her body weight.**

CHAPTER TWO

A GROUNDED RIDER

GROUNDING EXPLORED

If you are standing up and push downward through your feet, you will feel the ground forces that push back at your feet and travel upward through your body. If you are lying on your back, you will feel this as increased muscle tone in your back. If you lie on your stomach, you will feel increased muscle tone in your abdomen. And if you are lying on a side, you will feel the increased muscle tone on the side touching the ground. Think about water careening downward from a height, then seeking its own level. Feel the earth push back upward against the force of the waterfall. Imagine you can inhale and receive that energy.

Even crawling on the ground can help you feel this connection to the physical forces of the earth as they push at you. To enhance this feeling, I suggest the following imagery exercise (fig. 2.1):

Stand up and imagine your brain is extremely heavy, so heavy your body is unable to support it up in your head. Close your eyes and visualize your brain slowly sinking toward your center of

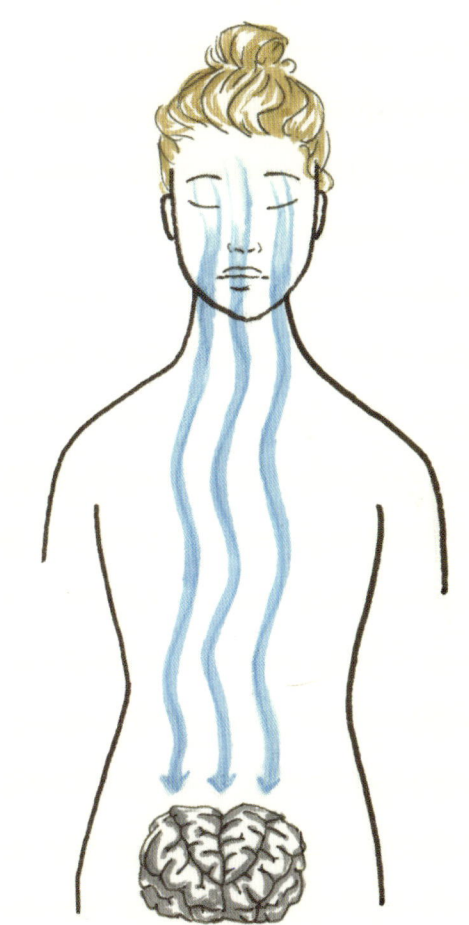

2.1 Sinking Brain

gravity. You can rest your hands just below your navel if it helps you get the sensation of where your center of gravity is located. Now push your feet downward into the floor and be aware of an upward-lifting feeling through the arches of your feet, through the inner sides of your legs, and through your pelvis. Note any other areas of your body that feel affected by this action, and label each sensation (for example, tingly, strongly supported, light as a feather). Labeling these sensations often enhances the benefits of imagery exercises. Allow the grounding forces to flow through you freely. Do not try to control or direct them. You are grounded when you feel settled, with an upward pull in your front line and a downward pull in your backline. You will feel attentive toward the moment, rather than the past or the future. If you are mounted, you will feel any gripping release.

GROUNDING IN THE SADDLE

Before you put on your riding helmet, press a fingertip into the top of your head and press another fingertip between your eyebrows for one minute (fig. 2.2). Next, cover your ears with your palms firmly enough to generate "the sound of the ocean." This is a sound similar to the one you hear when you press a seashell to your ear. Breathe slowly and deeply. It will sound like the

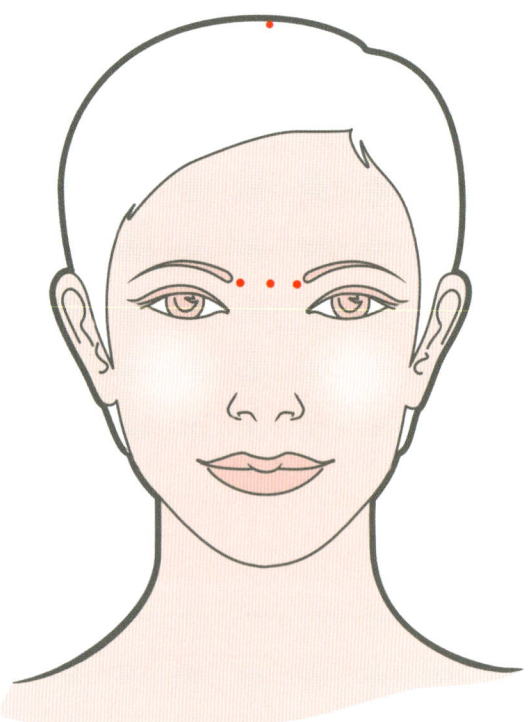

2.2 Locate and simultaneously apply pressure to the acupressure points between your eyebrows and on the crown of your head.

wind at the seashore! These steps will help you feel grounded before you mount up. Once you are in the saddle, take the thumb of each hand and press downward at the slightly webbed area between each finger of the opposite hand for five seconds. Exhale as you do this.

Now close your eyes briefly, if it is safe for you to do so, and feel every spot that makes contact with the saddle and stirrups. Which part of your body feels the most settled (top, bottom, left, right, front, or back)? Finally, take three deep, slow breaths, audibly sighing "ahhh" on each exhale.

GROUNDING EXERCISE 1:
Shaking Out Unwanted Energy

Step One: Stand or sit and shake your arms, hands, and fingertips as if you were shaking water off them. Visualize that you are also shaking off all unwanted energy, such as fear, frustration, or anxiety.

Step Two: Now rub your hands briskly together to create warmth, and place your fingertips together as if you were holding a large grapefruit. Holding this shape, place your hands in front of your center. Feel the new, tingly electromagnetic energy between your fingertips.

Step Three: Allow your fingertips to separate from each other a little—they might feel like magnets that want to connect with each other again. Breathe slowly, pausing after each inhale and each exhale. This exercise will ground you nicely anywhere, anytime.

GROUNDING EXERCISE 2:
Sacrum Sink

Step One: At the halt, have a friend hold the reins to allow you to concentrate and submit to the grounding (fig. 2.3).

Step Two: Place your hands on your sacrum while you visualize it dropping to the earth's core. You should feel your sacrum drop a little when you do this.

Step Three: You can also practice the Sacrum Sink unmounted. Put your hands on the back of a railing or piece of furniture and press down with your hands and feet as you release through the sacrum. A sigh can help this imagery: *Ahhh!*

2.3 Sacrum Sink

GROUNDING EXERCISE 3:
Barefoot Grounding

Step One: Remove your shoes and socks and simply stand or walk barefoot on grass, dirt, or sand.

Step Two: Feel the sensations of your feet meeting the earth. This is a particularly potent exercise after a thunderstorm has passed through—breathe in fresh, rejuvenating air.

GROUNDING EXERCISE 4:
Crawling

Crawling on the ground or a mat as a young child might is quite grounding and also serves as a super neuromuscular reset. Have fun with it!

Step One: Start out with *ipsilateral movements* (moving left arm and left leg at the same time, for instance).

Step Two: Then crawl, using *contralateral movements* (left arm and right leg move together).

GROUNDING EXERCISE 5:
Growing Roots

Step One: Stand outdoors and imagine there are roots growing out of your feet, downward into the earth.

Step Two: Inhale and imagine calm, peaceful, green light entering through the roots and spreading upward throughout your body.

Step Three: Exhale all unwanted or excess energy and thoughts back down through the roots into the ground.

Step Four: Repeat for several cycles until you feel a calm, refreshed connection to the earth.

Try this exercise before a horse show! It's a great way to center your mind.

---

chapter takeaway ✓

It's good for a rider to get a sense of the earth's ground reaction forces as they push back at us. It helps you feel as if you have roots, connecting you to the present moment in space and time. This allows you to better focus on yourself and your horse.

PART 1

CHAPTER THREE

Positive Tension is the Key

MUSCLE TONE AND POSITIVE TENSION

Muscles work primarily by their pulling action. Groups of muscles form chains when they work toward the common goal of either creating or resisting movement (stabilizing). Muscle chains are part of fascial lines that you will learn to balance through exercises presented in this book. The concept of positive tension is an integral part of establishing the muscle tone needed to ride well. Let's take a closer look.

In fig. 3.1 A, you see a section of a dryer hose bending to the side. This represents a rider who takes the shape of a "C"-curve. The left and right sides are not pulling with the same degree of tension, resulting in an unwanted side bend in the torso. The side that is bending has too tight a tone and is locked short. The longer side is overly stretched and is locked long. This corresponds to a misaligned rider who lacks balance in the muscle tone of her left and right sides. This affects her horse because she struggles to weight

3.1 A Tension vs. Positive Tension

each seat bone equally, and her pelvis, rib cage, and head are apt to drift out of alignment. Both the clarity of her aids and overall performance are diminished.

3.1 B–D Tension vs. Positive Tension

In fig. 3.1 B you will notice an unequal pull on the ends of the dryer hose, resulting in unwanted movement. The top is pulling sharply upward, while the bottom exerts little, if any, pull. This corresponds to a rider who lifts up through the crown of her head without grounding her sacrum. Instead, to find her balance, she must use leg grip, press on the stirrups or, perhaps unknowingly, use the reins to steady herself.

Next, fig. 3.1 C shows the two ends of the hose in a vigorous tug-of-war with each other. This visual corresponds to an overly tense rider who struggles to ride smoothly and follow the horse's movements. This extreme tension sets the rider up for injuries and deviations in postural alignment.

Finally, in 3.1 D we see both ends of the dryer hose exerting a gentle pull in opposite directions, like a friendly tug-of-war game that no one wins because the pressure in each direction is equal. There is no movement. This is an example of an *isometric pull*, and *this* is *positive*

tension! Positive tension is a healthy tension reflecting balanced, well-toned muscles in a state of readiness. While positive tension can be considered a hold of a lengthened position, it is not as vigorous as a stretch. A rider in positive tension could receive a stimulus from her horse and easily react, or she could give an aid without either underreacting or overreacting.

Positive tension is a healthy tension stemming from the body's inner strength and balance. If you use positive tension throughout your body to counteract gravitational and other physical forces, it results in *self-carriage*. Self-carriage is about holding up and controlling your own body weight; it includes supporting, directing, and maintaining your body's direction, speed, movement patterns, postural patterns, suppleness, and even its energy level. This is the same type of self-carriage many riders are working on establishing in their horses! It is therefore not surprising to learn that when a rider maintains an appropriate amount of positive tension, directing and carrying her own body weight strategically as she sits upon her horse, the horse is invited and welcomed into his own self-carriage.

But positive tension and self-carriage are not about holding specific muscles in a friendly tug-of-war indefinitely. Since the rider straddles a moving horse, she should strive to match his movements until she is ready to give an aid and make a change. Remember that positive tension is more about creating mild to moderate isometric holds than about movement, yet subtle movements in the rider need to happen in order to follow the horse. In other words, some body parts move subtly while others hold their position in a mild to moderate way. How does a rider know what to move and what to hold? It is largely a matter of feel! I examine this in depth in chapter 5 (see p. 42). Following the exercises at the end of this chapter will also help improve the rider's sense of feel.

POSITIVE TENSION EXERCISE 1:
Sandpaper Boards

This exercise utilizes sandpaper as a proprioceptive device to help you get a feel of positive tension. I am fond of using grade #60 sandpaper, stapling a couple of strips of it to two short boards, as can be seen in this photo. Heavy cardboard and duct tape to secure the strips also works.

Step One: Place the boards a couple of feet apart, making sure the sandpaper (or duct tape) has a front-back orientation (fig. 3.2 A).

Step Two: Place your feet on the sandpaper, and then tension your knees and thighs in an outward (lateral) direction while simultaneously tensioning your inner calves and feet toward each other in an inward (medial) direction. The sandpaper does not allow for movement, resulting in a low to moderate level of *positive*

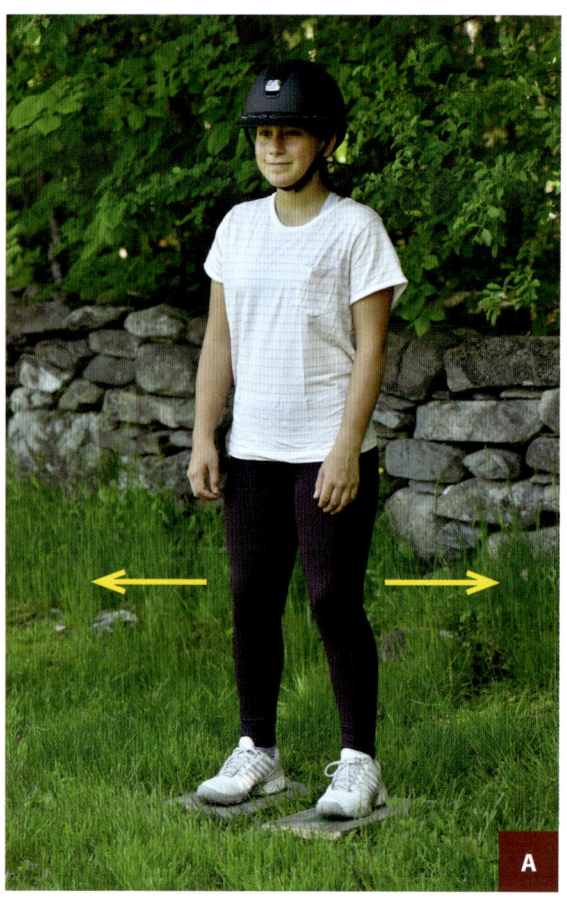

3.2 A & B Sandpaper Boards

tension. You will feel how that tension gives you great muscle tone. This is the type of tone that promotes strong riding, laced with stability and suppleness!

Step Three: Rearrange the sandpaper boards so that one is ahead of the other, about hip-width apart (fig. 3.2 B). This mimics a situation like a turn, where you might place your outside leg *behind* the girth and inside leg *at* the girth. It also encourages a diagonal connection from the inside foot to the outside arm (think *inside leg to outside rein*).

Step Four: Experiment with generating positive tension by aiming each leg *toward* the other as if they were a pair of scissors about to close. Do this isometrically, without visible movement.

Step Five: Now try the opposite "movement," and tension each leg *away* from the other as if they were a pair of scissors about to open.

Notice the varying sensations in each case. When you are mounted, your trainer or a helper can hold the boards under your feet, or you can imagine it instead—which is nearly equally effective.

POSITIVE TENSION EXERCISE 2:
Goldilocks Zone

This is an exercise to help you learn when you don't have enough positive tension.

Step One: Deliberately make yourself feel loose and floppy so you can recognize that feeling if you experience it in your riding (fig. 3.3 A). This could be a loose, floppy isolated body part, or it could appear as a general lax tone throughout your entire body. It is important to feel and recognize a loss of positive tension so you can make a self-correction. Not only is it extremely difficult for

3.3 A Goldilocks Zone

a horse to balance under a loose, floppy rider, his rhythm and gaits will also be negatively affected as his rider flails in unwanted movements.

Step Two: Demonstrate an overly tense, forced position (fig. 3.3 B). This creates a stiff rider who is unable to follow the movements of her horse and bounces around in a misaligned position. Riders may experience this excess tension as a full body tension, or it could be isolated to a body part such as one or both elbows. It is important for you to become aware of this type of tension so you can release it. There are numerous suggestions throughout this book on how to achieve this. It typically involves centering, grounding, and visualizing, coupled with deep, slow, rhythmic breathing. Humming and singing are also very helpful.

3.3 B & C Goldilocks Zone

Step Three: Find a state of positive tension that is "just right" (fig. 3.3 C). Your horse may sigh with relief when he feels this positive tension, particularly if you've been riding either too lax or overly tense. Your muscles should now feel a mild to moderate activation, as they did in the exercise with the sandpaper boards (see p. 26). This degree of activation is desirable because you can ride in balance and self-carriage without interfering with your horse's movements. And that encourages your horse to carry himself better.

POSITIVE TENSION EXERCISE 3:
Diagonal Connections

Step One: Stand with your body in the shape of an "X" (fig. 3.4 A). Grasp one extra-long exercise band across one of the diagonals of your body. (Alternatively, you can grasp two, from each foot to the opposite hand.) Feel each of the diagonal lines exert a pull from one of its ends to the other. This mimics the functional *myofascial lines* that are of particular importance to riders—the diagonal connections helping to keep you centered and stuffed in positive tension.

Step Two: Experiment using just one band at a time to see if you have as great a feel on one line as on the other. If one side lacks full feel, I recommend you avoid the temptation of doing more work on the weaker side. Concentrating on the weaker side is more likely to cause a new imbalance, as your weaker side shifts to become your stronger side. Instead, I suggest you work both sides in equal tension for equal amounts of time.

Step Three: Work on your diagonal functional lines but with the exercise bands along the front of your body (fig. 3.4 B). These myofascial lines work in conjunction with the back functional lines depicted in fig. 3.4 A and are equally important to develop.

Step Four: Continue your functional myofascial band work with the bands in an ipsilateral (same side) position (fig. 3.4 C). The bands start at the inner edges of the midfoot and run up through the inner knee before heading diagonally up toward the same-side armpit and then

3.4 A Diagonal Connections

3.4 B–D Diagonal Connections

overhead. I have found the musculature of many equestrians to be significantly weak here. The gains in their riding are noteworthy when they strengthen these ipsilateral functional lines (the outcome of many of the exercises in this book)!

Step Five: Wrap an extra-long exercise band around your whole body in a spiral fashion (fig. 3.4 D). Make sure one end touches the area between your ear and the occipital bone (located at the base of your skull behind your ear) and ends with it under your opposite foot, just in front of your ankle from its outer edge to its inner edge. There is a myofascial line that takes a similar spiral route and is highly involved in stabilizing your body. Riders depend on this line to keep themselves strong and stable in the saddle.

Step Six: Hold the band in positive tension for about a minute, and then reverse the band's position to do the other spiral line.

> **chapter takeaway** ✓
>
> A rider without positive tension easily falls out of alignment. She will struggle to weight each seat bone equally and to maintain her verticality. Positive tension is created when muscles or muscle chains exert a gentle pull on each other in opposite directions. It's like a friendly game of tug-of-war that no one wins. This healthy tension stems from the rider's inner strength and balance. It manifests outward in a state known as self-carriage.

CHAPTER FOUR

BREATHING AS A FUEL PUMP

WHOLE BODY BREATHING

Breathing uses muscles from different parts of the body, including your upper chest, rib cage, and diaphragm. In fact, the deepest breaths include actions from all three of those areas. If you put one hand on your upper chest and the other hand on one of your sides, during inhalation you will feel the highest ribs drawn up, the lowest ribs sinking down, and the whole rib cage pushed outward and slightly expanded. These are critical actions for effective breathing, and it is unfortunate that some people are taught to put a hand on the lower belly and expand only that area. I urge you to use all parts of your torso for both inhalation and exhalation. I call this *full body breathing*. The body moves when you breathe (fig. 4.1).

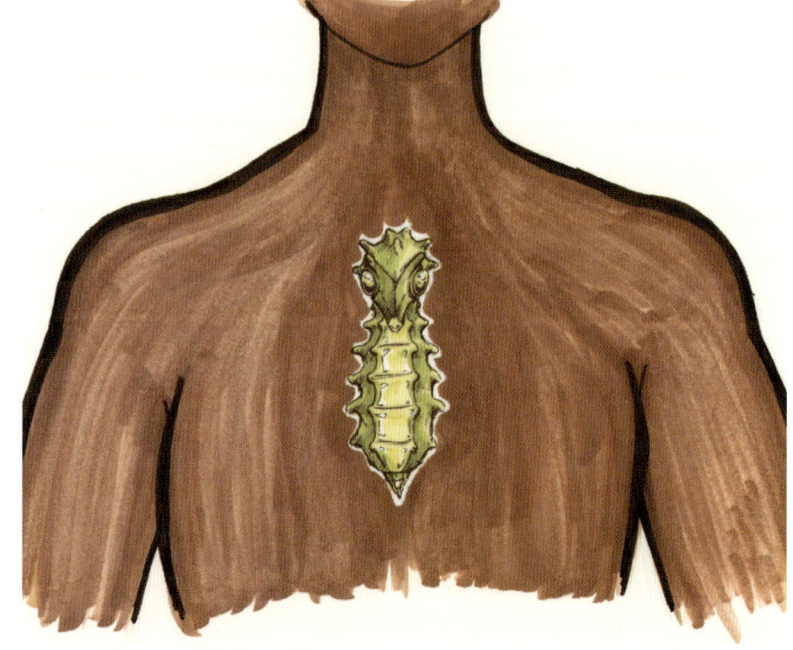

4.1 The shape of the *sternum*—sometimes called the *breastbone*—reminds me of a seahorse, so I envision a little bony seahorse holding my ribs together! Just as a seahorse would do, when the top (head) of the sternum nods forward, the bottom (tail) swings backward towards the spine. This imagery automatically enables the sternum to make microadjustments as you nod slightly with the movement of the seahorse. This exercise will enhance your breathing as well as your riding.

Deep breathing does *not* mean sucking in as much air as possible, nor does it mean breathing more rapidly. Doing either of these things creates (negative) tension and actually reduces the cellular exchange of oxygen. Our breathing is most efficient when it remains soft, quiet, and unaltered from its natural pattern. When you align your bones well, the diaphragm rises and falls in a fluid manner. This gives an inner massage to your organs.

It is also important to incorporate short, smooth pauses into the breathing cycle. There is a short pause after inhalation, but it is a natural pause, not a manipulation. There is a slightly longer pause after exhalation. This should feel anticipatory, like the pause of a symphony. This serves as an invitation for fresh air to enter the lungs gently and smoothly, in a rejuvenating fashion. It is during these pauses that the body is encouraged to deliver oxygen to the cells, a process known as *cellular breathing*. When you inhale "gobs" of air, or inhale too quickly, cellular breathing is diminished. This is extremely undesirable, because cellular breathing creates a sense of energy, fluidity, and elasticity throughout the body, and keeps cells healthy via fluid exchange. When you breathe slowly, rhythmically, and with pauses, your cells get nourished, and their waste products are carried away.

I strongly advise my clients to breathe through their noses for both the inhale and the exhale as much as possible. This warms and filters the incoming air in a way that mouth breathing cannot. In addition, mouth breathing activates stress hormones (fight, flight, or freeze), which negatively influences how you interact with your horse.

Good breathing supports good posture, which in turn supports good riding. Horses are keenly tuned in to our breathing; this is true whether we are mounted or not. Our emotions, intents, and energy are conveyed to them through our breaths. The quality of our breath makes it impossible for us to hide what we are feeling from our horses. They totally get us, even from a distance.

THE RIDER'S FUEL PUMP

Breathing air into the lungs is not like blowing up a balloon. Air enters the lungs due to a vacuum created by the contraction of the diaphragm muscle. Your lungs (and heart) slide around during breathing, and these organs need exercise to be fully functional.

Your posture will either enhance or compromise your breathing. When you stand and move well, your breathing encourages your spine to lengthen. This enables the lumbar spine (lower back) to support your diaphragm's efforts. It works both ways: posture affects your breathing, and full body breathing gives rise to good posture.

During inhalation, the chest cavity increases in volume from top to bottom, side to side, and front to back. These areas are reduced in volume during exhalation. The abdominal cavity is also affected and undergoes a shape change (but not a volume change) from top to bottom, side to side, and front to back. The spine goes into slight extension on an inhale and slight flexion on an exhale. Effective breathing stems from making good shape changes—in other words, maintaining good posture. The muscle predominantly responsible for the shape changes of these cavities is the diaphragm.

The diaphragm is not symmetrical; this is one of numerous examples as to why we struggle with our body's symmetry. Specifically, the diaphragm is higher on the right side of the body, due to the liver pushing it upward. Additionally, the heart (located above the diaphragm) pushes this muscle downward on the left side of the body.

The diaphragm divides the torso into two cavities. They are the *thoracic* (upper) and *abdominal* (lower) cavities of the torso. The diaphragm's central tendon allows for its vertical movements in the body, rather like a telescoping umbrella handle that enables the up/down movements (fig. 4.2). Because of its proximity and attachment to the heart's pericardium and the lungs' pleura, the vertical action of the diaphragm has a strong effect on the movements of the organs within both the upper and lower torso cavities. In addition, the body's organs can offer both resistance and stabilization to the diaphragm.

When you ride, you are subconsciously coordinating movements between your body's organs and your breath. Riding has an extremely positive effect on the well-being and function

4.2 The diaphragm is rather umbrella-shaped due to the organs it surrounds and supports.

of your organs. It's just what your health care provider ordered!

When the diaphragm rises and falls, it is called *vertical breathing*. The diaphragm rises on the exhale and descends on the inhale. Vertical breathing promotes oxygen delivery to your cells (cellular breathing). A rider is well-advised to tune in to the vertical aspect of her breathing by putting one hand on her belly button, slowly inhaling with a pause at the top of the inhale, and then slowly exhaling with a pause at the bottom of the exhale. If she does not feel her belly button rising (on the exhale) and sinking (on the inhale), she has a compromised breathing pattern. She has also closed the door on forward movement of her horse, because proper vertical breathing with good postural alignment plugs the rider into the horse's energy receptors, located on his back under the saddle. This up and down diaphragmatic movement coincides with the movement of two other key diaphragm-like muscles. One is located in your throat and the other in your pelvis. We will explore these other two muscles later in this book. For now, understand that all three of these muscles produce a powerful "fuel-pump action" that attracts and nourishes forward movement of your horse. If your horse falls behind your leg, it is quite likely your fuel pump is not operating optimally or rhythmically. Riders: pay attention to your breathing! Regular breathing exercises will pay off with better riding performance.

BREATHING EXERCISE 1: Checking for Verticality

This exercise will help you practice vertical breathing, an essential skill that will help you breathe deeply and "plug in" for a better connection with your horse.

Step One: Stand facing a full-length mirror.

Step Two: Take deep, slow breaths, and keep your front line soft. Do not bring your belly button toward your spine, as this will disrupt your core and impair breathing.

Step Three: Notice that when you inhale, your belly button descends. When you exhale, it rises. That's your diaphragm working effectively. This up-and-down action works as a fuel pump, encouraging forward energy in your horse.

BREATHING EXERCISE 2:
Assistance of the Tongue

This exercise builds on, and can be done at the same time as, Breathing Exercise 1 (p. 35).

Step One: As you inhale, rest your tongue softly on the bottom of your mouth.

Step Two: As you exhale, lift the tip of your tongue upward and press it to the roof of your mouth, in the space just behind your two upper front teeth, with gentle to moderate pressure.

Step Three: If you are riding, notice how the action of your tongue supports your diaphragm and other deep core myofascia. As sections of the deep core rise upward, it encourages a horse to respond when you ask him to lift his back, use his abdominals, and develop self-carriage.

BREATHING EXERCISE 3:
Do Re Me

Here's an exercise that uses sounds to assist your proper breathing and deep core support. It can be done while mounted or unmounted.

Step One: Inhale naturally and without force.

Step Two: On the exhale, sing, *"Do re me fa so la ti do,"* slowly from low note to high note.

Step Three: As you do this, visualize your diaphragm moving upward as you sing, and your organs sliding around to accommodate the diaphragm.

Step Four: Try this exercise again, but instead of singing, "purr like a cat." Continue to go from low note to high note as you visualize the diaphragm rising.

Which method gave you greater awareness of the vertical movement of your diaphragm? Which method does your horse prefer? He will likely respond better to one of the options you try than he does to others.

BREATHING EXERCISE 4:
Standing Diaphragm Stretch

Please do not overlook stretching your diaphragm! In particular, if you use your abdominal muscles in an effort to stabilize your spine (such as moving your belly button toward your spine or sucking in your gut), you will not be able to use your diaphragm throughout its full range of motion. This causes the diaphragm to become both weak and tight. When fibers of the diaphragm shorten, they may also become thicker, causing a negative effect on both your breathing and your riding performance.

Step One: Shake your whole body vigorously, then stand and clasp your hands overhead (fig. 4.3).

Step Two: Tension your hands as if they were trying to pull apart but can't.

Step Three: Maintain this engagement of the arms. Inhale and hold your breath.

Step Four: Rapidly "pump" your tummy muscles (squeeze/release) 10 times.

Step Five: Slowly and gently exhale fully.

4.3 Standing Diaphragm Stretch

Step Six: Repeat Step Four.

Step Seven: Return to your natural breathing and posture, and release your arms.

BREATHING EXERCISE 5:
Lying Diaphragm Stretches

This is one of my favorite diaphragm stretches because there is such an exhilarating, visceral feeling to it.

Step One: Lie down on your back (fig. 4.4).

Step Two: Side bend by moving your upper torso and legs sideways in the same direction, then hook one leg over the other.

Step Three: Grasp your ear lobes with your fingers and gently to moderately pull your ears forward from your head.

Step Four: Stick out your tongue as far as you can with your mouth wide open.

Step Five: Open your eyes wide. Pop them right out!

Step Six: Inhale slowly through your nose.

Step Seven: Exhale slowly as you roar like a lion. Louder! Do this five times.

Step Eight: Release, bend toward your other side, and repeat.

4.4 Lying Diaphragm Stretches

BREATHING EXERCISE 6:
Hands-Free Balloon Breathing

This is a fabulous exercise for breath control and developing awareness of the "outward expansion feeling" as you exhale, which is an important feature of core stabilization (we will address this in later chapters). Skip this exercise if you have a latex allergy.

Step One: Stand with feet about hip width apart. Insert the tip of a balloon into your mouth (fig. 4.5).

Step Two: Extend your arms out to your sides at shoulder height, palms facing down.

Step Three: Breathe in through your nose and exhale out through your mouth into the balloon. Be sure not to touch the balloon with your hands!

Step Four: When the balloon is over halfway full, close your eyes, because it may pop!

Step Five: On the exhale, feel how your abdominal expansion pushes outward on the abdominal wall. Deflate the balloon (you can use your hands to remove it from your mouth), and repeat the previous steps to inflation.

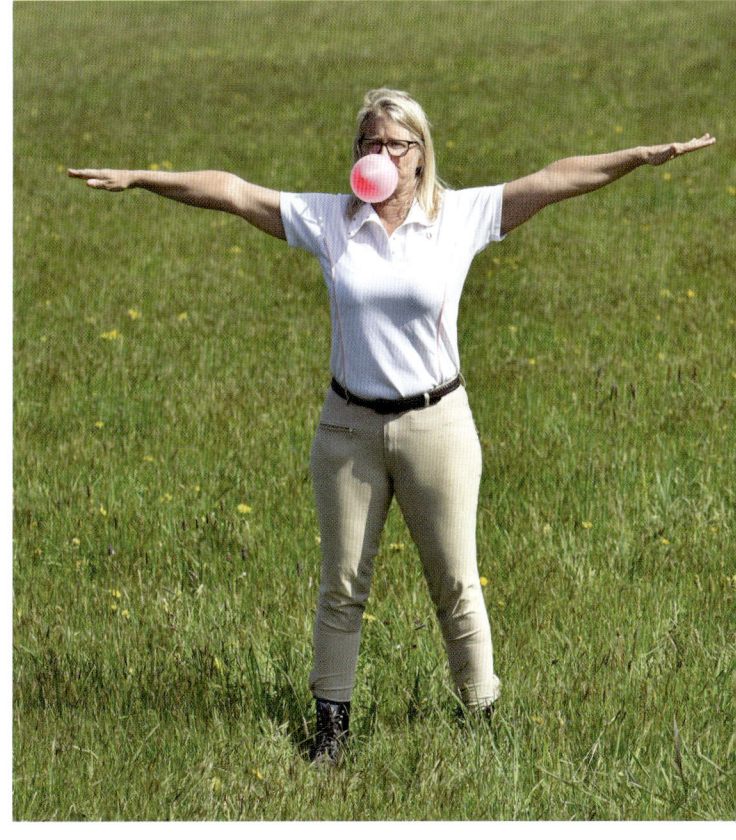

4.5 Hands-Free Balloon Breathing

BREATHING EXERCISE 7:
Backpack Breathing

For this exercise, start with what feels like a moderate amount of weight in a duffel bag or backpack, and build up slowly. Fill the bag with objects of your choice (ankle weights work well). Test out the weight; you don't want it to feel easy, nor do you want to struggle to lift it. Then get ready to increase your lung power!

4.6 Backpack Breathing

Step One: Lie down on your back. Use a lumbar cushion or pillow under your knees if needed for support or comfort (fig. 4.6).

Step Two: Place a moderately loaded duffel bag or backpack on your torso. The bag should be large enough to cover the area between your collar bones and pelvis.

Step Three: Breathe slowly and deeply for several minutes, making sure the pack rises and falls with your breathing.

Step Four: Repeat this exercise standing up with the pack on your back. Squat or bend for a minute or two as the pack rises and falls with your breathing. Breathe fully and slowly. Do not round your spine as you do this. Keep the natural curves in your spine. If this exercise is difficult you can place your hands on a table for support.

BREATHING EXERCISE 8:
Playing Instruments

To help improve posture and breathing at the same time, play a wind instrument! Don't worry if you don't have one—harmonicas are widely sold and will do nicely.

Step One: Practice playing a tune on any wind instrument.

Step Two: Now involve your stability and balance muscles as you play and stand on one leg (fig. 4.7). This is a great way to warm up for riding!

Step Three: Make sure you spend an equal amount of time standing on the other leg. Doing so will help you keep your myofascial chains in balance.

Step Four: Anyone for a dance as you play a tune?

4.7 Playing Instruments

chapter takeaway Use *whole body breathing* with a pause after your inhale, and a slightly longer pause after your exhale. This will enhance *cellular breathing*, which has a positive influence on your energy level and suppleness.

FOUR: BREATHING AS A FUEL PUMP | 41

CHAPTER FIVE

PROPRIOCEPTION AND FEEL

PROPRIOCEPTIVE PROPS

There is a portion of the neuromuscular system that enables the body to recognize where it is in space-time; we call this awareness *proprioception,* and the sensors and receptors responsible for monitoring it *proprioceptors*. Proprioception involves sensations and feedback from organs, muscles, bones, joints, fascia, ligaments, tendons, cartilage, and fluids. The proprioceptors monitor changes in position, stretching, vibration, intensity, pain level, temperature, shearing forces, compression, and even intent. The highly specialized receptors of the organs are termed *interoceptors*, and these detect even minor changes in blood oxygen level and blood pressure. Through our proprioceptors, we become aware of our movements, the space we take up, the relative positions of our body parts, and how close or far away we are from others or from external objects.

The vestibular system (located in the inner ear) aids in finding balance and adds information

5.1 Here are an array of Franklin Method Balls and other props. When used in conjunction with different exercises, these props significantly help a rider develop her sense of feel and awareness of her position. Every rider I have used these with has made great gains in her proprioception and performance. They are well worth the investment!

to the proprioceptors by deciphering where you are in relation to gravity. Visceral sensations from our organs add even more information. These systems all work together to form the perception of movements and position in space.

One of the jobs of a proprioceptor is to report this information to the central nervous system. For most of us, our proprioceptors can benefit from "waking up." Workouts for proprioceptors include a variety of props that differ in texture, density, and temperature. Props can be used either mounted or unmounted to develop a sense of feel and awareness of posture. Eric Franklin developed an extraordinary system of awakening proprioceptors through his Franklin Method® and Franklin Method Balls. There is even a dedicated set of Franklin Balls just for equestrians. As an equestrian coach, I use these extensively, and you will find them throughout this book (fig. 5.1).

The Founder of the Franklin Method®

Eric Franklin is a dancer and world-famous movement educator. He's the author of a number of books that make extensive use of imagery to improve alignment, posture, movement, body awareness, and athleticism. He developed a line of proprioceptive props that can be coupled with imagery to help enhance the sense of feel and the learning of new skills, increase confidence, relieve tension, and develop of a sense of timing. He offers a package of products specifically for equestrians. You will see his Franklin Method Balls and other props in numerous photos and in many exercises of this book. Many equestrian trainers utilize these props because they are effective at developing the rider's seat and body position. They also help a rider to recruit, stabilize, and strengthen her core.

THE ART OF FEELING

The sport of riding is a thrilling dance between *knowing* and *feeling*. You *know* riding theory from the outside in, and ideally, you *feel* your riding practice from the inside out. But the latter often falls short due to lack of tools in the rider's toolbox. Riders need specific training on how to develop a sense of feel. Developing feel is so important that I frequently tell my riders, "If I cannot help you learn how to mix your thinking with your sense of feel, I have given you nothing of lasting value. And you will always be dependent on me." My intention is to leg up my riders toward independence and not to use any one system or mode of thinking as a crutch.

Typically, what separates a mediocre rider from a highly effective one is a good sense of feel. Well, what does "having a good sense of feel" mean? It means the rider can sense subtle changes in how she supports and holds her body weight and body parts, as well as subtle shifts in her horse's postures and movements. She can answer questions such as:

- Are both seat bones weighted equally?

- Is my horse connected and listening for the next aid?

- Is my horse lifting his back in a way that fills out my seat?

- Is my horse stepping under his center of gravity?

- Does my horse show bascule (create a roundish arc) over his jumps?

- Does my horse maintain a steady rhythm?

If the answer to any of those questions is "No," the efficient rider catches it at or before it starts. Due to her keen sense of feel, she receives

Body Pulses

For a super mounted or unmounted exercise that leads to an increased sense of feel, try this: Identify a specific body part, such as your left big toe. First, using your fingertips, and then later without them, feel the pulse throbbing in that big toe. In the beginning, it helps if you gaze at the body part using focused, but soft, eyes. With practice, you will graduate into being able to do this, without touching, for any part of the body. Here is a list designed to get you started.

Practice "feeling a pulse" (first with touch, then without) in your:

- Heart area
- Right elbow
- Left kneecap
- Right pinky
- Right collarbone
- Left hip
- Left outer wrist
- Top of your head
- Tailbone

I encourage you to form your own list, and pay special attention to areas that are problematic for you (for example, unevenly weighted seat bones or tension in inner elbow crease). The more feel you have of your own body, the better you can feel your horse's movements, including his more subtle ones.

the subtle clues that things may be going amiss, and she fixes them promptly. Even the corrective aid she gives depends on her sense of feel, as she decides which aid to give, how to position it, and with what intensity.

One of the best ways to start to get in touch with your sense of feel is to become aware of how emotions manifest themselves physically. For instance, when you get a spasm in your hamstring, what emotion were you feeling just prior to the tightness? What were you feeling when the pain first hit? What did you feel in the aftermath? As another example, suppose you do a lousy turn-on-the-forehand. No matter the level of training or capability of your horse, identify *your* tense and unhappy body parts before, during, and after the maneuver. Did you start the turn in a worried state of mind? If so, perhaps you were worried about doing a lousy turn-on-the-forehand! Try to identify where your body tends to store your stress. Don't think, but feel, the areas of your body that are somehow affected by the stuffing of emotions in your favorite stress-storage-muscle. These areas can be quite distant from each other—and your horse feels it all! In chapter 12, "Letting Tension Go" (see p. 119), I make suggestions as to how to release emotional tension stored in muscles prior to your ride.

DEVELOPING PROPRIOCEPTION AND FEEL EXERCISE 1:
Photo Imagery

The Photo Imagery Exercise will awaken your ability to imagine and feel. You can then transfer this skill to the saddle to improve your riding.

Step One: Look at any photo. It could be one from this book, or another of your choice. However, do not select one of you and your horse (yet).

Step Two: Imagine you are someone in the photo.

Step Three: Verbalize where in your body you feel a change in sensation such as warmth, tension, or tingling. Imagine the part of the body that feels the change is "lighting up."

Step Four: What is the emotion associated with the part of the body that lights up in Step Three? Figuring this out will help tie your emotions to your body sensations.

DEVELOPING PROPRIOCEPTION AND FEEL EXERCISE 2:
Eyes Shut Touching

The Eyes Shut Touching Exercise will sharpen your sense of how far away you are from physical objects. In the saddle, it will help by giving you better-defined aids and improved coordination.

Step One: Place an object such as a small bean bag or grooming glove on a chair or bench.

Step Two: While looking at the object, touch or tap the part of your body you are trying to wake up. For example, tap your left seat bone.

Step Three: Now turn your back to the seat, and attempt to lower until you touch your left seat bone to the object. No peeking!

Step Four: If you miss, prop yourself up so your left seat bone is directly sitting on the object. Stand and repeat Step Three around five times.

Step Five: Practice this exercise using a variety of textured and smooth props of varying sizes, colors, and shapes. This will improve your coordination in the saddle.

DEVELOPING PROPRIOCEPTION AND FEEL EXERCISE 3:
Hot Water Bottle Balancing

Here is a chance to feel some of what your horse experiences when he attempts to balance under your shifting weight.

Step One: Place a partially filled (1/2 to 2/3) hot water bottle on your head, using an ear-to-ear placement (fig. 5.2). (Make sure it is well sealed!)

5.2 Hot Water Bottle Balancing

Step Two: Balance under the water bottle without touching it. Try this at first standing still, then at the walk.

Step Three: Now try walking backward, sideways, or over uneven ground while balancing under the shifting object. Try a "jump" if you are ambitious!

Step Four: Repeat this exercise using a front-back or diagonal orientation of the hot water bottle. You will probably find a horse's job is not easy!

DEVELOPING PROPRIOCEPTION AND FEEL EXERCISE 4:
Feel Your Seat Bones

Here is an exercise you can do mounted to wake up the proprioceptors in your seat bones.

Step One: Once mounted, put a Franklin Ball or other suitable prop under each seat bone (fig. 5.3).

Step Two: Close your eyes and notice any sensations.

Step Three: Discover any emotions that are tied into your sensations.

Step Four: Remove the prop from your right seat bone, leaving you sitting with your weight unevenly distributed.

5.3 Feel Your Seat Bones

Step Five: Repeat Step Four on the other seat bone.

Step Six: Remove the props. With eyes closed, check for any differences in the feel of your seat bones, right versus left.

Step Seven: Repeat Step Six with your eyes open.

DEVELOPING PROPRIOCEPTION AND FEEL EXERCISE 5:

Mounted Hand Proprioception

Here's an exercise that will help you get in touch with your hands and fingers. The Mounted Hand Proprioception exercise can be done in either your mounted or unmounted warm-up time. It will improve your ability to sense and receive your horse's energy through the reins.

Step One: Position a spiky Franklin Ball or other suitable prop between your hands, while still holding the reins (fig. 5.4). Alternatively, have a friend hold your horse so you can concentrate.

Step Two: Roll the ball slowly in all directions. Imagine you are softly squeezing out liquid tension from your hands and fingers.

Step Three: Focus on deep, rhythmic, whole-body breathing.

Step Four: Take the ball in one hand and tap all parts of your other hand, including your fingers, with it.

Step Five: Repeat with the opposite hand.

Step Six: Remove the prop and shake your hands out vigorously. Then stop the shaking and sigh: *Ahhhh*! Your horse will benefit from the soft feel now established in your hands.

5.4 Mounted Hand Proprioception

DEVELOPING PROPRIOCEPTION
AND FEEL EXERCISE 6:

Distance Proprioception

This is a great way to warm up before practicing Exercise 7, which focuses on ring geometry (see p. 50). To practice Distance Proprioception, you will need two thin objects to stand on, such as two pieces of cardboard.

Step One: Place a thin object, such as a rubber disk, on the ground and stand on it. Place another thin object about 10 steps away.

Step Two: Stand on one of the objects and put on a blindfold.

Step Three: Use your best guess and your senses to take 10 steps toward the other object. Did you land on it?

Step Four: If you did not land on the other object, pace it out with your eyes open, then try again.

Step Five: If you landed on the second object, pace out a longer distance, and then try the increased challenge!

5.5 Distance Proprioception

FIVE: PROPRIOCEPTION AND FEEL | 49

5.6 Ring Geometry Proprioception

DEVELOPING PROPRIOCEPTION AND FEEL EXERCISE 7:

Ring Geometry Proprioception

For this exercise, an eyepatch can be worn in various ways, such as: covering the right eye (to increase your sense of feel); covering the left eye (to sharpen your step-by-step thinking); or between the eyes (to enhance your peripheral vision and ability to use imagery for improved ring geometry). You should also have a blindfold or second eye patch handy in case you want to challenge yourself. For accuracy, it may be helpful to "draw" the points or figures you are trying to highlight into the ring surface before beginning this exercise. Use your heel or the edge of your boot. Cover it back up when you are done visualizing where you plan to travel. The Ring Geometry Proprioception exercise will help you sense exactly where you are in the ring and improve your ability to make more accurate figures while mounted.

Step One: Position yourself in the area of the ring you would like to know and feel better, such as along a wall, a turn, or the centerline (fig. 5.6).

Step Two: Cover your right eye with a patch. When this exercise becomes easy, you can progress to the other eye patch options listed at the beginning of this exercise.

Step Three: Now walk a course of imaginary jumps, go down the centerline of the arena, or walk the entire boundaries of the ring—whatever it is you wish to get to know better and improve in.

Step Four: Every so often, kick the sides of the arena (or a jump standard) to get in physical touch with the ring's parameters. This is an important step as it will boost your ability to sense exactly where you are in the ring at all times.

DEVELOPING PROPRIOCEPTION AND FEEL EXERCISE 8:
Flag Walk

5.7 Flag Walk

For this exercise, wear an eye patch between the eyes, just over the nose. This eliminates your central vision, leaving you to rely on only your peripheral vision. I love this exercise because of the way it awakens your sense of feel. Use imagery to envision yourself completing the maze with coordination and grace!

Step One: Set up a maze using tiny flags or other suitable markers.

Step Two: Put an eye patch between your eyes so that it cuts out your central vision. You should only be able to use your side (peripheral) vision now.

Step Three: As you walk through the maze, notice your body's tendency to drift one way or to change speed (fig. 5.7). What emotions and body sensations are associated with these irregularities? Did your breathing change? If you repeat the exercise, notice which sensations are unchanged and which are new. Do not try to alter the sensations. Honor whatever feelings come up.

Step Four: Now try the maze again, walking sideways or even backward! Notice how your sensations may change as you switch directions.

---

chapter takeaway

You can improve your riding by developing your proprioception and sense of feel. This can be done, mounted or unmounted, using a variety of props. These props will help you take your knowledge of riding theory and integrate it into your riding practice.

PART
1

CHAPTER SIX

Vision and Visualizing

A RIDER'S VISION

Your vision and focus of attention are closely related. Both are vibrant and constantly changing in response to internal and external cues. Closing your eyes fosters increased sensitivity in discerning your emotions and other senses. For instance, you can detect vibrations more keenly, and thus your hearing feels sharper. A simple test to highlight how closely your vision and balance are related is to try standing on one leg with your eyes closed!

Your brain receives signals from each of your eyes simultaneously, but fuses what the right eye sees with what the left eye sees (fig. 6.1). Your right eye has a different way of framing the environment than your left eye does. The left eye sends its view of the world to the right side of your brain (which prefers to look at the whole picture). Your right eye sends its information to the left side of your brain (which prefers step-by-step details). And even though the left and right sides work together, they are not always

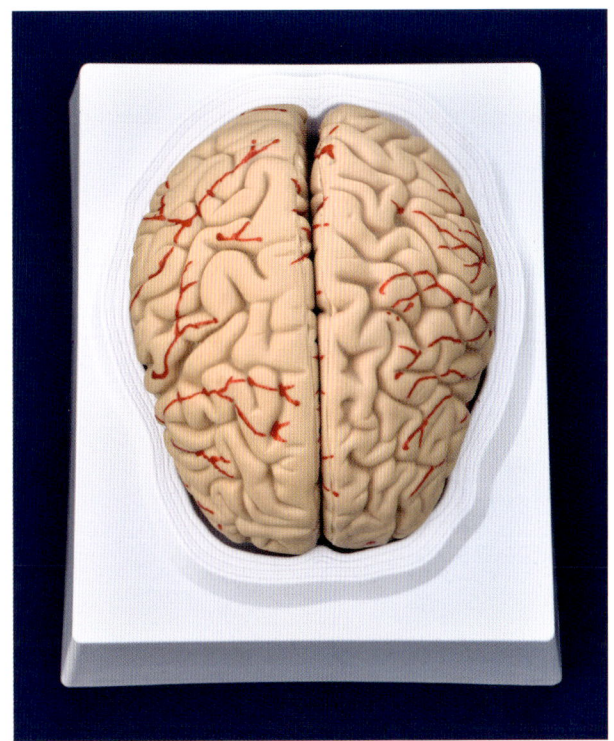

6.1 Notice the middle strip along the center line of the model brain in this photo. This is called the *corpus callosum*. When information is shared between hemispheres of the brain, it has to cross over this section. This crossing-over pattern enables you to see the "whole picture" with all of the details. This crossover is enhanced by physical exercises that cross the mid-line of your body. Several sample exercises can be found beginning on p. 58.

harmonious about it and compete for control! The side that wins out becomes the dominant side of your brain. This is why we tend to be labeled as either *logical* (left-brained) or *gestalt* (right-brained) in our thinking.

We are posturally drawn to where we look. The muscles in your body prepare themselves so they are ready to move where the eyes are looking. When you hold your head properly over your spine, your head and neck are making small changes to help your eyes face in the best direction for your vision and your balance.

Weightlifters often look to the ceiling when they lift, which encourages an extension of the spine. Desk jockeys frequently stare ahead at their computers with their heads following suit by drifting forward into a slump. Most riders I serve start out with a downward cast to their eyes. The rider who looks down at her horse, or even the ground, is inviting her posture to take a literal nosedive. Try looking out to the horizon while using your peripheral vision to support your central vision. It will boost your balance, position, and performance. When I help students bring their riding position into correct alignment, most riders are quite surprised that they need to cast their eyes upward in order to look straight ahead.

Pony Tail Vision

The occipital area of your brain, located at the back and bottom part of your head, is associated with vision. The occipital muscles can be portrayed as a ponytail (fig. 6.2). This "ponytail" of muscles often gets tight from stress or overwork. It helps to imagine loosening the clasp of the ponytail by frequently massaging this area as you look with your eyes up/down, left/right, and in a clockwise circle/counter-clockwise circle. As you massage this area, keep switching your gaze rapidly from a near object to a faraway object. For those who work on a computer, this is quite beneficial as a nice screen break!

6.2 Pony Tail Vision

It's important to develop your ability to use central vision and peripheral vision independently, as well as operating together. You will have a chance to practice this skill later in this chapter. I call your central vision your "sharp eye" and your peripheral vision your "soft eye." When intense focus is needed, such as gazing ahead to a challenging jump or polo goal, it's important to recruit your sharp eye, to maintain a narrow focus. But most of the time, it is wise to use your peripheral vision to support your central vision. Doing so widens your field of vision, and encourages supple joints and fluidity. When your peripheral vision supports your central vision, you will have a more comprehensive sensory picture, enabling you to have a better sense of feel. Most riders come to me utilizing mainly their sharp eyes, without a supporting use of their soft eyes. To correct this, I give these riders lots of homework focused on getting in touch with their peripheral vision.

Using the gaze of your eyes puts your body in the strongest position to ask for and then make a smooth, balanced turn. Note that I did not advise you to turn your entire head! This is because your spine extends up into your neck; if you turn your whole head, it disrupts the stability of your spine by pulling it out of neutral position. Plus, turning your whole head recruits mainly your sharp eyes, whereas maximal use of the eyes recruits your soft eyes to support your central vision. For a safer and more stable turning position, use the eyes maximally, and only turn the whole head when it is truly needed.

EXPLORING IMAGERY

Imagery is a powerful form of visualizing. Imagery differs from "simple visualization" in that it has the added dimension of identifying emotions and sensations associated with that which is visualized. Imagery utilizes all the senses and prompts a deep, visceral reaction. It encourages both psychological and physiological responses. Here is a sample list of some possible sensations, awarenesses, and other perceptions you may experience when you gaze at or picture an image:

- Body parts may feel tingly, compressed, warm, numb, relaxed, or even stressed.

- Emotions may shift; for example, you may feel more or less confident, anxious, determined, mellow, or joyful.

- You may automatically initiate an action, such as closing your eyes, holding your head, wringing your hands, changing your position, clearing your throat, or yawning.

- Your state of consciousness may be affected; you may feel more or less alert, fatigued, meditative, mindful, or distracted, for a few examples.

Music boosts the power of imagery. I believe equestrians and their horses would benefit if they rode to music or sang when they rode. Another way to enhance imagery is giving it the background scene of your choice, such as a waterfall or tropical island. Add pleasant aromas and sounds, such as the smell of lilacs or the trill of a songbird. All these pieces help your body and mind connect and work as a team.

Our brains light up more extensively while practicing imagery than when we simply watch a video or observe a rider in a clinic. Therefore, I advise you to use imagery as you observe others. Imagine it is you who is riding and tap into the sensations the image pulls up. Athletes can boost their performance by imagining a scene where they are successful, and couple that with sights, sounds, smells, and feelings of pride and exuberance. There is a visceral component to successful imagery, where you feel your guts cheer, dance, and shout out with your amazing success!

The areas of your brain that are activated during *imagined* movements are similar to the brain areas activated by *actual* movements. In this way, movement and posture are well supported by using imagery. Consider that a young child might think, "I ride, I sing, I dance," as they move about. But an adult is more apt to think, "I toe out, I slouch, I am crooked." In this example, the child is more focused on the whole, and the adult on the parts. To restore better movement and posture, riders typically throw themselves into what they think of as an "ideal" position. This is not imagery, and does not produce a well-aligned, supple rider! Instead, this forces the body into a stiff, artificial pose. By using imagery instead, the rider invites the body into a supple, natural posture, with fluid movements. It puts you in touch with your body-mind connection and opens the doors to your sense of feel.

VISION AND VISUALIZING

The exercises of this section are quite helpful in assisting riders with their efforts to look ahead instead of down. Looking down at your horse causes small adjustments in your body weight that in turn puts more emphasis on weighting your horse's forehand. Additionally, looking down at the ground tends to catapult you to the spot of your gaze.

Several of the following exercises involve crossing over the mid-line of the body, which, as I've already mentioned, influences the left

6.3 Taffy Eyes

A Tip for Forward Gaze: Taffy Eyes

I developed Taffy Eyes as an image to use with clients who could benefit from looking up to the horizon. Try to imagine that your eyeballs are attached to their sockets with taffy that can stretch far away (fig. 6.3). Imagine placing both your eyeballs on the horizon; it will feel as if you are riding to the horizon as though magically drawn there!

To enhance this imagery, ask yourself the following questions:

- Where do I feel tight when I look at this image?
- Where do I feel relaxed in my body?
- Did my breathing rhythm or depth change?
- Is my posture different? Am I more folded, side-bent, or vertical?
- Did I make any spontaneous movements?
- Did my level of focus or anxiety change?
- Did this image sharpen or dull my senses?

and right hemisphere connectivity of your brain. Improving this connectivity enhances your riding because it links your logical, thinking brain area to your creative, feeling brain area. This will help you sprinkle the theory of good riding into your physical riding practice—and that will boost your performance.

VISION EXERCISE 1:
Eye Crossovers

The Eye Crossovers exercise connects your feelings and other senses to your vision.

Step One: As you walk (mounted or unmounted), shift your gaze to the right for a few seconds, then to the left, also for a few seconds. Do not turn your whole head.

Step Two: Now halt or stand still. Begin to make full, slow eye circles—once clockwise, once counterclockwise. As you do this, imagine you are in a peaceful setting. Include all the sounds, sights, smells, emotions, and tastes of this peaceful place.

Step Three: Walk again, and repeat the eye movements of Step One. Notice your sensations and any changes that took place.

VISION EXERCISE 2:
Palming the Eyes

The Palming the Eyes exercise will bring warmth and attention to your eyes. This is a good exercise to do after spending time looking at your phone. It's restful and restorative.

Step One: Shake your hands out and release old energy. Pretend your hands are wet and flick the water away.

Step Two: Now rub the palms together briskly until warmth is generated.

Step Three: Cup your warm palms over your eyes. Don't press on your eyeballs. Be gentle! Hold for one minute.

Step Four: On an exhale, sigh deeply. *Ahhhh….* Relax your arms.

VISION EXERCISE 3:
Shifting Eyes Balance Poses

When you are trying to balance in a pose, your vision adds substantially to your sense of balance. To check this out and to develop your stability, try the Shifting Eyes Balance Poses. This exercise will help you keep your balance in the saddle.

Step One: For safety, position yourself near the corner of a wall, and get ready to catch yourself as needed. Assume a "balance pose," such as an in-line stance with one foot directly in front of the other (heel to toe), or simply stand on one foot.

Step Two: Cross your arms or place your hands on your hips.

Step Three: Begin to move your eyes around in all directions at varying speeds.

Step Four: Move your head from side to side as well as up and down. Your head is the primary mover here. Allow your eyes to shift without controlling them.

Step Five: Keep your head still, close your eyes, and continue the balance pose. Use imagery to root yourself and stabilize.

Step Six: Repeat this exercise with the other foot leading.

VISION EXERCISE 4:
Near-to-Far Focus Flutters

A beneficial exercise for your vision is to change your focus from near to far and back again. Your eyes get tired of being locked into one position. That is one reason why it's a good idea to take breaks from close-up work such as sewing or computer time. Practice using both sharp and soft vision for each position you are focused on. This exercise will improve your ability to use different aspects of your vision when you ride.

Step One: Position yourself where you have a long-range view of something in the distance.

Step Two: Stand or sit, and place the index finger of your dominant hand about 18 to 24 inches in front of you.

Step Three: Using both eyes at first, repeatedly shift the focus of your eyes from the point of your finger to the spot you selected in the distance. Vary the speed of eye movements from slow to fast. Repeat with one eye closed, then switch.

Step Four: Next, move your finger up and down as your vision continues to shift from near to far.

Do not move your head for this step—only move your hand. (To increase the challenge, you can also do this step using only one eye and an eye patch on the other eye.)

Step Five: Now keep your hand with the pointed finger still. Move your head from left to right, and also from up to down, as you repeatedly shift your gaze from your fingertip to the distant point. Close one eye and repeat, then switch.

Step Six: Repeat all the steps of this exercise using the index finger of your non-dominant hand.

VISION EXERCISE 5:
Bouncy Ball Glow

The Bouncy Ball Glow exercise is a fun way to link your coordination with your vision. You will need a glow-in-the-dark, high-bounce ball and an eye patch; find an area with a hard floor and dim light. As you practice this exercise, expect your reaction time to improve and your reflexes to sharpen. I love giving this exercise to my clients who are working on tempi changes because it improves coordination of their aids, boosting their horse's performance!

Step One: Put an eye patch over your right eye. Start to toss the ball from left hand to right hand and back again. Do this for a minute.

Step Two: Next, bounce the ball on the ground, alternating hands. If you start by holding it in your right hand, catch it with your left hand, and vice versa.

Step Three: Move the eye patch to cover the left eye and repeat all the steps explained above.

Step Four: Finally, move the eye patch to position it between your eyes (above your nose). Repeat the exercise. This time, you will need to rely on your peripheral vision. Practicing this step is a great way to develop soft eyes!

VISION EXERCISE 6:
Sharp Eyes

The Sharp Eyes exercise will help you to develop your central vision for the times you need extra focus. Note that in general, sharp eyes are *not* good to use while riding because they tend to put the body into a tense, harsh mode. But you may need sharp eyes periodically when approaching a challenging jump, or to get a better look at something questionable on the trail, for a few examples. To do the Sharp Eyes mounted exercise,

6.4 Sharp Eyes

you will need two strips of black construction paper, approximately 6 inches long and 2 inches wide, and first aid tape. Ride in a safe, enclosed area such as a dressage ring or indoor arena. Do not ride in the company of other horses when you do this exercise—your focus will be too narrow to stay safely out of their way.

Step One: Before mounting, place two strips of black paper on either side of your nose, such that you are limited in your visual focus to only that which is directly in front of you. Secure the black paper with first aid tape on your forehead and under your chin.

Step Two: On the horse, select a point within moderate distance to focus on. Later, you can choose other distances (fig. 6.4). As you ride, imagine a big jump or wide ditch in front of you that you want to take a better look at. Notice the parts of your body that feel tense as you do this. Identify any emotions or sensations accompanying this.

Step Three: Follow up this exercise by doing Vision Exercise 7: Soft Eyes, which will reunite your central and peripheral vision so you are balanced and safe. *Do not* stay in sharp-eye mode.

VISION EXERCISE 7:
Soft Eyes

I love what this exercise brings to a rider's ability to feel and follow her horse, as well as give clear aids and influence him effectively. For this exercise, you will need one strip of black construction

6.5 Soft Eyes

paper (about 2 inches by 6 inches) and some first aid tape. As with the Sharp Eyes exercise, stay in an enclosed arena without any other horses. Get ready to "wake up" your peripheral vision!

Step One: Prior to mounting, place one strip of black paper over your nose, taping it to your forehead and under your chin. You should still be able to see on both sides, but that which is directly in front of you is blocked out.

Step Two: In the saddle, notice your sensations and emotions (fig. 6.5).

Step Three: Use imagery to enhance your feel of connection to your horse. For instance, you can imagine you are a cloud softly blowing in the breeze, or perhaps you are riding on the beach.

Step Four: Make a note of what this exercise felt like, and what it brought to your riding. This is a great exercise to do when you feel stuck in progress on a movement or in a level with your horse. It tends to soften the "stuck" emotions and enables you to "let them go."

> **chapter takeaway**
>
> **Our bodies are drawn in posture according to the gaze of our eyes. When you hold your head over your spine, your head and neck are making small changes that help your eyes face in the best direction for your vision and balance. It behooves a rider to look forward toward a horizon.**

CHAPTER SEVEN

MOVEMENT PATTERNS AND MOBILITY

MOVEMENT EXPLORED

Movement—and the accompanying awareness of sensations generated by it—link the body and the mind. For best athletic function, it is wise to incorporate a wide variety of types of movement throughout your day. We are born to learn to crawl, walk, run, climb, jump, push, pull, swim, bend, lift, carry, catch, throw, kick, skip, balance, shuffle, twist, swing, hop, lunge, squat, roll, stretch, row, dance—and of course, ride! Motion is created and controlled by muscles deep in the lumbar and pelvic areas. These muscles are either directly attached, or strongly linked, to our head, arms, and legs. Our breathing promotes coordinated use of our movement muscles.

Functionally, the lower body specializes in weight balancing, locomotion, and keeping our center of gravity in a vertical line over our base of support. These are actions that enable a person to move out into their environment. The upper body specializes in reaching, grasping, and breathing. These are actions that bring the external environment to the person.

Consider mounting a horse. Both the upper and lower bodies become involved and work together to get you safely astride. Connecting and coordinating upper and lower body movements through specific full body exercises that challenge stability will give riders a sound foundation for their sport. This book emphasizes many exercises of that nature.

If you want a reminder of how to walk or move properly, watch a young child who is not yet of school age bend, pick things up, throw, move around objects, reach, and grasp. In general, toddlers have amazing gluteal muscles simply due to their daily movements. They don't need specific exercises to activate or develop their glutes—it's inherent and natural.

Once children start school and are required to sit a lot, their movement patterns alter and they begin to lose their correctness and quality. Modern lifestyles have distanced older children and adults from the way we were designed to move. But trying to recreate early childhood movement patterns often unlocks adult-level tension and pain.

One of my favorite exercises is crawling forward and backward. It releases "all the steam from my internal tea kettle" in a way that regular working out or stretching doesn't touch. If you watch young children crawl, you will notice they use a different speed and style based upon their energy level, mood, and intent. At times, they seem to spring forward as they push backward with each leg, using power and zest. Other times, the crawl may resemble more of a saunter or even a swagger, appearing as an outer expression of their inner mood, thoughts, and energy level.

When you bring your inner self into your movements this way, you avoid "stuffing" your feelings. Your body releases pent up energy and allows it to flow through you and out. This is a gift to our horses, because they both exude and receive energy so intricately and sensitively. Our pent up, "stuck" energy is terribly tough on them. So before you walk to a paddock to catch your horse, breathe out negative energy and "flick it out" as you shake your fingertips. Perhaps focus on the people, animals, and things you love and that bring you joy. Releasing negative energy will help you present yourself to your horse as a respected partner and a treasured friend.

NEUROMUSCULAR FUNCTIONING

The quality of your movements is largely dependent upon your neuromuscular coordination, which is how well your nervous system communicates with and controls your muscles as they either move or hold a position. It is the nervous system that creates our reaction time and the quality of our coordination, and this is why *neuromuscular retraining* is an integral part of my approach for riders. Notice that neuromuscular retraining is part of my Equestrian Training Pyramid (found in the Appendix of this book, see p. 263).

Neuromuscular retraining connects your brain to your movements, and teaches the muscles how and when to engage, as well as when to relax and lengthen. Coordination can be improved by practicing correct movement patterns in a slow, controlled fashion. The movements should be done both forward and backward in order for neuromuscular changes and movement patterns to become permanent. It is the super-slow movements characteristic of this technique that our brains pay attention to! I am most fond of the methods used by Moshe Feldenkrais, Thomas Hanna, and Sarah Warren. Check the Bibliography and Recommended Reading section (see p. 265) for sources of information on their methods.

FLUIDITY OF MOVEMENT

Exercise is not just about increasing your heart rate or building your muscles. Every time you move, you are circulating body fluids, including blood, which delivers oxygen and nutrients to your tissues. With the assistance of the lymph system, blood also captures and expels cellular waste. Varied movements power this system best.

Expressing your body's underlying fluidity through your movements is as much an art as a science. But how are fluidity and graceful movements achieved? There are many ways, but one option is to take Tai Chi classes. Tai Chi gives you a good sense of how to move fluidly from your center. Another option is to use proprioceptive props coupled with imagery (see chapter 26, p. 243). This is a combination that lures you into graceful movement as you express your creative self. For example, here are a few ways imagery can help you improve the quality of your own walk (*not* on horseback!):

- Put your thumbs on your side-pocket area. Imagine smooth, glare ice under your feet, and glide through your walk as if you were ice skating. Feel the glutes that are under your hands light up!

- As you walk, imagine your legs are swinging freely in your well-oiled hip sockets to the beat of a metronome.

- Walk as though you are in chest-high warm water, with gentle water jets circulating. Embrace your fluidity!

MOBILITY

Mobility is a measure of how well you move. Do you move with control, balance, strength, agility, and grace through aligned positions? Or are your movements choppy, weak, stilted, or stiff? Do you experience strain and discomfort during movement? Mobility takes that into consideration as well. *Mobility* is *not* the same as *flexibility*, which is the capacity to move through a maximum range of motion. In the case of flexibility, it's the *quantity* of movement that is considered. A rider should pay some attention to her flexibility, but she will benefit even more if she focuses on her mobility.

Another way to look at it is that *optimal mobility balances flexibility with stability*. Why is that so? Well, if a joint can move through a wide range of motion but doesn't know when to stabilize or stop moving, an injury is likely to occur. This is a *hypermobile* situation. You can have hypermobility in just one joint, or it can be widespread over your entire body. Stretching can be risky or even dangerous if you have hypermobility. A hypermobile joint has muscles that know when to move but don't know when to guard or hold. This is part of joint proprioception. Luckily, most of us can improve our joint proprioception through exercise that incorporates unilateral (one-sided) movements and/or unstable surfaces. Numerous options for such exercises are presented in this book.

What follows are a few things you can do to help improve your mobility and the quality of your movement patterns. Take note that these exercises emphasize movements in all directions: front/back, left/right, up/down, rotate/side bend.

MOBILITY EXERCISE 1:
Target Practice

This exercise uses specific parts of your body to touch a "target" in all directions at all speeds. It has a beneficial effect on your mobility and coordination.

Step One: Put a piece of painter's tape on a wall.

Step Two: Choose a body part to touch to the "target" on the wall. Some examples that are good for equestrians might be: right seat bone, left shoulder blade, ball of the right foot, left tricep (back of the arm). It's like playing Twister but on the wall, and you use only one body part at a time. So, if you are trying to get in touch with your shoulder blades, try to touch your shoulder blades (one at a time) to the tape on the wall. Do not stare at the tape while doing so—glance at it, turn around, and attempt to tap one scapula to that spot on the wall.

Step Three: When the above version of "Equestrian Twister" is going well, try it again with your eyes closed, or put on a blindfold. Make sure you have selected a safe area.

MOBILITY EXERCISE 2:
Standard Hip Hinge

Hip Hinge is a critical exercise for mobility training because this movement pattern is needed and used multiple times a day. When it is not done correctly, it can cause injury. This exercise is worth spending time on to get the recommended form cemented into your neuromuscular system. Before you start this exercise, tap the back and sides of your pelvis with your fingers.

Step One: To make the hip hinge or "bowing" movement, start with feet hip-width apart. Fold at the leg creases (where the legs join with the torso), keeping your knees softly bent (fig. 7.1).

Step Two: Support the fold with your lateral lines by tensioning (not moving) the knees and thighs in an outward direction. This is an *isometric activation*.

Step Three: When more support is needed, add a second line of tension by aiming (but not moving) the inner calves and feet as if they were going to slide together, while continuing to hold the outward tension of Step Two. You should feel your inner calves and thighs pulling softly in an upward direction toward your torso.

Step Four: Be sure to keep your back aligned in a neutral position, keeping its natural curves. Do not deliberately round or arch your back. Keep your pelvis neutral; do not tuck or tilt it. I suggest getting a friend to observe you to make sure your back and pelvis are straight.

Step Five: "Anchor" the lower ribs by tucking them back toward the spine (see p. 140).

Step Six: Your hips should stay square to the front. Check to make sure they have not shifted to one side.

Step Seven: Repeat this exercise slowly several times , focusing on the glutes powering the move.

MOBILITY EXERCISE 2:
Single Leg Hip Hinge

The Single Leg Hip Hinge exercise builds strength, stability, and mobility. You will need a light object, such as a curry comb, small ball, or spray bottle, to lift up and down.

7.1 Standard Hip Hinge

7.2 Single Leg Hip Hinge

Step One: Start with feet about hip width apart and place your object on the ground in front of you (fig. 7.2).

Step Two: Transfer your weight primarily onto one leg and "root down" until you feel stable.

Step Three: With all your weight supported by the chosen stance leg, fold at the leg crease as you did for the Standard Hip Hinge (see p. 67).

Step Four: While keeping your hips even in height, extend the non-stance leg behind you as you fold forward. Extend the leg as much as you can comfortably do so. (You may not be able to reach as far with the leg as shown in the photo — that's fine!)

Step Five: Lift through the back of your neck, keeping your head and neck well-aligned with your spine. Don't allow the head to fall forward.

Step Six: Check to make sure you have not locked the stance knee. Keep a soft bend in it.

Step Seven: Grasp the object and come back to a vertical stance, keeping your weight fully supported by your chosen stance leg. Once your upper body is tall, lower the raised leg to the ground.

Step Eight: Repeat this exercise on the original side about five times. Switch sides and repeat.

MOBILITY EXERCISE 3:
Nose Plant Squats

I love this exercise as a way to teach proper squat form. Many people recruit their quads and hamstrings for squatting but neglect to engage their glutes. This exercise fixes that tendency!

You will need a thin strip of foam for this exercise to protect your nose. Place the foam along the length of your nose for protection.

Step One: Face a wall and place your toes 3 to 12 inches away from it (fig. 7.3). Position your hips, kneecaps, and toes to face forward, unless that elicits pain, in which case you should adjust to a position that is comfortable.

Step Two: Bend your knees and draw your hips back behind you, leading with your tailbone. Sink down toward the ground in a squat.

Step Three: Your face should stay parallel to the wall for this entire exercise. Protect your nose by pressing it against the wall through the thin piece of foam. No chins poking forward here!

Step Four: Engage the gluteal muscles at the back of your pelvis and also at the multifidus muscles at the back of your waist. Visualize these muscles pulling your sides toward your spine, hugging your spine to stabilize it.

Step Five: Keep your body weight over your heels. When you have lowered into a squat as much as you can while still keeping your nose pressed to the foam, push through your heels to stand back up.

Step Six: Perform this exercise slowly, and repeat to fatigue.

7.3 Nose Plant Squats

MOBILITY EXERCISE 4:
Bow to Squat

Bow to Squat is a super way to train the lower body with a correct movement pattern and mobilize the hips. It will encourage a balanced partnership between your glutes, hamstrings, and hip flexors. These muscles help riders stabilize their seat and maintain a correct leg position in the saddle.

Step One: Stand with feet hip width apart and the knees softly bent (fig. 7.4 A).

Step Two: Slide your buttocks backward as you maintain a neutral spine. Drop your arms toward the ground as you hinge from the hips into a bow.

Step Three: Keep the head and neck in line with your spine. Don't look up!

Step Four: Pause at the end of your range of motion. When you reach your end range of motion, your body will naturally come to a stop.

Step Five: Weight your heels as you sink your buttocks downward into a squat. Do not deliberately press your knees together. Pause again in this squat position (fig. 7.4 B).

7.4 A & B Bow to Squat

Step Six: Push through the heels and come back to standing. As you do this, engage the muscles at the sides of your hips by tensioning (not moving) them in an outward direction. This will give you some strength and stability, and will also help protect your back.

Step Seven: Repeat the bow-to-squat pattern at different speeds. Always pause for a few seconds in both the bow and the squat phases.

MOBILITY EXERCISE 5:
Football Shoulder Drops

Football Shoulder Drops are a favorite among my clients! They teach you to first, free up your thorax (upper torso) and second, to properly move it, whether mounted or on the ground. While doing Football Shoulder Drops, your lower back provides stability, and your upper back receives and transfers the physical forces acting upon you. Practicing this exercise helps keep your back healthy, and it will facilitate your ability to move with your horse. It is helpful to tap your fingers along your collar bones a few times before starting this exercise.

Step One: Step your feet slightly wider than hip-width apart.

7.5 Football Shoulder Drops

Step Two: Bend or fold at the waist and rest your elbows just above your knees.

Step Three: Drop your right shoulder and the right side of your rib cage toward the ground. Keep your knees in place without sliding them around.

Step Four: Lift the right shoulder and right side of the rib cage back to the starting position.

Step Five: Repeat steps three and four for the left shoulder and rib cage.

Step Six: Alternate between dropping the right and left sides for about a minute.

Step Seven: Now, stand with feet shoulder-width apart. Put your hands on your upper ribs just below the collar bones. Slowly turn your head left and right. Feel how your thorax is performing very subtle football shoulder-drop movements (as described in steps three and four). This is the same degree of movement you want in your thorax while riding. The movement is subtle!

Step Eight: Try walking (unmounted) while allowing this free, alternating action of the upper rib cage as in Step Seven. Notice that when your right leg glides forward, the left side of the thorax glides forward. The left arm should not swing deliberately, nor should the left hand initiate the movement. Instead, simply allow the thorax to move; the left arm is passive and goes "along for the ride." The action you feel is generated by the thorax.

chapter takeaway ✓

The quality of your movements, both in and out of the saddle, is largely dependent upon neuromuscular coordination. Coordination can be improved by practicing correct movement patterns in a slow, controlled fashion.

The ways in which you move and position your body all day long mold and sculpt it as if it were a piece of clay. Exercise is helpful and supportive of your health, but the concept of movement is far more encompassing than just exercise. Make a fist and imagine it is the sum total of all your movements throughout 24 hours; time-wise, your daily exercise session may well represent only the tip of one pinky, whereas movement does not need a dedicated time slot. Shake! Wiggle! Squirm!

CHAPTER EIGHT
POSTURAL PATTERNS AND SELF-CARRIAGE

CHARACTERISTICS OF GOOD POSTURE

Our posture presents who we are to the world. If your chin juts forward and your chest puffs out, you may well give the impression of being overconfident. However, if your head is lowered and your chest sinks, you would likely present as someone "down in the dumps." Consider also the person who stands with her bones well-aligned, as described in chapter 1 (see p. 7). She is likely to be interpreted as someone who is centered and calm, but ready for action. This type of posture is ideal for a rider.

Our postural tone is a reflection of our state of readiness. It represents the background tension of a muscle before its full contraction. This underlying tone varies from person to person such that there is a continuum of tone from limp to rigid. We will explore this concept further later in this chapter.

Well-aligned posture promotes deep, healthy breathing patterns, which are nourishing to your organs and body tissues. Further, well-aligned posture supports good physical health and mental clarity, as well as your ability to balance and stabilize. Good posture is characteristic of a lengthened, neutral spine, which allows your nerves to send messages more freely between your body and brain. When you maintain good posture with a lengthened, neutral spine, your internal organs have optimal space, and are not compressed. Your body feels free to move in any direction, at any time.

On the other hand, poor posture often results in injury, compromised breathing, and fatigue. It contributes to poor movement patterns, which in turn give rise to aches and pains. The person who slumps, side bends, or pushes her hips forward cannot breathe well. She typically breathes in a shallow manner, or too fast or too slowly. She frequently skips the pauses at the end of each inhale and exhale. She is also apt to become winded when she rides, particularly at

PART 1

> *"The mind is like the wind, and the body is like the sand; if you want to know how the wind is blowing, you can look at the sand."*
>
> –Bonnie Bainbridge Cohen, *Exploring Body-Mind Centering* (North Atlantic Books, 2011)

faster speeds. Her internal organs are crowded and compressed, with compromised functioning. These conditions create a body that would rather rest than move.

Let's take a closer look at good versus bad posture.

Let's consider someone with muscle tone that is too loose (fig. 8.1 A). She appears ready only for a recliner and maybe an iced tea! She is slumped in a way that crunches her organs and collapses her core. Because her spine is curved forward, it makes it hard for messages to get through to her brain. I hope a rider with this posture is not about to get on a horse!

In contrast, some people look like they were just told to "stand up straight!" and as a result, over-correct (fig. 8.1 B). This rider is now locked into spinal extension (including hyperextension

8.1 A–C Slumped (A), hyperextended (B), and well-aligned posture (C).

of the lower back). This is a forced, overly tense position, but many riders fall into this over-corrected pattern. They think their spine is lengthened in this extended position, but it is actually shortened!

The best way to create space and length in the spine is by preserving the spine's natural curves (fig. 8.1 C). You want to be well-aligned along a vertical plumb line. This rider gives me the feeling she is ready for any action or activity—including mounting up!

Improving your posture is about so much more than taking a yoga or Pilates class, working out at the gym, getting chiropractic adjustments, or going to a massage therapist. Although all these actvities can be supportive and helpful, doing these things alone won't help you improve your riding much. To truly improve your posture, you need to study and change your habitual movement and posture patterns as you go about the daily business of life. You must develop a mindful awareness of where your body is in space, as well as the ensuing self-correction to bring yourself into alignment. It's a 24-hour-a-day job, because even your sleep position counts.

If you have the tendency to over-correct (see fig. 8.1 B), consider what verbs you use to bring yourself into improved posture. If you "throw," "force," "push," or "pull" yourself into position, you are quite likely overdoing it. Instead, use verbs that result in smoother movements, such as "ease," "knit," "tuck," or "draw," when you think about moving body parts into position. Support these words with imagery that brings in a quality of softness. For example, imagine your horse is a cloud that you have climbed astride.

Let's take a look at how posture on the ground can influence posture when you ride.

RIDING POSTURE TIPS

In chapter 1 (p. 7), we learned that good riding is not about maintaining a fixed position. But this is often how a rider approaches the process of refining her posture on horseback. Inevitably, most riders have an imagined "ideal position" they try to artificially force upon their bodies. Yet we all have different body proportions, sizes, shapes, joint ranges of motion, positional awareness, and proprioception, not to mention mobility styles. There is no single mold! So re-sculpt your imagined position into one that starts exactly as you are today. Then gently tweak it, bit by bit, to achieve improved balance of your body and mind, which will enable you to bring your most supple self to your horse. Let go of any judgment your mind tortures your body with. Judgment and rigid expectations do not serve you or your horse well. You can't succeed, enjoy, or connect with your horse when you "ooze with the sludge" of negative energy! Instead, aim to reframe with a positive upswing approach, and enjoy the harmony it creates.

Ground-To-Saddle Examples

The posture and movement patterns you automatically assume on the ground do have a major effect on your riding posture (figs. 8.2–8.5). Here are some examples of how that might factor in:

- If you stand with your knees "locked" or hyperextended, it often causes the rib cage on one or both sides to collapse. Hyperextended knees also compromise your ankle and hip suppleness. All this gives rise to a rider who looks and feels stiff.

- If your hips drift forward when you stand, your body assumes a banana shape. I've seen this pattern so frequently among trainers that I have dubbed it the "trainer's stance." When the hips drift forward of the ribcage in this way, the lower back hyperextends and the tailbone tucks under. This position gives rise to chronically contracted muscles, particularly the *psoas* and the *hamstrings*, compromising the fluidity and function of the pelvis, legs, hips, diaphragm, and spine. Your breathing becomes strained. If this is your habit, work on keeping your hips back over your ankles ("seat over feet") instead.

- If you look downward as your head and neck drift forward, you have misaligned your spine and encouraged compressive forces to head straight for your lower back. *Ouch!* Instead, try to keep your head back over your spine and your face parallel to an imaginary wall in front of you. Raise your eyes up, but don't poke your chin out. Be especially careful of this habit during daily activities such as texting, cooking, raking, sweeping, driving, writing, and reading. Much of modern life encourages a forward-and-downward head position. By the way, this forward deviation of head placement encourages your horse to put weight on his forehand. It also impedes his forward motion. (For more tips of this nature, please see chapter 15—p 147.)

- If you sit, stand, and move with too much arch behind your waist (you can fit a fist or more behind your waist when standing against a wall), you will struggle with being able to follow the movements of your horse. You may also be troubled by pain in the spine or the hips due to a concussed and compressed spine. I advise you to keep well-anchored floating (lower) ribs. (See chapter 14—p. 139—for specifics.)

- If you have too flat a back (you can't fit a flat hand in sideways between the back of your waist and the wall), your tail is apt to tuck under. Your horse will feel that! This pattern often results in a weak upper back, as well as spinal instability. Your front line will become tight. Your balance and breathing will be negatively affected. You will struggle with being able to give clear aids to your horse. You may well feel stiffness and pain either during or after your ride. (For in-depth information, check out chapter 13 and chapter 18—pp. 126 and 175.)

- If you walk by jutting a heel forward, with your foot positioned ahead of your hips, you are using your *hamstrings* instead of your *glutes* to move, and your *base of support* (lower legs and feet) is ahead of your *center of gravity*. This is unfortunate, because the glutes are the proper muscles to push you along and propel you forward. When the glutes are active, your center of gravity stays directly over your base of support. Glute activation is important for riders because the upper glutes are a fabulous support for your lower back. (For further tips on glute activation, see chapter 11—p. 107.)

- If one or both hips jut out or sway to the side when you walk, your pelvis and hip muscles are not in full control! The force of this lateral

8.2 This rider is not well balanced and is putting a lot of weight on her horse's forehand. Notice how her head is jutting forward and her lower ribs are protruding in front of her. She is going to get jostled around and her lower leg has swung back due to hinging at her knees.

drifting pushes the pelvis and hips to the outside, often creating a side bend such as a "C"-curve. This movement pattern can also lead to pain from conditions such as sciatica or sacroiliac joint problems. In the saddle, this habit shows up as unequally weighted seat bones. Remember: *Where the pelvis goes, the hips*

8.3 Here, the rider sits behind a vertical plumb line and her coccyx (tailbone) is pressing on her horse's back. *Ouch!* When her horse steps off, she is going to be behind the motion, and particularly at the trot and canter, she is apt to balance using her reins or stirrups.

8.4 The rider has low muscle tone. Her body will have many extraneous movements, and she will not be able to stabilize herself well. Because this rider has collapsed her front line, her horse will be resistant to forward motion.

8.5 This rider's pelvis has drifted sideways. One seat bone will feel heavy to her horse, while the other will feel very light. It will be harder for him to balance or understand the rider's aids, and her posture may well create tension and confusion for him.

8.6 A & B *Ahhhh!* **Here we see a well-aligned rider who can communicate clearly with her horse and support his efforts to balance under her. In the view from the back, you can see she is sitting in a laterally balanced fashion, weighting both seat bones equally—or as close to it as possible.**

follow. Learning to activate the side glutes will help. (Refer to chapter 11, p. 107, for specific exercises.)

If you are striving for your mounted posture to be balanced, supple, and stable (figs. 8.6 A & B), I highly suggest you enlist the assistance of a qualified equestrian ground coach. Alternatives include bodyworkers who are skilled in The Alexander Technique, Rolfing, or similar disciplines. It can help to ask for the following:

- A functional movement scan.

- A postural assessment.

- A set of corrective posture and movement exercises.

This is a fabulous way to support your riding because your myofascial imbalances show up clearly and can be addressed.

SELF-CARRIAGE

Self-carriage for a rider is her capacity to support her body weight independent of balancing on her reins, bracing on her stirrups, pinching with her legs, or relying on a misaligned position. None of these are intentional actions, and the rider is typically surprised when an observer or horse show judge points them out to her. The following exercises will help you develop more awareness about your self-carriage and give you strategies to begin to fully support and control your body weight.

SELF-CARRIAGE EXERCISE 1:
The Pokes

Imagine yourself as a stuffed sock. Self-carriage for a sock would mean it is equally stuffed throughout in a way that balances out its weight. Figure 8.7 shows two socks; the one in the model's left hand is well-stuffed, and the one in her right is under-stuffed, resulting in misalignment. The stuffed sock represents a rider with self-carriage versus the under-stuffed one without. Which rider would you rather carry if you were a horse? Keep this image in mind while doing the poking motions of the following exercise.

Step One: Look in a mirror or ask an observer to locate the parts of your body that are "under-stuffed."

Step Two: Using one pointing finger, poke into an area that is "well-stuffed" so you can feel the

8.7 The Pokes Imagery

underlying muscles respond. Keep your finger in place there. When you poke these muscles, you should feel the muscles "punch back" a little bit. Do this a few times to get the sensation down.

Step Three: Repeat Step Two for an area of your body that is "under-stuffed." Poke the under-stuffed area until you feel the same sensation you identified earlier in your well-stuffed areas. It may take several pokes to "wake up" the underlying muscles—but you can only improve your self-carriage if you wake up your sleepy muscles first.

SELF-CARRIAGE EXERCISE 2:
Posture Breathing

This exercise will help you use breathing to make you feel taller and more "stuffed" in self-carriage. When done while mounted, Posture Breathing can help to lengthen your spine.

Step One: Imagine you are breathing in the first scent of early spring air, and inhale gently through your nose.

Step Two: As you inhale, direct your breath into all the spaces of your body. Feel the breathing process as much in your toes as you do in your nose.

Step Three: Exhale with a quick, sharp breath, as if you were fogging up a mirror. Try making a quick "*haaaa*" sound as you do this.

Step Four: Gently exhale any remaining air through your nose, emptying your lungs fully.

Step Five: Your next inhale should feel spontaneous. Allow it to happen on its own. As this happens, turn your attention to your spine and feel how it lengthens and decompresses with the inhalation. This type of breathing will encourage a bit more space between the vertebrae. Sense that you are taller. Creating an image of your taller self will help!

Step Six: As you exhale, be sure to maintain that upright feeling. No collapsing! You have just taught your body-mind to link your breathing with your posture and self-carriage.

SELF-CARRIAGE EXERCISE 3:
Human Lead Rope

"Walking yourself" using a "human lead rope" is a great way to train your rib cage to hold itself in position and help support your body weight (fig. 8.8).

Step One: Secure a long dog leash or a lead rope with a large clip (or attached carabiner) around your lower rib cage. It should lie just under your lowest floating ribs. Make sure it is fairly tight. Reach behind you to hold the end of the rope. Slide your hands upward so you are pulling the rope taut with your hands over your head.

Step Four: As you pull upward, feel your rib cage lift upward and forward. (This is good for people who slouch and slump.)

Step Five: Now that you have tried both options, select the one that feels best for you. If you tend to arch your back and poke your ribs out, follow the directions of Step One. If you tend to collapse the rib cage and slump, select the placement of the lead rope in Step Three. Ask an observer to help make the determination if you are unsure.

Step Six: With your lead rope in your preferred position, take yourself for a walk! Make sure to go forward, backward, and sideways with your steps. If that goes well, try some "leg-yielding," "half-pass," and perhaps even some "cavalletti."

8.8 Human Lead Rope

Step Two: As you pull upward, feel your lower rib cage aim backwards in the direction of your spine. Allow this to happen. You have just "anchored" your rib cage! (You will learn more about this in chapter 14—p. 139.)

Step Three: Turn the leash around so the vertical part of the strap is along your mid-line in front of you. The back part of the strap should lie at the lower end of your rib cage. Pull upwards tightly.

SELF-CARRIAGE EXERCISE 4:
Overhead Wall Press

Overhead Wall Press puts your body into an isometric holding pattern that will connect your upper and lower halves to your deep core myofascia. It is hard work, but the benefit is improved self-carriage and riding posture. Challenge yourself to develop your postural muscles and boost your core endurance by doing as many sets of Overhead Wall Press as possible.

8.9 Overhead Wall Press

Step One: Stand facing a wall, placing your toes 12 to 24 inches away.

Step Two: Walk your hands up the wall while keeping your head neutral. Stop when your hands are in a comfortable position overhead. Don't look up at your hands—feel them on the wall (fig. 8.9).

Step Three: Actively press your hands into the wall, sliding the shoulder blades upward. Hold this position for seven seconds, then push back into standing again.

Step Four: Take a breath or two before starting at Step One to repeat this exercise. Keep repeating until your muscles feel tired and you get a sense they have worked hard enough.

SELF-CARRIAGE EXERCISE 5:
Single Leg Wall Push

This exercise is more exertional than it looks! The Single Leg Wall Push helps support your self-carriage by building strong postural muscles throughout your body. Be sure to train both sides of your body for an equal amount of time. When practicing this exercise, it is important to follow the body positioning cues given in the steps that follow—otherwise, you will be strengthening a misaligned position.

Step One: Stand with your back facing a wall. Step about one leg's length away from the wall.

8.10 Single Leg Wall Push

Step Two: Extend both arms overhead, without looking up at them. Keep your head in a neutral position.

Step Three: Hinge at the hips and kick one leg up behind you. Place your foot flat on the wall, toes pointed down. Your gaze should now be toward the ground, with your head and neck in a neutral position. If you are just learning this exercise, position yourself in a corner or near a counter to touch or grab with your hands if you lose balance.

Step Four: Keep looking down at the floor as you extend your arms fully out in front of you (fig. 8.10). Push down into the floor with your stance leg while pushing into the wall with your other foot. Keep the legs fairly straight, but soft in the joints.

Step Five: Keep your hips and rib cage square to the ground.

Step Six: Hold the Single Leg Wall Push for seven seconds, then reverse the steps and come back to standing. Take a couple of slow, deep breaths.

Step Seven: Repeat all steps on both sides to fatigue—when a muscle is getting sore or is on the verge of perhaps doing too much. This exercise will be a blast-off toward improved human self-carriage.

8.11 Back to Blades

SELF-CARRIAGE EXERCISE 6:
Back to Blades

It's time to pay attention to the muscles in between your shoulder blades. They are an important part of self-carriage.

Step One: Stand with feet hip-width apart and turn your head to the left.

Step Two: Place the back of your right hand behind your waist on your lower back.

Step Three: Using the muscles between your spine and right shoulder blade, gently draw the right shoulder blade toward the spine.

Step Four: Keep these muscles engaged and hold the scapula (shoulder blade) toward the spine for seven seconds. Release the squeeze for three seconds. Repeat on the right side to fatigue.

Step Five: Repeat Step Four and complete an equal number of sets for the left side.

SELF-CARRIAGE EXERCISE 7:
Side Superhero

Get your sides involved in self-carriage through the Side Superhero move. It has an extra bonus of helping to stabilize your core. Find a comfortable spot for this exercise, such as a pad or yoga mat, and feel free to insert a pillow at the side of your waist, as well as under your hip, for comfort.

8.12 Side Superhero

Step One: Lie on the side of your choice.

Step Two: Simultaneously lift both legs and the upper torso 1 or 2 inches off the ground.

Step Three: Hold this position for seven seconds, then release to the ground for three seconds.

Step Four: Repeat steps one through three to fatigue. Complete the same number of sets on your other side.

---

chapter takeaway ✓

Your posture presents who you are to the world, whether you are on the ground or on the back of a horse. Investing in your ability to support and direct your body weight has a big payoff. Your improved self-carriage encourages and invites your horse to develop his own self-carriage!

PART 2

FINDING YOUR POSITION

The 12 chapters of this section help riders understand how their bodies are joined together by connective tissue. We will explore the fluid nature of a rider's body, and how that sense of fluidity enhances her ability to ride well. You will learn more techniques to "wake up" sleepy muscles, as well as how and when to rest them. Our stress is often stored in our muscles, so I will offer ways to release that tension so as to bring the best of yourself to your horse. I will teach you how to achieve both outer and inner fitness. Finally, I will discuss the roles of both the teacher and the student of horseback riding, along with some of the lessons I have learned from over 50 years of teaching horses and humans.

CHAPTER NINE
THE SECRETS OF FLUIDITY

OUR FLUID NATURE

We are made up of trillions of cells, each containing cellular fluid. If we are healthy and active, those cells function and communicate with each other via a steady flow of fluids through their cell membranes. This is a balanced, gentle system (not forced and harsh), involving blood and lymph, and synovial (joint), cerebrospinal, cellular, and intercellular fluids, among others. Blood is circulated throughout the body thanks to the pumping action of the heart, but other fluids in your body do not move in this manner. For instance, it is the deliberate movement of your body throughout the day that creates the optimal flow of fluids through the lymph system. During times of the day when you are sedentary, such as while working at a desk or while driving, or even more significantly, while recovering from injury, the lymph system can stagnate. Imagine what it is like when a brook becomes stagnant; this same type of effect can impact our bodies when lymph and other fluids aren't moving freely. Since we are largely fluid-based beings, keeping our fluids circulating supports our health and well-being. This chapter offers you tips on how to keep body fluids flowing, even during times of rest or lower activity.

If you don't move enough or drink enough water, the cells and tissues in your body become "sticky" and lose their ability to be "springy." This results in sagging posture (and dismal riding). Fluids bring your cells nourishment, but also cart away waste. They regulate your body temperature, protect your organs, keep digestion optimal, help you think clearly, and lubricate joints. Eating a healthy, balanced diet will likely supply you with most of your required electrolytes, but I recommend bringing a water bottle to your workouts and sipping it throughout. Hydrating during exercise allows your body to absorb fluids as you move around and is more effective than gulping down half a bottle afterward.

A fountain of youth and vitality secretly flows within all of us. It is the placement and flow of fluids to and from our organs that gives rise to this freely flowing vital energy. When you have good posture, you give length and space to the body's cavities containing your organs. Poor posture shrinks that space, causing our vital energy to become stagnant and blocked—and we become old before our time!

Our *personal flow* is a feeling of wave-like fluidity that springs subconsciously from all our senses. We strive for flowing movements. But it's equally important to strive for fluid thoughts and positive affirmations. An example is being open to other ways of doing things, including training horses and riders. It's easy to lock into a single system that appears to work for us and our current horse(s). But horse and rider training is evolutionary, not stationary, in nature. Body shape, athletic condition, and state of mind for both horse and rider are in a constant state of change. I encourage you to step outside your comfort zone and embrace fluidity in your approach to learning and training. In the end, *you* get to pick what to weave into the current training plan for you and your horse.

FLUIDITY OF THE RIDER

Coordination is when your body parts move in flowing harmony. Nerves, fascia, joints, bones, muscles, tendons, and ligaments all pull toward a goal that is centered around movement (fig. 9.2).

In general, the more joints that are softly bending, the smoother the movement. To remain fluid, don't extend your joints or lock them straight. Overly extended or locked joints block energy flow and produce stiff, robotic movements. Remember that fluidity of a rider, whether

Bit of Advice

To help keep your lymph system in good working order and support its ability to carry away waste products from cells and tissues, try dry brushing with a good quality skin brush (fig. 9.1). Brush your full body, a section at a time, but always toward the heart. You shouldn't push down hard—it's not a massage. But this gentle action will encourage your lymph to move.

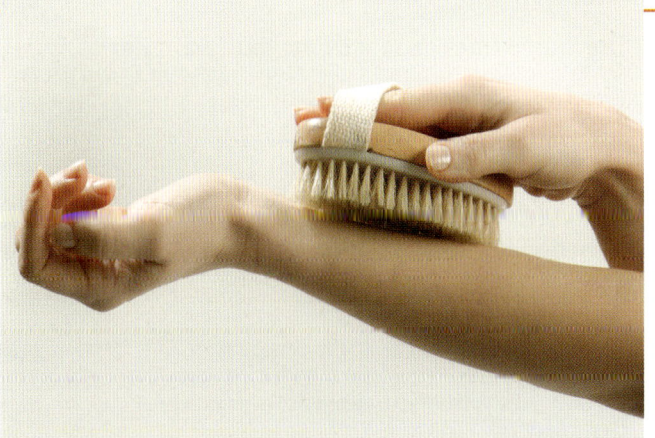

9.1 Dry brushing in the direction of your heart will help your lymph system eliminate toxins and waste products from the body's tissues.

9.2 Imagine warm, gentle waterfalls flowing from the tops of your shoulders down your back. Close your eyes and feel a descending sensation as your shoulder blades and sacrum relax and drop. It is helpful to imagine these gentle waterfalls when you ride, as it will help dissolve any tension that your back is holding.

following, asking, or influencing her horse, involves no abruptness.

Here are some ways for a rider to support her fluidity and suppleness:

- Hydrate before, during, and after exercise. This is best done by taking sips of water, not gulps.

- Warm up and start exercising slowly. Before exercise, your blood is mainly in the vicinity of your organs. Your warm-up will draw some blood flow to the muscles you are starting to exercise. Pulsing actions are particularly helpful for a warm-up. Pump the muscles you are trying to activate as if they were a fist doing a squeeze-then-release.

- Keep moving throughout your day. Healthy creatures squirm! Walk, wiggle, stretch, kick a pillow, crawl—anything, but don't keep still for too long. If you have a desk job, I suggest that every 15 minutes you shake, tap, shift, march in place, or otherwise *move*. Prioritize your health and well-being.

- Weave the exercises of this book (or others of your choice) into your day. Isometrics are especially suitable for this as they can be done anywhere and require no equipment. The exercises you select should be something you look forward to and are apt to actually do. This is the best way to build a sustainable program.

- "Ride a wave" either mounted or unmounted (fig. 9.3). Use imagery to enhance your sense that your horse is moving as strongly and fluidly as an ocean wave. Incorporate all your senses, including the sounds of seagulls, the scent of saltwater spray, the roar of waves, and the feel of power moving smoothly beneath you. Allow your mind and body to become as supple and strong as the wave you are imagining.

What follows are exercises to help you keep your fluids flowing. You'll find ideas for those with sedentary jobs or long commutes, as well as those who are sidelined in rehab.

FLUIDITY EXERCISE 1:
Bounce Away

Step One: To stay fluid throughout the day and move your lymph, it pays to keep a stability ball (or rebounder) close by.

Step Two: Sit and bounce to your heart's delight! Your immune system will thank you, because this bouncing action is superior at moving body fluids around.

FLUIDITY EXERCISE 2:
Basketball Bounces

Step One: Find a ball with bounce, such as a properly inflated basketball.

9.3 Imagine your horse is a wave you are riding. Flow with the powerful forces by remaining centered, strong, and supple.

Step Two: Try to bounce it when your fingers are stiffly extended and joints are locked open.

Step Three: *Hmmm…* try again, this time with flowing, supple joints. *Ahhhh!* Notice the implications of this exercise for a rider doing a sitting trot.

FLUIDITY EXERCISE 3:
Slither and Shake

Step One: We are inclined to initiate movement from our arms and legs, keeping our torsos fairly still. So do the reverse. Keep your arms and legs still as you slither and shake your torso!

Step Two: Try this sitting, standing, kneeling, crawling, or in almost any other position you can imagine. It's a super exercise to break up a long drive.

FLUIDITY EXERCISE 4:
Bubbling Spring Acupressure

I credit Sally Swift and her *Centered Riding* books for inspiring the use of *Bubbling Spring* acupressure for riders. This refers to triggering an acupressure point in each foot to help "wake up" your sense of fluidity (fig. 9.4). Manipulation of this acupressure point is also said to benefit the kidneys and rejuvenate the spirit.

Step One: "Undress" a foot and sit down.

Step Two: Cross the bare foot over your other leg.

Step Three: Using your thumb, press the Bubbling Spring point for about a minute.

Step Four: Visualize blood, lymph, and body fluids flowing freely throughout your foot as you do this. Feel the warmth of your circulation.

Step Five: Breathe deeply and rhythmically.

FLUIDITY EXERCISE 5:
Elegant Mansion Acupressure

The *Elegant Mansion acupressure point*, also known as *K27*, benefits the kidneys and improves the flow of fluids (fig. 9.5). It's more physically accessible than the Bubbling Spring point described in Fluidity Exercise 4 and can be done while mounted. Manipulation of this point is said to relieve anxiety and enhance breathing.

9.4 The *Bubbling Spring acupressure point,* also known as *Point K1*, is located on the center of the sole and at the base of the ball of the foot. It's between the two toe pads and lies right on the spot where a rider's foot touches the stirrup.

9.5 The *Elegant Mansion acupressure point*, located about an inch below the collarbones and beside the sternum (breastbone), is accessible for a mounted rider. Pressure on this point assists your breathing effort and is said to relieve anxiety.

FLUIDITY EXERCISE 6:
Roll 'Em

You can do this exercise even when sitting in a chair or on a sofa. It's all about "rolling" to keep your fluids moving, your joints supple, and your movements youthful.

Step One: Start to roll your body—hips, trunk, shoulders. Let your arms and legs go along for the ride.

Step Two: Vary your speed from slug-slow to fox-fast.

Step Three: To engage your core for even more benefits, laugh as you roll!

Step One: Locate the hollows about one inch below the collarbones and beside the sternum (breastbone).

Step Two: Using your thumb, press fairly firmly but not harshly on these two points as you take five slow breaths.

chapter takeaway

Tap into the secret fountain of youth inside you by learning to move throughout the day in a way that encourages internal fluid flow. Sip small amounts of water frequently rather than waiting for a deficit and then chugging it. Use imagery when you ride to bring forth a fluidity to your posture and movements.

CHAPTER TEN
FASCIAL CONNECTIONS

FASCIAL CONNECTIONS EXPLORED

Fascia is a connective tissue primarily made up of collagen. It's abundant in the body and gives structural support to soft tissues and joints, as well as bones, muscles, ligaments, tendons, nerves, blood, and organs. As you age, you produce less collagen and begin to lose muscle mass. Lower collagen production causes your skin to get saggy and your joints to "feel their age." The good news is there are ways to maximize your collagen production, even as you age. (I refer readers who are thirsting for more on this topic to Scott Hogan's *Built from Broken*, published by SaltWrap in 2021—see Bibliography and Recommended Reading, p. 265.)

When I use the term *myofascial*, I am referring to both *connective tissue* and the *muscles* connected and intertwined with it. In his book *Anatomy Trains* (Elsevier, 2020), Thomas W. Myers beautifully details a number of discrete myofascial chains running throughout the body. These chains interconnect and run in all directions of the body, including up, down, left, right, front, back, center, diagonally, and in spiral fashion. It is these chains that need to balance with each other in order to achieve desirable posture and correct movements. When the chains are not balanced, your connective tissues can yank your muscles and bones into misalignment.

I find Myers' approach fascinating and utilize it frequently when I train my clients. But I also find that my riders get confused and overwhelmed by learning the details, going into left brain mode and minimizing their ability to feel. Instead, I focus on the work of ensuring their myofascial chains are balanced, and they can just concentrate on their riding. It's a win-win situation.

You began to get a sense of these myofascial chains in back in chapter 3 (see p. 23). This chapter will shed more light on the subject.

Fascia functions as a sensory organ. It's quite rich in both nerves and proprioceptors. Additionally, the connective tissue has a crimped (wavy) arrangement that enables it to store "bouncy" energy. When fascia gets neglected from lack of proper movement or injury, it gets "sticky" and less wavy, and its capacity to release energy declines. Training your fascia improves both its elasticity and its capacity to store energy. The energy stored in fascia is released during movement. Children are loaded with healthy, bouncy fascia; adults can rejuvenate theirs with proper training. The exercises included in this chapter will help with this.

There are sliding and gliding elements in fascia. But when you are stressed, the nerves in fascia tend to tighten it up. So you will not be apt to slide, glide, and stretch well when you are worried. This has obvious implications for your riding, particularly if you compete. When your fascia is in this super-tense state, it creates dysfunctions in your proprioceptive, postural, movement, and neuromuscular systems. *Yikes*—just thinking about that can create more stress! So, breathe more slowly and deeply, with proper pauses (explained in chapter 4—see p. 32). Focus on your breathing as you imagine long chains of reddish muscles connected by white, wavy, springy fascia. This healthy condition of your fascia is conducive to being strong, stable, supple, coordinated, and all the other physical attributes that support your ability to ride well. This imagery of healthy fascia is a powerful tool for riders.

How do you know if your fascia is in good shape? Well, if you have great posture and full range of motion in your joints, if you feel springy and bouncy rather than dumpy and saggy, your fascia is most likely in great shape. But what if it's not? There are numerous tips coming up in this chapter, but for a moment, let's consider a couple of quick techniques to help encourage the fitness of your fascia.

- First, if you watch your horse after he takes a nap, you'll see that he frequently does something called a *pandicular stretch*. (Yes, this is named with reference to panda bears!) The horse tenses his body as he moves in full range of motion throughout a stretch. One of the classic equine pandicular stretch moves involves keeping the rump high as the head, neck, and forelegs dip down. This stretch is a great reset to the neuromuscular system, as well as being quite nourishing to the fascia. It wakes the body up and prepares it for movement. This special pandicular stretch is key for maintaining healthy posture. It moves fluid around and gently invites "stuck" fascia to start releasing its hold. (Like layers of plastic food wrap, fascia sometimes "sticks" together.) In addition, it helps alleviate chronic muscular tension.

Pandicular stretches are sometimes called *resistance stretches*; I have listed some

Self-Assessing Your Fascia

A full assessment of your myofascial chains by a qualified bodyworker or fitness professional is most desirable. They can evaluate how your myofascial chains are functioning, determine imbalances, and help you restore them. But you can get a sense of your own musculature chain balances (see p. 99) by doing a quick self-assessment. Here are the steps:

Step One: Lie on the ground with your hands resting on and pushing into your thighs and your lower legs at a 90-degree angle to your thighs (fig. 10.1 A). Hover your head a 1/2 to 1 inch above the ground, keeping your face parallel to the ceiling. Start a stopwatch and see how long you can hold this position. This measures the strength of your front fascial lines. Stop the time if you fall out of alignment, feel any pain, or are too fatigued to go on. Record your score.

Step Two: Lie on your belly (fig. 10.1 B). Start your stopwatch to see how long you can hold this position. Stop the time if you fall out of alignment, feel any pain, or are too fatigued to go on. Record your score. This measures the strength of your back fascial line.

Step Three: Now try a side plank position, supported on your left forearm (fig. 10.1 C). Be sure to keep your head back in line with your spine. Again, start a stopwatch—record your score.

Step Four: Finish your assessment with a side plank supported by the right forearm (fig. 10.1 D). Again, be careful about holding the head in alignment and not out in front of you. Start a stopwatch. Record your score.

Step Five: Now you are going to compare your scores by using the length of time you were able to hold each position without stress, strain, or pain. To be in good balance, your scores from Step One (front line) should be equivalent, or very nearly so, to your scores from Step Two (back line). Your scores from Steps Three and Four should also be equal, or very nearly so. Finally, your scores from Steps Three and Four should be 75 percent or less than your scores from either Step One or Step Two. In other words, it's not a good idea for your sides to take over your front or back lines.

10.1 A–D Self-assessing your fascia: Step One (A), Step Two (B), Step Three (C), Step Four (D).

Step Six: Now you can make a plan. Let's say your scores were the following:

- Front line: 60 seconds
- Back line: 42 seconds
- Left side plank: 57 seconds
- Right side plank: 22 seconds.

To help correct this unbalanced profile, you would plan on doing more exercises or activities for your back line and right side. But you also would need to increase your front line, because your left side is trying to "overtake" it. This is a case where a personal trainer or qualified professional can be of support and assistance.

examples later in this chapter and have included several sources of information in the Bibliography and Recommended Reading sections at the end of this book (see p. 265).

- Another simple technique to improve the health of your facia is the use of a *foam roller*. Gently compressing the fascia with this tool is similar to slowly squeezing the water out of a sponge. It brings in fresh blood and fluids to the area rolled, while encouraging the removal of waste products. The roller also helps to break up stuck areas of fascial tissue and restore flexibility. As you use a fascial roller, you may find small, painful spots on the muscle fibers. These are called *trigger points*. Trigger points can happen when a muscle is overworked, or otherwise becomes stressed or shortened with reduced blood flow. Rolling slowly over the trigger point in all directions can unlock the area, improve fluid flow, and relieve pain. There are a number of types of rollers and ways to roll. Experiment, and do what works best for you! If you have no experience rolling, I highly suggest a system called the Melt Method® by Sue Hitzmann (see Bibliography and Recommended Reading on p. 265).

FASCIA AND THE RIDER

Balancing fascial lines is an essential component of athletic performance because it drives proper posture, movement, functioning, strength, suppleness, and stability. Luckily for equestrians, Mary Wanless has detailed all the myofascial chains and their implications in her fabulous book *Rider Biomechanics* (Kenilworth, 2017). In it you can find a wealth of information about the various chains and how they relate to your riding posture and performance.

Let's explore how these chains might affect a rider. Firstly, we are not perfectly symmetrical beings. For example, the liver is on our right side and pushes upward on the diaphragm from below; the diaphragm is also not symmetrical; it is larger on the right. There are numerous other examples of our natural asymmetry, all of which affect all us in different ways.

Consider a rider with a slight "C"-curve (side bend) to the right. She could be compensating due to subconscious discomfort from *visceral asymmetry*, resulting in a shortened right side and lengthened left side. Or maybe the "C"-curve is due to her habit of standing with one leg bent and the other leg straight. Or possibly, it's due to the way she's been slinging her pocketbook over her shoulder for decades. There are numerous other reasons for why this "C"-curve could

When Do You Use Your Myofascial Chains?

The Superficial Back Line

What is it? The *Superficial Back Line* is a line of muscles and connective tissue that forms the posterior (back) surface of your body. It helps hold your body upright. You use your *Back Line* when:

- You suddenly realize you are slumping and straighten up.
- Your horse puts the brakes on unexpectedly.

The Superficial Front Line

What is it? The *Superficial Front Line* is a line of muscles and connective tissue that forms the front (anterior) surface of the body. It balances out the back line and protects your organs. You use the Front Line when:

- You get out of bed in the morning.
- Your horse suddenly bolts.

The Lateral Lines

The *Lateral Lines* cover the sides of the body. They give surrounding support to the front and back lines. You use your Lateral Lines when:

- You realize you're in a bit of a "C"-curve and straighten up.
- You find and rescue a lost seat bone that drifted to the outside.

The Spiral Line

The *Spiral Line* literally spirals around your body, wrapping you in support. You use it when:

- You realize you are tilting your head sideways and self-correct.
- You are asking your horse to side-pass.

The Arm Lines

The *Arm Lines* are front, back, superficial, and deep myofascial lines that run through your arms, connecting them to other lines. When do you use your arms?

- When you are driving to the barn.
- When you hold the reins and receive your horse's energy.

The Functional Lines

The *Functional Lines* go diagonally across your body in a big "X." These lines are designed to help you move athletically. When do you use your Functional Lines?

- When you are playing horseshoes.
- When you are performing a leg-yield with your horse.

The Deep Front Line

The *Deep Front Line* is the deep core myofascia responsible for centering you. It travels just in front of your spine, giving the lumbar section good support. When do you use your Deep Front Line?

- When you breathe.
- When you are riding and your trainer asks you to correct your forward head posture.

happen. But the horse she rides is not concerned with the cause; what jumps out at him is the unevenness of her weight on her left seat bone compared to her right seat bone. That's a big deal, and it's worth periodically reminding yourself what that might feel like to a horse. To create a similar effect in your own body, just place some ankle weights on your head in an unbalanced fashion. This asymmetrical weight distribution is challenging and at times, unsettling, for both horses and people. No matter what the cause, this particular asymmetry is best addressed by bringing body-mind awareness to the imbalance through a series of myofascial exercises (see p. 102).

Fascial chains function and work together, not in an isolated fashion, and this is why whole-body movements (or even simply visualizing them) work best for nourishing fascia and shoring it up. The functionality of our fascia is also well-served by lengthening or stretching the parts that have shortened. But stretching fascia isn't the same as *standard stretching* (maneuvering your body in a way that allows gravity to help with the stretch—for example, bending to touch your toes and holding that position for a minute is *standard stretching*). Consider the difference as explained by Bonnie Bainbridge Cohen, founder of Body-Mind Centering®, in *Sensing, Feeling, and Action* (Contact Editions, 2012):

When you stretch a muscle you don't change the mind of its length. You use other muscles, or body weight, or some mechanical force to make it longer. You use an external force to stretch the muscles, but you don't actually change its inner length. But a "lengthening contraction" is a process of releasing and of changing the muscle internally. In fact, if you put a stretch on a spastic muscle you will just tighten it.

When I started this type of work, my physical and neurological issues had wreaked havoc with me. They had half a lifetime's experience delivering body-wide, broad, painful spasms. There were times when I could not rise out of bed, and when I did, I needed to rely on my cane or a walker. Imagery was a huge help to my understanding of how to release and create space within my clenched muscles. I imagined myself as being nearly microscopic in size. And I was, of course, riding a near-microscopic horse. (I had been grounded for years, but still rode avidly in my day and night dreams!) It was a Pony Express image, and I was charged with the mission of delivering a message to the taut, painful muscles inside my crippled body. The mini and I would charge in through my skin at full gallop and halt abruptly at a sore, bound-up spot. I put my tiny hands on the spasming spot and said, *You've done your job of shortening very well. Now it's time for you to release and rest.* And I imagined the muscle sighing and melting into a warm, semi-solid, sleep state. One by one, the spasms slowly dissolved; it's been 15 years at this point with no spasms, no cane, and no walker. Imagery is that powerful.

It was at about this point in my recovery that I first learned about fascia. It took me quite a while to understand the difference between lengthening and stretching. Lengthening is more like creating space between bones when body parts are held in a neutral position, whereas stretching is often utilized in either extended or flexed body positions. And I discovered there are three special types of (nontraditional) stretching that fascia loves.

1 *Pandicular type stretches*: These are the resistance stretches explained earlier in this chapter (see p. 95). The muscle being lengthened is both relaxed and strongly activated at the same time. It is also put through its full range of motion. Several examples of other pandicular stretches are included in this section.

2 *Bouncy, ballistic stretches*: Your fascia will benefit from tiny bounces near the end range of motion. In this section, I will detail several of these movements that your fascia will love!

3 *Massage with a foam roller, hand-held roller, Franklin Tough Ball™, or lacrosse ball*: Using any of these tools, take super slow movements, first side-to-side, then up-and-down, then circular. It should feel like you are squeezing water out of a sponge. This rejuvenates fascia by promoting a liquid exchange in fascial tissues. It helps move lymph and cellular waste products away. Fresh fluid from your blood plasma is then free to enter. The slow, steady pressure of the roller helps to relieve muscle and tissue tightness, and your mobility increases.

How often should you do fascial exercises? With fascial work, it is critical to give your body a chance to flush the old, problematic waste products out and replace them with fresh, youthful tissue. Therefore, I highly recommend athletes practice fascial exercises twice a week, to include all three types of exercises just mentioned. When trying to improve the health of your fascia, it takes this type of consistency to rebuild a strong fascial network and reclaim some youthful movements.

MYOFASCIAL EXERCISE 1:
Pandiculars

Be sure to keep the same level of tension throughout this and other pandicular stretches. Stop at your natural endpoint and never push through pain. You will need something solid to lean on for this moving exercise (fig. 10.2 A). A kitchen counter works well, as does a sturdy chair. In the end position (fig. 10.2 B), be sure to keep pressing down into the counter as you also press your feet down into the floor. To add length to your calves, step on a half-foam.

Step One: Stand and press down into a counter or the back of a chair, keeping your arms fairly straight without locking your elbows.

Step Two: Step far enough away from the counter to allow for bowing forward (with your head coming between your arms).

Step Three: Tension your entire body—in other words, squeeze your whole body like you would squeeze your hand into a fist. Aim for 50 to 70 percent of your maximal tensioning capacity.

Step Four: Slowly go from standing, to bending. Begin the movement from your center, and keep pressing the arms downward because that will add to the proper tensioning of the exercise.

Step Five: Work up to being able to sustain this exercise for one minute.

10.2 A & B Pandiculars start position (A) and end position (B).

MYOFASCIAL EXERCISE 2:
Standing Straddle Bend (Pandicular Type)

The Standing Straddle Bend focuses on the tops of the hamstrings, where they connect to your seat bones. This area of our hamstring tends to tighten up thanks to our modern lifestyles—we sit and drive frequently, and it is easy to become sedentary due to common conveniences. Be sure to keep a soft bend in your knees. If you straighten behind the knees, you will not be lengthening the correct area of your hamstrings. Be sure to isometrically squeeze the legs together and backward without moving them, and stand clear of walls or objects.

Step One: Stand in an open area with your legs wide. Point your feet very slightly outward (fig. 10.3 A).

Step Two: Bend forward at the hips and grasp your lower legs just above the ankles (fig. 10.3 B).

10.3 A & B Standing Straddle Bend set up (A), and bending phase (B).

Step Three: Tension your body in this position to 50 to 70 percent of its maximal tension.

Step Four: Pull your torso toward your legs as your legs tension both toward each other and backward. The legs should not move, as if they are stuck in mud.

Step Five: Do not hold still; instead, continually move in and out of the bend. Keep grasping your lower legs just above your ankles; as you move, you will feel the resistance in your fascia. Don't stand up until the exercise is complete.

Step Six: Practice this resistance stretch flow until you can sustain it for one minute.

MYOFASCIAL EXERCISE 3:
Side-Tap Walk (Bouncy Type)

Make this a bouncy move. You can Side-Tap Walk in place, or take the pattern on a walk. Both versions are beneficial. Keep your body stiff for this exercise and go through the steps at a quick pace.

Step One: Start with feet hip width apart and raise your right arm overhead, keeping it fairly straight. At the same time, extend your right leg to the outside and tap the outside of the leg

10.4 Side-Tap Walk

or hip with your fingers. Keeping the left side straight, lean toward the left. This is not a "C" curve (fig. 10.4).

Step Two: Take a normal step with the right foot as you bring your right arm down by your side.

Step Three: Repeat Step One, this time using your left arm and leg.

Step Four: Continue this exercise for a minute or two.

MYOFASCIAL EXERCISE 4:
Wall Springs (Bouncy Type)

Here's a bouncy type exercise for the upper body. Yes, you'll be "bouncing off the walls" on this one! Wall Springs are a great exercise for the fascia of your shoulder girdle. You should feel a good "zing" with each bounce.

Step One: Stand facing a wall with feet hip width apart. Start about 2 feet away, adjusting your feet later as needed.

Step Two: Rub your hands together to create warmth and awareness.

Step Three: Separate your fingers.

Step Four: Fall forward toward the wall, pushing off from it with your hands until you are standing upright again (fig. 10.5).

Step Five: First try pushing off the wall with hands positioned wider than shoulder-width. Alternate with push-offs where your hands are about shoulder-width apart.

Step Six: If possible, continue this pattern for about a minute.

Step Seven: Shake your arms out well.

10.5 Wall Springs

MYOFASCIAL EXERCISE 5:
Rolling Out

There are numerous kinds of *fascial rollers*. It's worth trying out different kinds because it all boils down to personal preference. For example, I suggest using a golf ball for your feet (fig. 10.6). You may feel occasional discomfort when you roll, but never push to the point of pain. Listen to your body and use tolerable pressure. Some areas of your body will need softer rolling, and some will welcome a firmer touch. Do not roll over your bony parts, and note that fascial rolling is not advised for small children. Leave two to three days between rolling sessions.

Step One: Equestrians often benefit from rolling out feet, hands, legs, back, and hips.

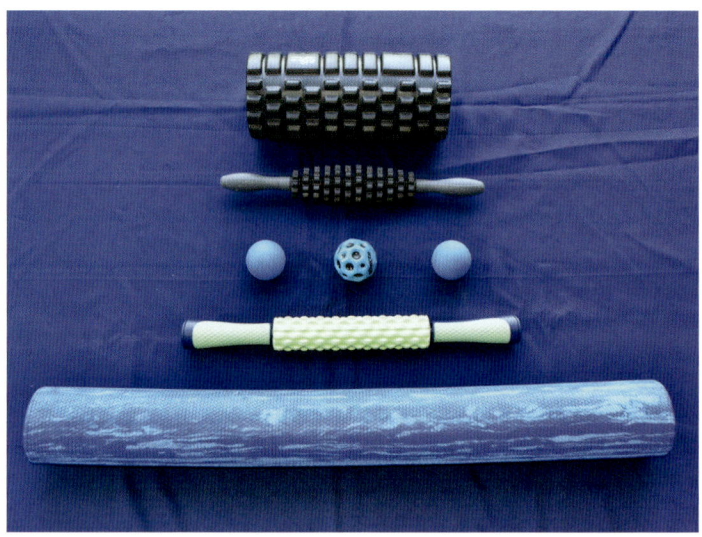

10.6 An array of fascial rollers.

Taking care of your fascia through specific, twice weekly exercises will help rehydrate and rejuvenate body tissues. This is important work, as regular exercise can restore and balance the body's myofascial chains. Balancing these chains is important to help you achieve your best performance when you ride. You may not know you have imbalances, but I guarantee, your horse can tell!

CHAPTER ELEVEN

MUSCLE ACTIVATION AND RECOVERY

MUSCLE MYTHS AND FACTS

Muscle Myth 1: Bringing your belly button toward your spine will stabilize and strengthen your core.

Fact: *Ouch!* I hurt all over when I hear those words! First, please know if you follow that advice, you are 1) collapsing your rib cage and core; 2) interfering with your breathing; 3) compressing your abdominal organs (affecting the floor of your riding seat); and 4) restricting your horse's ability to move and balance himself.

Although abdominal muscles are often recruited to stabilize the core or tone down too much arching (*lordosis*) of the lower back, they are inefficient at it and it's problematic to do so. These muscles typically attach to the sternum, ribs, or pelvis; there is no direct connection of those muscles to the spine. Using abs in isolation to stabilize the spine actually pulls the body out of alignment—thus *destabilizing* the spine.

Further, it also impedes *thoracic mobility*, a key player in being able to follow a horse's movements well. As you shall see in chapter 18 (see p. 175), it is those muscles with a direct connection to the spine or the deep core myofascia, *not* the abdominals, that have the greatest beneficial effect in stabilizing the core.

Muscle Myth 2: The longer the isometric hold (such as in a front plank), the better the payoff.

Fact: This couldn't be further from the truth! Extensive studies by world-renowned spine and core expert Stuart McGill have shown that holding an isometric move for longer than seven seconds impedes blood and fluid flow to and within the affected areas (as explained in his book *Low Back Disorders*, published by Human Kinetics in 2016). This deprives the area of oxygen delivery and waste removal. If you are a body builder, this practice builds bulky, visible "Popeye-type" muscles. But that type of musculature does not serve equestrians—first, because longer, leaner muscles are more conducive to riding well, and second, in terms of daily functioning, "farm kids" (who use full-body movements with shorter duration holds) often outperform body builders (who use isolated movements with longer holds).

Seven seconds of holding and three seconds of resting best constitutes one isometric repetition. It is the number of those reps you can do (*core endurance*) that best predicts functional success, *not* how long you hold a specific move.

Muscle Myth 3: When your muscles shake, it means you've had enough exertion and should stop.

Fact: Muscle shaking is actually a great sign; in particular, your *stability muscles* are quite fond of shaking while they work. Shaking is their way of letting you know they are awake, alert, and doing their job.

Muscle Myth 4: Riding and barn chores are enough of a workout to be balanced, healthy, and fit for riding.

Fact: *Oops!* This line of thinking can get you into trouble farther down the road. You're only as fit as your postural and movement patterns are correct, day in and day out. So if you ride several horses a day, muck out, stack hay, scrub water buckets, and pour grain with a forward head position, or a weak spiral line, or unbalanced myofascial chains, or a destabilized spine, or with shallow irregular breathing, it won't make you a better rider. It will also predispose you to injury.

Muscle Myth 5: You should strive for full activation of key muscles when you ride.

Fact: *Full activation* of a muscle or muscles would be extremely detrimental to your riding. You would be excessively tense, and risk upsetting your horse. Even constant, *unmounted* full muscle activation is unhelpful. It is best to let your body develop at its own pace and express its wisdom by letting it decide how much to activate each muscle. This is how the body learns to protect you from injury (including falls off horses).

Muscle Myth 6: Certain muscles, such as the inner thigh muscles, should not be activated when you ride.

Fact: Some equestrians fear developing certain muscles they believe should not be used when riding. This often includes the *adductors* (muscles that attach to the pelvis and legs and bring the hips and legs inward toward the body's mid-line), the *upper trapezius* (which raises the shoulders toward the ears), and the *hip flexors* (responsible for lifting and bending the legs toward the trunk). But when these muscles are neglected, the result is imbalances of the myofascia. Functionality and performance are diminished. So while certain movements, such as raising the shoulders toward the ears, are not desirable when mounted, they should be part of your ground (resistance) training. Otherwise, in this case, the *trapezius* muscle of your back will not function properly. And because the *trapezius* also functions (lower down) as a key postural muscle, your riding position will be affected in a negative way. Quite a number of clients just starting out with me have weakness in their upper, mid, and lower *trapezius*. (You can find "trap" strengthening exercises in chapter 16—see p. 157.)

Overdeveloping the inner thigh muscles is a common fear—of course, no one wants to grip their horse like a clothespin. But the same muscles that move the thighs inward are also part of our deep core myofascial chain, which pulls upward with each exhale. When used in this way, these muscles actually invite a horse's back to lift, then support it in the lifted position. In reality, these are important riding muscles that are typically not trained. You will learn more about these in chapter 27 (see p. 251), but to get a sample feel of the upward lift, try the unmounted exercise on p. 111.

Muscle Myth 7: Horses don't like big butts.

Fact: Another set of muscles equestrians tend to fear are the glutes, muscles located at the back and sides of your pelvis. The glutes are quite active in movements such as bending and squatting; they should also be active when we walk or run, but frequently, they are not. Instead, the glutes are often *deactivated* thanks to modern lifestyles, and especially from sitting. I will explore this further in a minute.

What many riders don't realize is that the glutes also help stabilize your lower back and control pelvic tilting and rotation. In fact, they are an integral part of the rider's leg aids. Riders typically understand they should not clench with the buttock muscles, as doing so puts distance between the seat bones and saddle. While it is true there should be minimal action of the lower glutes when you ride, it is often the hamstrings (which attach directly to our seat bones) that tend to pop us out of the saddle. The *higher*, *deeper*, and *side* glutes (yes, three different types!) are *all* important to activate when you ride. Conscious activation is critical, because our glutes tend to "go to sleep" every time we sit—and they are infamous for "staying asleep," even when the alarm is ringing! Unfortunately, not using our glutes effectively predisposes us to fatigued muscles, back troubles, injuries, and potential joint replacements (not to mention serious imbalances in your myofascial lines). Developing the glutes will result in big payoffs in a rider's ability to stabilize her torso during movements such as medium and extended trots. It also will solidify the connection between the rider's legs and the horse's hind legs. We will learn more about the specifics later in this chapter.

MUSCLE ACTIVATION EXPLORED

A muscle needs to activate before it will function properly for movement. Modern living, inertia, and poorly designed chairs, sofas, and car seats all stifle our ability to move. Movement itself can help activate muscles, but some muscles are notoriously hard to activate. We've already seen how the glutes are examples of this. When the glutes don't activate, our spine is subject to excessive compressive forces, in turn giving rise to weak, inflexible, sleepy, painful areas that hurt or spasm when you move. Moving as much as possible within your pain-free range will substantially help your athletic performance and your body's ability to function. But you can get even better relief if you activate a muscle prior to initiating the exercise or movement. Let's take a closer look.

Muscle activation refers to a state of readiness of a muscle to contract, hold, or elongate. Equally important, it also involves a muscle's willingness and capacity to deactivate, thus avoiding over-tension or spasms. When a muscle in a myofascial chain resists deactivation, it tends to shorten the chain length.

Ideally, you should sense that all your muscles are there for you, ready to fire (or relax) at a moment's notice. If you watch an Olympic athlete such as a ski racer, she will often shake and tap her legs, sides, and hips before she takes off down the mountain. She is *activating* ("waking up") the muscles she is about to call upon. She will often choose specific muscles to activate by prioritizing the weak links of a chain. This is a smart, and very effective, training tool. Here are some actions that will "wake up" a muscle:

- Shaking
- Tapping
- Rolling
- Poking
- Wiggling the overlying skin
- Squeezing the muscle on and off in pulsing fashion
- Pointing to a muscle and bringing your attention to it with your thoughts

MUSCLE ACTIVATION EXERCISE 1:
Adductor Lifts

You will need two strips of coarse sandpaper, stapled or duct taped onto cardboard or a piece of wood approximately 15 inches long by 12 inches wide for this exercise. The sandpaper helps hold your feet in place.

Step One: Stand on two sandpaper boards set about hip-width apart (fig. 11.1 A).

Step Two: Tension (don't move) your knees and thighs in an *outward* direction as you simultaneously tension your feet and inner calves *toward* each other. Keep your feet stuck to the sandpaper so that nothing moves.

Step Three: Close your eyes, breathe, and visualize an upward movement of energy from the arches of your feet to the inner edges of your calves and thighs. This upward sensation continues into your torso, particularly when you exhale.

Step Four: Now try this exercise with your feet in a staggered position (fig. 11.1 B). This will enable you to feel your inner thighs lift as if one of your legs is at the girth and the other is behind the girth while riding.

11.1 A & B Adductor Lifts standard (A) and staggered (B).

MUSCLE ACTIVATION EXERCISE 2:
Left Side Activation

What follows are examples of how a rider might use muscle activation prior to riding in order to wake up a sleepy left side.

Step One: Sit centered on your seat bones with your right leg fairly straight and the left leg bent (fig. 11.2 A). Your right heel should be placed firmly on the mat as you hug your bent left leg and pull it toward your torso. You can now roll

11.2 A–C Left Side Activation

from side to side to accentuate the feel of your left seat bone.

Step Two: Place a weighted vest (or other source of weight—a 5 to 10 pound ankle weight will do) on your left shoulder as you tap the sides of your left rib cage and hip with your fingers to "wake up" the underlying muscles (fig. 11.2 B).

Step Three: If your rib cage tends to slide off to the right side relative to the position of your pelvis, slide your rib cage to the left so it is better centered over your pelvis (fig. 11.2 C). Direct your attention to your left side and tap with your fingers to "wake up" the muscles that lie there.

MUSCLE ACTIVATION EXERCISE 3:
Glute Poke and Punch

Step One: Poke a finger into the muscle you are about to use. Try poking into the back of your pelvis, keeping your finger in the "poke" position.

Step Two: Now, let the muscle "punch back" into your finger. It should feel like the muscle in the pelvis squeezes and bulges out a little. (The back of the pelvis is *loaded* with glutes.)

Step Three: Lighten your touch while keeping your finger in place, then relax the muscle you just activated. The job of the finger held lightly in place is to check and make sure the muscle is now *deactivated* and resting. *A deactivated muscles* should feel like it is not working, potentially even weak.

Step Four: Repeat this exercise while poking into each side of your pelvis. Make sure you have both *activation* (bulging) and *deactivation* (releasing) in the muscle.

MUSCLE ACTIVATION EXERCISE 4:
Triceps Shake and Wiggle

Most riders would do well to activate their triceps (the muscle on the back of the upper arms) because typically, our biceps tend to overpower them. The Triceps Shake and Wiggle exercise will invite your triceps to step up to the plate!

Step One: Shake out your arms in a moderately vigorous way for about a minute.

Step Two: Take your left hand and put it underneath your right upper arm. Slide and shift around the skin there until you create warmth.

Step Three: Shake your arms again, then repeat the exercise on the other side.

MUSCLE ACTIVATION EXERCISE 5:
Independent Body Parts

One of the biggest challenges of riding is to moderately activate specific muscles as you tone down or deactivate others. Use the activation methods explained earlier in this chapter to assist you in these next challenging exercises. For deactivation and release, it is best to use imagery. Imagine the muscle or body part turning into a soft, billowy cloud, or melting like an icicle or a pat of butter on a warm homemade muffin. Try some of the following moves to practice activating and deactivating muscles simultaneously:

- Tighten the right leg crease area (where the leg joins the torso) as you release and deactivate the muscles around the right seat bone.

- Tighten the top of the left shoulder (between the top of your left arm and head) without tightening the arm, elbow, wrist, or fingers.

- Tighten the backs of the thighs without tightening the muscles at the back of the pelvis. Also, do not lift the kneecaps or tense the front of the thighs.

- Tighten the muscles of the pinky fingers without tightening muscles in the wrist, elbows, or arms.

- Tighten the muscles of your heels (yes, they have them!) without tightening or clenching your toes or kneecaps.

- Tighten the muscles around your ears and eyes while releasing and deactivating the muscles of your jaw.

MUSCLE ACTIVATION EXERCISE 6:
Glute Activation Walk

Many people pull themselves along with their hamstrings when they walk, but it is more correct to activate your glutes and push yourself forward. There should be a glide to your stride, similar to ice skating.

Step One: Tap the sides and back of your pelvis to wake up your glutes.

Step Two: Taking smaller steps than you would usually, land a little more toward the mid-foot. Your heel may touch first, but avoid a hard heel strike (fig. 11.3).

11.3 Glute Activation Walk

Step Three: Do not allow the leading leg to extend in front of your hips. Instead, establish a bit of a forward lean from the ankles to hips. Keep your *center of gravity* (between the hips) over your *base of support* (feet).

Step Four: Keep your legs fairly straight, with a soft bend at the knees. Do not hyperextend or lock the knees.

Step Five: Feel the firmness of the glutes with your hands. Don't consciously contract them.

11.4 A–D Eventer Bekki Read of Round Robin Farm in Tunbridge, Vermont, demonstrates lower ribs poking outward and upward due to a failure of the rib cage muscles to activate (A). This puts a lot of stress on the lumbar region. To activate her lower rib cage muscles, Bekki drops a stirrup and raises the same-side arm (B). She then pulses the lower rib cage muscles as if she was pumping a fist. This exercise should be repeated on the other side. Bekki holds her hand on her rib cage as she moves it forward, backward, left, and right relative to her pelvis (C). This increases her awareness of the rib anchoring muscles. Thanks to her effectively activated rib anchoring muscles, Bekki jumps with well-aligned ribs and a supported lower back (D).

Your glutes will contract on their own if you took a correct step.

Step Six: As one leg steps forward under your center of gravity, the other leg swings backward as it would if you were skating.

Step Seven: Place one hand on the pelvis on the side of the leg swinging behind you. Feel the pelvis push backward. Imagine a little duck's foot pushing backward as if it was propelling a duck while swimming (see fig. 13.4—p. 130).

MUSCLE ACTIVATION EXERCISE 7:
Activated Riding

There are numerous ways to activate key muscles when you ride. The example shown in figs. 11.4 A–D focuses on activating the rib cage muscles at the beginning of a jumping lesson. Activated rib cage muscles support the rider's lumbar area.

REST AND RECOVERY

Your muscles rest and repair themselves as you sleep at night. This is a critical aspect of making a full recovery from the preceding day and being able to perform your best. A good night's sleep is an investment in your safety and well being. It helps you stay sharp and supports your response/reaction time. When you are tired, have been overtraining and perhaps not giving your body adequate time off, you increase the likelihood of injury.

Rest is important, but there are two types of rest to consider: *passive rest* and *active rest*. *Passive rest* is when you refrain from all activity; after a significant injury or surgery, this is usually advisable. But during passive rest, you are prone to losing strength and stamina as your muscles weaken and connective tissue shortens. This process weakens your bones and can pull them out of alignment. Your aerobic capacity declines. Circulation and lymph drainage are also negatively affected. Mental acuity declines, and your mood may suffer.

The second type of rest, *active rest*, is when you incorporate low intensity movements into your routine, encouraging healing without stirring up pain. For example, an injured or fatigued runner might walk or aqua jog instead of resting completely. In active rest, you can move and do low-intensity exercise frequently. Be vigilant that you do nothing to bother your injury or add to your fatigue. During active rest, I suggest you work on building core endurance. Your spine and core will love this and reap good benefits.

In her landmark book *The Thinking Body* (The Gestalt Journal Press, 2008), Mabel Elsworth Todd suggests an active rest pose known as

11.5 For constructive rest pose, lie on your back with knees bent and feet flat on the floor. Fold your arms across your chest. Breathe slowly and deeply to rejuvenate your muscles. Do this pose daily for 10 to 20 minutes.

constructive rest pose (fig. 11.5). This pose allows the shoulders and hips to sink deeply and rest in their sockets. Strive to do this pose daily for 10 to 20 minutes. Your muscles and joints will thank you.

Note that it is the constant use of a single position (whether held or in a movement) that creates dysfunction and ultimately pain in joints. They simply wear out! Repetitive movements also contribute to myofascial imbalances. Varied postures and movements are the hallmark of healthy, functioning bodies.

chapter takeaway ✓

A muscle needs to activate before it can properly produce a movement. Some muscles activate easily. But certain muscles, like the glutes, tend to "go to sleep" and can benefit from deliberate prior activation. This can be accomplished by bringing attention to the muscle by poking, tapping, or shaking it, or using some of the other methods explored in this chapter. It is much better to let your body dictate how much to activate a muscle than aspire to a prescribed percentage of activation. Following your body's cues promotes its functionality.

PART 2

CHAPTER TWELVE
LETTING TENSION GO

"Be yourself and the right people will find you."
— Life and Wellness Coach Sabrina Cadini

THE BODY AND STRESS

Life typically fluctuates from feeling harmonious and grand to being overwhelmed by stress or struggle. Milder emotions tend to be replaced by others with greater potency. It's a bit of a roller coaster ride!

When we don't let go of our stress, it settles in the body. It is reflected in our breathing, our posture, our movements, our health and well-being, and our decision-making. It is in the energy we present to our horses. When we are stressed, our muscles put a chokehold on our bones. Typical places to store stress include the jaw, shoulders, neck, hips, belly, and back.

When we hold tension in a body part, our postural shape changes, and it often raises our center of gravity. Breathing then becomes shallow and orients toward the chest. Digestion suffers. Neuromuscular and vascular balances are altered. Energy is diminished—and you stop thriving.

Once again, movement becomes key to unlocking the grip of heightened tension on our muscles. When we move or breathe less, we are restricting a muscle in its expression; the only choice it has left is to grip onto our bones, typically raising the body's center of gravity. But releasing downward can mitigate that effect. Try releasing the arms, the shoulder blades, the lower jaw, and the coccyx downward as you take a long, deep sigh. At the same time, cast your glance downward. *Ahhhh!* A sigh is an extremely potent release of tension—that applies to our horses as well as us!

To alleviate the effect stress has on your muscles, be aware of the trigger emotions behind the gripping. Some include feeling:

- Overwhelmed
- Fearful
- Loss of control
- Pressured
- Impatient
- Numb
- Alarmed
- Dread
- Unworthiness
- Angry
- Resentful
- Jealous

The next two sections of this book will give you some specifics on how to intervene before those feelings trigger gripping muscles. The body and brain need to learn how to work together. The muscles in the rider's body know they have to move to settle the brain down. Frankly, the mind finally quiets down when it realizes it is the body that holds the wisdom (fig. 12.1). It's movement of the body that enables you to let go of stress and step out of your own way. The questions and concerns come from your mind. The answers come from your body.

TECHNIQUES OF LETTING GO

There are so many variables to life and to riding: physical, mental, emotional, neurological, psychological, situational, energetic levels, and environment, for a few examples. It can be complicated, challenging, and even scary to have so many unknowns out of your control. When you add in expectations, accident history, performance anxiety, and faulty assumptions, it's easy to see why so many riders sometimes struggle with stress.

We all have different ways to process our stress, but here are some additional ideas worthy of your attention:

- *Shaking out body parts:* This can help release old patterns that have frozen into your body-mind system. It feels energizing but also relaxing as you shake because doing so distributes body fluids and enhances internal body space.

12.1 This overly tense rider's brain has run away with anxious thoughts. She is desperately trying to catch her brain and rein it back in! But it's the movements of her body that will quiet her anxious thoughts.

12.2 Heading out on a trail ride with friends is a powerful way to let tension go. Simply relax and enjoy nature.

- *Nature:* How lucky those of us who work with horses are to be close to the rhythms of nature! How long has it been since you went on a relaxing trail ride with a friend (fig. 12.2)?

- *Grounding:* Get in touch with your planet by sitting on a rock or the ground. Walk barefoot on the grass, and feel your connection right down to the core of the earth.

- *Breathing:* Slow, deep, rhythmic breathing is central to all modes of letting tension go. Full-body breathing can settle both you and your horse.

- *Mindfulness:* Bringing one's attention to the present moment is vital for the release of unwanted tension. Try placing your hands either on your heart or any area where you can readily feel your pulse. Alternatively, listen to the sound of your breath. Either of these actions help to capture your runaway thoughts.

- *Play:* Playful movements heal and help release "stuck," grippy muscles. Play should be an activity you really look forward to!

LETTING TENSION GO

It's important to start your ride from a platform of relaxation. Neither horse nor rider can perform well if not functionally relaxed. If some of your muscles are shortened and bound in *negative* tension, *positive* tension (see p. 23) cannot be achieved. It is up to the rider to set the tone! Invest some time in settling yourself before you mount up. Your horse will appreciate your improved focus, timing, and coordination. The centering and grounding exercises of chapters 1 and 2 (see pp. 7 and 19) will help your tension dissipate before you mount up. But here are some other exercises to help you release your tension even further.

TENSION RELEASE EXERCISE 1:
Playful Movement

You need a super quiet, tolerant horse, a bareback pad, and an experienced helper to hold your horse (remain halted for this exercise).

Step One: While steadying yourself with your hands, swing one leg forward over the horse's neck (you will be sitting sideways), then swing the same leg over your horse's hindquarters until you are facing your horse's tail.

Step Two: Bend forward from your hips and "melt" into your horse's back line.

Step Three: Remain quiet so you can feel your heartbeat and hear and feel your horse's breathing. Notice any rhythmic or synchronized movements as you become one with your horse. If this version of the exercise is too much for your horse, you can get a similar effect while standing on the ground. Simply place your ear to one of your horse's sides, and loop one arm over his back while you hear and feel his breath.

12.3 Playful Movement

TENSION RELEASE EXERCISE 2:
Thin Straw

Step One: Exhale slowly through a real or imagined thin straw, making a small circular opening with your lips.

Step Two: Next, inhale through your nose slowly and deeply. Pause at the top of the inhale, then repeat Step One.

Step Three: As you breathe in, visualize bright light and positive energy entering your lungs and traveling throughout your body. As you exhale, imagine your unwanted emotions and stress-provokers exiting.

Step Four: To enhance oxygen intake, do this exercise with your hands held high against a wall. Be sure to pause after both the inhales and the exhales.

TENSION RELEASE EXERCISE 3:
Meditation Walk the Course

This can be done using a dressage test or obstacle course, as well as any jumping course.

Step One: Center, ground, and bring yourself to the present moment. Feel your pulse and listen to the sound of your breath.

Step Two: Begin a walking meditation (in your ring, barnyard, or hay field, for example) by allowing sounds, sights, smells, and emotions to enter your awareness, but then flow through you and away.

Step Three: When your mind becomes active, simply allow those intruding thoughts to drift away.

Step Four: Re-ground and re-center as needed.

TENSION RELEASE EXERCISE 4:
Tighten and Shake

Step One: Tighten one hand into a strong fist and hold for three to five seconds.

Step Two: On an exhale, release the fist with an audible sigh. Shake your hand and fingers for a few seconds.

Step Three: Embrace the comfort of the relaxed muscles. "Thank them" for letting go.

Step Four: Do steps one through three with as many different sections of your body as you can. Don't forget your face and jaw!

TENSION RELEASE EXERCISE 5:
Barrel Roll

Step One: Lie down on a soft surface and visualize yourself as a barrel.

Step Two: Imagine you are about to roll down a gently sloping, grassy hill.

Step Three: As you begin to "roll down the hill," embrace your youthful joy and abandon life's cares. Laugh! Allow the joy of your laughter to settle like grains of salt sprinkling your bones.

TENSION RELEASE EXERCISE 6:
Base of Skull Point

The Base of Skull Point exercise makes use of an easy to access acupressure point. It can be done either mounted or unmounted.

Step One: Take one finger from each hand and press one finger's-width below the base of your skull, about half an inch outward from the spine.

Step Two: While holding the pressure, visualize a relaxing scene or your favorite vacation spot. Hold for about one minute. You can also try humming or a light chant while doing this.

---

chapter takeaway ✓

Life generates stress. This is true for us as well as our horses. But it's possible to mitigate the effects of stress through mindful awareness and playful movements. If we don't take active steps to release our stress, tension locks into the muscles of our body, and the muscles pull at our bones. Remember that questions and concerns come from your mind. Answers come from your body.

CHAPTER THIRTEEN
THE RIDER'S PELVIS

THE PELVIC ARCH

The well-aligned pelvis is a *neutral pelvis*. A neutral pelvis is one that is aligned with gravitational forces. The seat bones point directly down, and there is a hint of an anterior tilt, meaning your pelvis needs to be in a slight "ducky tail" (see fig. 1.13, p. 18). Remember, as we discussed in chapter 1, if you imagine your pelvis as a bowl containing water, there should be a steady *drip, drip, drip* out the front of it. However, many riders hold their pelvis with the water pouring out of the back end. Some hold their pelvis so that no water comes out at all. Still others have water *pouring* out the front end. But a *neutral pelvis* has a just a *drip, drip, drip* out the front end. And be careful your pelvis is not higher on one side, pouring water out the left or right. It is helpful to enlist a trained ground person to verify when you are truly neutral and aligned. You can't tell this accurately from a mirror.

When the pelvis is not held in a neutral fashion, you compromise your sacrum's ability to support and distribute the sizeable compressive load that travels through the spine. This applies whether you are mounted or unmounted, but the effect is amplified when you ride because of the additional physical forces of the horse's movements. This is one reason why your back may not be happy with you during or after a ride. Additionally, the pelvic floor muscles cannot function properly without a neutral pelvis; these muscles affect the floor of your seat in the saddle.

Unfortunately, part of modern living is being sucked into car seats and "comfortable" chairs, soft sofas, or relaxing recliners. These tend to tuck our pelvis under and drag our hips forward, causing the pelvis to become situated in front of the rib cage. This position is a recipe for how to hyperextend your lower back, crunch your neck and spine, and freeze your hips all at once! *Yikes!* The good news is you can free up the muscles that tense the pelvis into a tucked position (fig. 13.1).

NEUTRAL PELVIS EXERCISE 1:
Hoof Picks

Step One: Hold a hoof pick in each hand.

Step Two: Press the backs of the hoof picks at a point about an inch below the top rim of your pelvis, and a couple of inches away from the center of your spine.

Step Three: Slowly drag the hoof picks directly upward to the bottom of your rib cage.

Step Four: Feel the muscles of your back release, and allow your pelvis to slide into a neutral position. It will feel as if you have a slight "ducky tail."

13.1 Hoof Picks

PELVIC BALANCE

Some riders have a too forward tilt to their pelvis, and their weight is then too heavily balanced on the pubic bone. When this occurs, the horse cannot balance well under the rider which discourages him from moving forward. In this case, both the horse's and rider's backs will be quite stiff, compromising supple, swinging motion. Since the bowl-shaped pelvis connects the spine (our *stability*) to our legs (our *mobility*), it has a role in both stability and mobility. Therefore, the rider with an exaggerated anterior tilt to her pelvis will struggle with her posture, her gait, and her stability. Remember that the position of your pelvis affects the curvatures of your spine, so a pelvis that is not in a neutral position is likely to pull the spine's neutral alignment off. Double trouble!

There are extremely strong ligaments, tough tendons, powerful muscles, and supportive fascia that bind the spine, pelvis, and thighs with each other. When you sit on a horse, there is an arch that forms (like a bridge) between each seat bone and the sacrum of the spine. This strong arch supports the weight of the upper torso and balances the compression forces of the spine. In this way, the pelvis contributes to the proper and healthy functioning of the spine (fig. 13.2).

When you ride, your pelvis distributes your upper body weight to its two sides and through to the sacrum and your seat bones. The pubic bone (*ramus*) in the front of the pelvis completes the pelvic ring such that your upper body weight is distributed around the whole pelvis. Sitting in alignment requires a pelvis that is anchored through the floor of your seat. The rider's entire pelvis is anchored to the horse's movements in a supple way that transfers physical forces through her joints.

The floor of your seat is a triangle formed between your two seat bones and the pubic bone. This triangle should be nestled in the deepest, lowest part of your saddle when your pelvis is in a neutral position. When the pubic bone is not anchored to the pommel of the saddle, you will create instability by teetering on your two seat bones. This is one good reason to visualize a slight "ducky tail," because it enables the triangular floor of your seat to function as your solid, stable base. I often lay three strips of coarse sandpaper in a triangle, attach them together with duct tape, then place them on the saddle for the rider to feel the triangular nature of the floor of her seat. Only when all three of these points connect do the seat bones point directly downward. Maintaining contact with the floor of the seat enables the seat bones to "plug into" the "energy receptors" of a horse's back, and voila, you have a physical, as well as an energetic, connection with your horse (figs. 13.3 A–C).

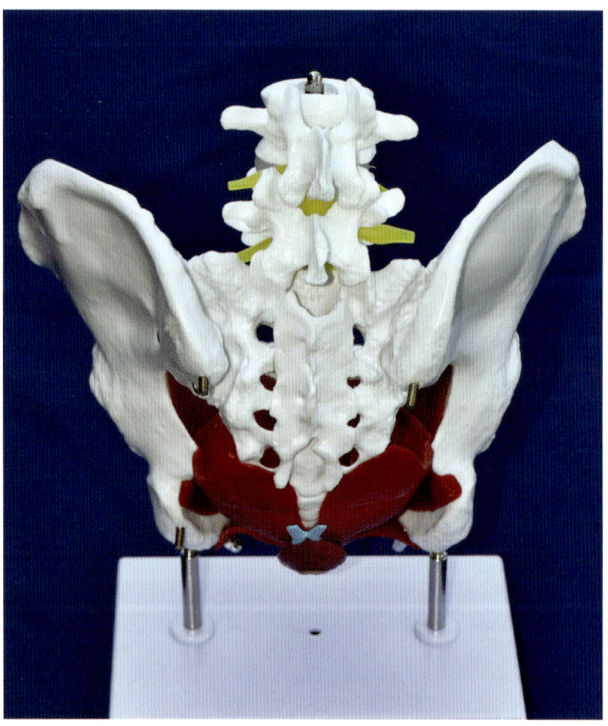

13.2 This is a model of a female pelvis. Note the archway created from the two *seat bones* (the base) to the *sacrum* (the large triangular bone at the back of the pelvis—the pelvic floor is indicated in red). This arch bears the task of supporting the weight of the rider's head and trunk.

13.3 A–C The pelvis *tucked under* is an unstable situation for both the pelvis and spine (A). It is also an uncomfortable position for the horse to try to balance under. Because the rider is "unplugged," it significantly interferes with energy transfer from horse to rider, as well as rider to horse. When the position of the pelvis is tilted too far forward, it is also quite an uncomfortable position for the horse, and an unstable position for the rider (B). It is hard for the horse to balance beneath her. But when the rider has good contact with the floor of her seat, essentially "plugging into" her horse's energy, she enhances her chances for a successful ride (C)!

It's helpful to visualize a ship's anchor in your pelvis, because the body's center of gravity is typically just in front of the sacrum (at about S-2). When we are stressed or lose our posture for other reasons, it is common for the center of gravity to become elevated to a higher point in the torso. But to ride in a stable yet supple fashion, it's best to keep one's center of gravity low, allowing the sacrum to descend. Imagining a heavy ship's anchor in your pelvis reinforces the anchoring of the floor of your seat (fig. 13.4).

Additional imagery can help encourage correct position and function of the pelvis when you ride. First, try this. Place your hands at the back-bottom edge of each pelvic half and walk forward a few steps. You will feel a kickback alternating from the left and right sides of your pelvis; this feeling is the result of your pelvic halves moving. Be sure to take short steps, because if either of your legs reaches out in front of your hips, you may not be able to feel this action. A reminder that it's a neutral pelvis that gives rise to the healthiest pelvic rotation and hip extension.

Now imagine each pelvic half has a little duck's foot attached to the bottom rim (fig. 13.5). Like a duck swimming in water, the foot (and pelvic half) kick rearward in a circular action in order to go forward. When a pelvic half aims rearward, it stabilizes the sacrum; this is highly desirable because it helps you find fluidity as well as deep core strength. But a word of caution here: When you are mounted, do not push and shove the "duck feet"/pelvic halves around. Simply allow each "duck foot" to fluidly follow your horse's natural movements. Pretend you are a duck paddling on a good-sized pond, and not one that is fighting currents in the middle of Lake Superior! You are sitting on your horse's precious back, and you have a responsibility to it. You should never push and shove on your horse's back with your pelvis, and especially do not push in a downward direction. The movement should feel more like you are body surfing a ripple or small wave. As the "water-wheel-hips" alternately rotate, there is a decisive "pull up" feeling

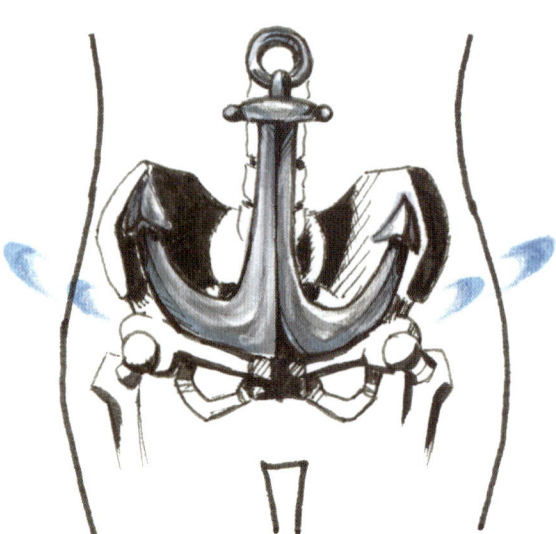

13.4 Visualize your pelvis as a strong, stable foundation, like a heavy ship's anchor in the saddle.

13.5 Imagine there is a duck's foot at the back/bottom of each pelvic half. The duck paddles rearward to swim forward in the water. This is the feeling you should get at the back of your pelvis when you walk or run. When you ride, the feeling is similar, but gentle and following the movements of your horse.

(especially when asking a horse to lift his back), and a passive "follow down." Allowing your pelvic halves to rotate independently will help you learn how to sit well to the trot.

PELVIC FLOOR MUSCLES

The *pelvic floor muscles* (PFM) attach to the pubic bone and the coccyx (tailbone) as well as to both seat bones. These deep fibers run front to back, from pubic bone to coccyx. It's mostly the deeper fibers that assist the upward action of the PFM during exhalation, and whenever the deep core myofascia is actively engaged (fig. 13.6).

Healthy pelvic floor muscles do three things:

1 They hold your organs up.

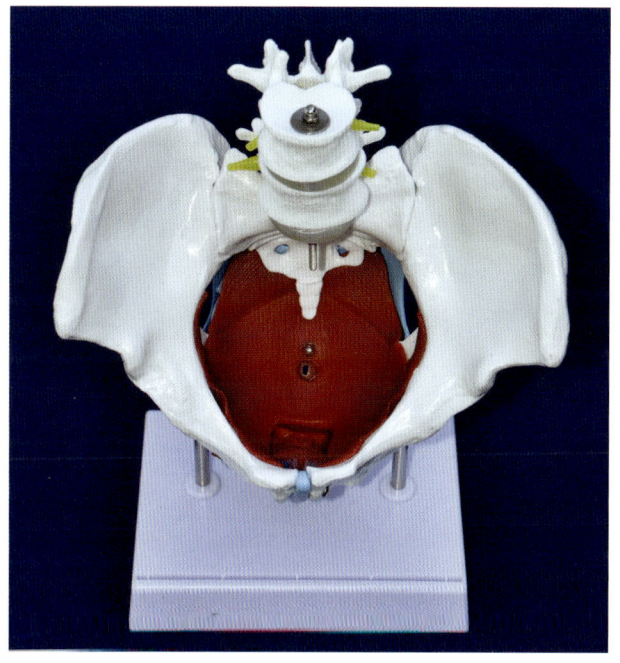

13.6 The pelvic floor (in red) and its myofascia support your center of gravity. The PFM acts like a hammock to the organs of the pelvis. When these muscles contract, they pull the pubic bone, coccyx, and seat bones toward each other. During this contraction, your spinal stability muscles are also activated.

2 They hold back the body's elimination (for instance when you sneeze, cough, or laugh).

3 They notify the spinal stabilizers of when it's time to activate.

If any of these three functions are compromised, your PFM may be weak. Weakness can occur due to the effects of aging, gravity, trauma, surgery, childbirth, or simply neglecting to strengthen this area. Sitting does not help you strengthen your PFM. But also consider the opposite; if you tighten or squeeze the PFM too much, they get overly tense and don't function well. For a rider, tight PFMs lock up and force her to rely on gripping, leaning on the reins, or balancing her body weight on her stirrups.

Ideally, the PFM should be moving upward and downward continuously, with a gliding sensation that is connected to your breathing. These muscles have a close association with your diaphragm. When you inhale, both the diaphragm and PFM glide downward. When you exhale, they glide upward. If you put one hand on your belly button, you should feel it rise upward with each exhale and sink back down on each inhale. This is because when the diaphragm contracts, it pulls downward, creating more space in the thorax for incoming air. Some people find it hard to feel this action when they are standing. In this case, I suggest trying a bridge position (fig. 13.7).

Pelvic floor muscles need both *elasticity* and *tonicity* to support breathing and daily functioning. Therefore, both strength and stretch work are important for this area. The following exercises will help you tone the pelvic floor muscles as well as keep them flexible.

Bit of Advice: Stabilize Your Pelvis

When you need to quiet down your seat and stabilize your pelvis, try this:

Isometrically tension the muscles that draw the pubic bone rearward toward the coccyx. Do not pull your belly button to your spine to accomplish this. The action described occurs lower down, more toward the bottom of the pelvis. Put one hand on your pubic bone to get a sense of where to feel this action. When you engage those muscles, you stabilize the pelvis. You may feel your lower belly spread out more. This action also encourages the spinal stabilizers to "wake up" and get to work! Make sure your belly remains soft. Holding the front line inward or tucking your pelvis (like a tail) underneath you will destabilize both your pelvis and spine.

13.7 In the bridge position (lie down on your back with your knees bent and your feet flat on the ground, and push down into your feet as you lift your hips off the ground), place one hand on your belly button as shown. You will feel it descend (toward your feet) on each inhale and ascend (toward your rib cage) on each exhale.

Kegel vs. PFM Exercises

You may be familiar with *Kegel exercises.* They are effective at developing and maintaining sphincter control for the process of elimination. But Kegels target the superficial muscles near body cavity openings. Although helpful for both men and women, these exercises will do little to improve the floor of your seat when you ride. When practicing Kegel exercises, you are typically instructed to stop the flow of urine midstream, or stop yourself from passing gas.

Compared to the Kegel exercises, PFM exercises tap into much deeper muscles. Note the difference between a typical Kegel exercise as just described, and the following (perhaps too graphic) PFM visualization: Imagine you are sitting on the toilet and just starting to release your urine or stools when you are suddenly shaken to the core by an ear-piercing howl of a coyote just outside the bathroom door. In response, you quickly suck it all back up into your body, intensely feeling an upward action deep inside, just in front of the sacrum and spine. *Those* are your PFM at work!

PELVIC FLOOR MUSCLE EXERCISE 1:
Power Buttwalking

The Power Buttwalking exercise will tone the floor of your riding seat, and it may also make you laugh (as it did for our model)!

Step One: Sit on a mat or comfortable, even surface. Stretch your legs out in front of you.

Step Two: While keeping your upper torso stable, begin to "walk" on your bottom by lifting each hip and pelvic half—first left, then right (fig. 13.8). Be careful to not lean from side to side with the upper body.

Step Three: "Walk" the outline of a square. In each corner of the square, buttwalk in place a few beats.

Step Four: After completing the square, "walk" 10 steps forward, 10 steps backward, 10 steps to the left, and 10 steps to the right. You can also try a leg-yielding type pattern!

Step Five: Once you have mastered the buttwalk with minimal leaning left or right, challenge yourself by buttwalking up and down hill.

PELVIC FLOOR MUSCLE EXERCISE 2:
Crawling on Forearms

In this variation of the crawl, you move your forearms and legs in diagonal pairs, like a trotting horse. The left forearm and the right lower leg will be on the floor at the same time, and vice versa. Keep the pace of this crawling exercise slow.

13.8 Power Buttwalking

13.9 Crawling on Forearms

13.10 Lizard Crawl

Step One: Find a comfortable surface (on a pad or mat if needed). Get down on your hands and knees.

Step Two: First practice a few crawling steps where you move in a same-side (*ipsilateral*) pattern. This means you will move your left forearm and leg at the same time, then the right side in a similar fashion.

Step Three: Now start the crawl in a diagonal pattern (*contralateral*—fig. 13.9) for a couple of minutes.

PELVIC FLOOR EXERCISE 3:
Lizard Crawl

Lizard Crawl is a slow, methodical exercise with huge benefits to the floor of your seat. Breathe deeply and slowly, and sigh as you move for added perks.

Step One: Lie on your belly on a comfortable but fairly firm surface.

Step Two: Slowly move each arm ahead of you while also moving the opposite leg in a slow swing out to the side (fig. 13.10).

Step Three: Keep your head and neck in a neutral position, eyes looking toward the ground.

Step Four: Also try some backward Lizard Crawling!

PELVIC FLOOR MUSCLE EXERCISE 4:
Baby Bounce Squats

When you practice the Baby Bounce Squat, make sure you keep a slight "ducky tail" (see p. 18). Don't sink so low that your pelvis tucks under.

Step One: Stand with your feet about hip-width apart.

Step Two: Draw your hips well back as you bend your knees and squat. Keep a slight but strong "ducky tail." If your pelvis starts to tuck under, stop—you've gone too low.

Step Three: Reach forward with both arms, while keeping a solid amount of weight in your heels. Keep your head and neck in line with your spine (fig. 13.11).

Step Four: Start tiny bounces (vertically) leading the moves from your hips.

Step Five: Your body will tell you when you've had enough. Listen, because your body holds the wisdom of knowing what you need and what is helpful.

PELVIC FLOOR EXERCISE 5:
Pop-Up Stance

You will utilize ground reaction forces in the Pop-Up Stance exercise to both strengthen and supple your PFM. This move will bring more verticality and less sideways movement to your walk as well as to your riding. This is called Pop-Up Stance because you *don't* deliberately lift one pelvic half—instead, you forcefully *push down*, causing the other pelvic half to automatically "pop up." The foot on the popped-up side will hover over the ground.

13.11 Baby Bounce Squats

Step One: Stand with your feet about hip-width apart.

Step Two: Forcefully push directly downward with one pelvic half. You should feel your leg and foot on that side push toward the core of the earth. Stay straight, and do not bend your torso.

Step Three: Allow the pelvic half/leg/foot on the opposite side of your body to pop up and hold the hovering foot here (fig. 13.12). Work up to a minute or two of the hovering hold. Be sure not to deliberately lift the leg or foot.

Step Four: Slowly swing the hovering leg forward about 6 inches, then rearward about 6 inches. Keep up this slow swinging for about a minute, without touchdowns if possible.

Step Five: Repeat on the other side.

PELVIC FLOOR MUSCLE EXERCISE 6:
Sounds for the Pelvis

The use of sounds can significantly increase the sensation of your PFM lifting on exhalation. This action will support your attempts to lift a horse's back up.

13.12 Pop-Up Stance

Step One: On exhalation, use a long "*hhhhh*," "*thhh*" or "*fffffff*" sound as you visualize the PFM climbing upward toward the rib cage. This sound also helps your spine stabilize.

Step Two: When you inhale, visualize the PFM returning downward as they relax. Don't aim for 100 percent relaxation, because they need some tone to support your organs.

PELVIC FLOOR MUSCLE EXERCISE 7:
Pelvic Connections

You are about to get a sense of how vastly different parts of the body are connected. Have fun with this new awareness!

Step One: Put each hand on the front of your pelvis such that you feel both top and bottom pelvic rims.

Step Two: Keeping your head straight and stationary, let your eyes glance up and down, plus to the left and right. Notice what happens to your pelvis. Think about how this action can apply to the advice that trainers often give concerning looking at the horizon.

Step Three: Repeat Step Two, but use both the eyes and the head this time. Look up, down, left, and right. Typically, this produces a more vigorous feeling than in Step Two.

Step Four: Move your hands to the back of your pelvis and tap the sacrum and coccyx areas (below the waist). Visualize your tailbone. While keeping the rest of your body still, try to slightly move only your tailbone—forward, backward, left, right, up, down, and in circles. No one should be able to see your hips, pelvis, torso, head, arms, or legs move. If you were able to do that, by golly, you just wagged your tail! This is a superb warm-up exercise for riding.

---

chapter takeaway ✓

To be in a neutral position, your pelvis needs a slight anterior tilt. This is the only position from which your sacrum can properly distribute the sizeable compressive load that comes through the spine when you ride. Like all other muscles, your PFM need to be supple as well as toned. Practice the supportive exercises in this chapter to help improve the health of your PFM.

PART 2

CHAPTER FOURTEEN
THE RIDER'S RIB CAGE

RIB ANCHOR EXPLORED

The floor of the rib cage is made up of the large, powerful diaphragm muscle. There are 12 pairs of ribs, all of which connect to the thoracic spine. The front of the rib cage connects to the sternum (breastbone) either directly (for ribs 1 through 7) or through cartilaginous extensions (ribs 8 through 10). Ribs 11 and 12 are called "floating" because they do not connect to the sternum at all; the floating ribs move rearward as you inhale. To feel this motion, place one hand on a floating rib and the other hand at the top of your rib cage or sternum—and breathe. As you inhale, feel how the floating ribs move toward the spine, while the upper ribs and the top of the sternum have an upward-outward action.

Because the ribs attach to the thoracic spine, the thorax is quite stable and not very flexible; it does a good job of supporting the spine. But if the thorax is not well-positioned in alignment with the head and pelvis, or is held with too much tension, the entire body—from head to toe—will be affected. Developing thoracic mobility is key to keeping the lower back and shoulders healthy. But the rib cage is an area that frequently is locked up, poked out, or sucked back and under. None of these positions are desirable. Instead, the ribs should move with your breathing, your walking, and your riding. They should have some degree of stability and strength, but they also need to be supple.

One reason the rib cage is prone to stiffening is because people try hard to achieve what they feel is an "ideal" posture. Unfortunately, the "chest out and high" posture is *static* rather than *dynamic*, and *forced* rather than *natural*. It results in rigidity of the rib cage as well as a number of other joints, such as the hips, knees, ankles, and shoulders. Ideally, you should feel a slight rotation of the rib cage as you move about.

Try this: Put one hand on each side of your rib cage toward the top, a bit below the collarbones. Turn your head to the left and right. Feel the subtle action of the ribs as they naturally rotate a bit with the turning of your head. This is *not* side-bending—it's a tiny twisting action that involves a bit of sideways movement. If you stop this important rotation, your rib cage will likely lock up, poke out, or suck under. And if you lock out your rib cage when you ride, you won't be able to follow the movements of your horse. You may well struggle with rigidity and bouncing.

Fortunately, you can learn to use your rib cage to anchor your lumbar spine, giving you a nice strong "dressage back." Unfortunately, many riders try to achieve a dressage back by tucking the pelvis under, leaning behind the vertical, or both. If you put your hands on your floating ribs (the front, lower section of your rib cage) and cough lightly, you will get a sense of where and how to anchor the ribs (figs. 14.1 A–C).

It is good to create space in the thoracic area. However, it's incorrect to simply "lift" the rib cage in an upward direction off the pelvis. If only the rib cage lifts, you are not generating positive tension. Remember from chapter 3 that to create positive tension, you need a gentle pull from both ends of a body part (see p. 23). But how to do that? Although I could explain the process, I'm choosing not to do that for two reasons. First, doing so would overly engage the left side of your brain. But there also is a way you can experience the feeling of good thoracic space and

14.1 A–C Notice how the lower ribs on this rider pop upward and create a big arch at the back of her waist (A). This is an unstable situation, and she is at risk for back trouble. When the rider's hands guide her floating (lower) ribs downward into the ground, her pelvis must stay neutral and not tuck under as she "anchors" her ribs (B). When you first learn this exercise, bending your knees is advisable. With practice, you will be able to do this even when you bring your arms overhead (C). With this improved rib cage position, you will find strength in your back.

movement without so much effort. For most of us, the rib cage and thorax are well-placed when we walk backward. We've had a lifetime to interfere with and mess up our forward walk, but our backward walk is typically a sound movement pattern. When you walk backward, your rib cage will come into place dynamically, and you'll feel it rotate slightly from side to side as you move.

This action is automatic—and it's also the correct position and motion of the thorax when you ride. When you allow these small, alternating rotations while keeping your rib cage anchored, you are supporting and stabilizing your lower back and anchoring yourself to the movements of your horse when you ride. This allows for a safe transfer of physical forces through your spine.

THE LIFT OF THE STERNUM

To review, the *sternum* is sometimes called the *breastbone* (see fig. 4.1 on p. 32, where it is depicted as a seahorse). The sternum operates much like a vertical seesaw, such that when the top tilts forward (such as during inhalation), the bottom will be aiming back toward the spine. It is important for a rider to understand the mechanics, because trainers sometimes advise you to "lift" your sternum. But the sternum rises on inhalation and descends on exhalation. This combination of rising and tilting forward, then lowering and tilting back, gives rise to an oblique, spiraling-type of motion. If a rider has minimized the motion of her thorax, the motion of her sternum will also be reduced, and there won't be proper space created for the heart and lungs, impeding the rider's breathing. On the other end of the spectrum, if a rider forces her sternum to rise, it will result in an unnatural, chest-high-and-out position. This will lock up her pelvis, hips, arms, and shoulders. So, what to do?

To find the middle ground, try to *think with passive verbs rather than active verbs.* Instead of *Lift the chest*, think *Allow the sternum to rise with each inhale as you feel the sacrum sinking and grounding.* For a tactile adjustment, it may be helpful to press the blunt end of a hoof pick at a point about halfway up the sternum, then drag it upward to the point where the sternum meets the collarbones. This activity can also be done while riding, using two fingers instead of a hoof pick, and is a good way to feel the correct placement and action of your sternum.

But by far the most effective way I have found to teach the proper motion of the sternum is through the use of sounds. I discovered this by accident while visiting at a client's farm. One day, her pet goose wandered close to me, turned sideways, and began the most vibrant, passionate honking I have ever heard. But the beauty of this serenade was that I had a close-up view of the movement of her sternum. It was as if she knew humans needed her as an example of how to properly lift one's sternum! Needless to say, I tried honking myself a few times and was sold on it as a teaching technique. I now use this as standard protocol for my lessons. And yes, even Grand Prix dressage riders are honking loudly as they ride! Another benefit of the honk is that you can, with practice, transition to a "silent honk"—and it is just as effective.

The rib cage is at its best when it's both stable and supple. The following exercises will help you achieve good rib cage function and develop new awareness of the subtle workings of the ribs.

RIB CAGE EXERCISE 1:
Rib Cage Trainers

Step One: Place a strap that is at least 3 inches wide and about 5 or 6 feet long at the back and bottom of your rib cage. Hold it out in front of you with both hands. The strap should feel snug.

Step Two: Move the bottom ribs back toward the strap until you feel solid support on the ribs. Hold for seven seconds and release.

Step Three: Repeat steps one and two to fatigue. Make sure you stay upright for the duration of this exercise. Do not fold or bend.

RIB CAGE EXERCISE 2:
Chicken Wing

Chicken Wing will wake up and strengthen your rib anchoring muscles.

Step One: Get on your hands and knees, with your knees directly under your hips, your right palm planted under the shoulder.

Step Two: Bend your left arm at the elbow, palm resting on the back of your head (fig. 14.2 A). Turn your gaze in the direction of the bent arm.

14.2 A & B Chicken Wing

Step Three: While keeping your arm bent, draw your raised elbow under your torso (fig. 14.2 B). Aim for the space between the opposite arm and leg.

Step Four: Repeat on both sides, drawing your elbow up, then down, to fatigue.

RIB CAGE EXERCISE 3:
Rib Cage Pulls

Rib Cage Pulls bring new awareness to how the placement of your ribs affects your sternum and spine.

Step One: Deliberately make a "C"-curve (side bend), drawing your right shoulder and hip to the right, and pause, while standing, sitting, or riding.

Step Two: Feel how the ribs on the short (right) side are being pulled into the spine. Continue to stay in the side bend.

Step Three: Now feel how the ribs on the longer (left) side feel pulled toward the sternum.

Step Four: Slowly straighten your body until you feel an equal pull on the ribs toward both the spine and the sternum. *This* is the positive tension you want for riding.

Step Five: Repeat all steps of this exercise for a left "C"-curve (side bend).

RIB CAGE EXERCISE 4:
Mounted "C"-Curve Iron Out

This exercise is perfect for "ironing out" your C-curve when you are mounted. It's also a great warm-up exercise (fig. 14.3).

The following description details the steps to counteract a *left side bend*. To counteract a *right side bend*, simply reverse them.

14.3 "C"-Curve Iron Out

Step One: Start at the halt. Raise your left arm high in the air as you drop your left stirrup and relax the left leg downward. Try to feel a lengthening in your left side.

Step Two: You can try this at the walk, and potentially also at the trot and canter. Use your judgment and stay safe.

Step Three: Repeat on the right side (even for a left "C"-curve problem). You will make faster gains in your efforts to straighten if you do both sides for equal amounts of time.

RIB CAGE EXERCISE 5:
Mounted Arm Sliders

Mounted Arm Sliders benefit the rib cage and involve both pushing and pulling in a balanced fashion. They will also keep you mindful about squaring your hips. You will need an unmounted helper for this exercise.

Step One: Halt your mount, keeping your hips square to the front. If you are not sure your hips are square, ask your unmounted helper to check.

Step Two: Ask your helper to hold your horse and let go of the reins.

Step Three: While keeping your hips square to the front, position your arms as if they were pulling back on an archer's bow. The front arm pushes forward as the arm in back pulls rearward. Hold for about five seconds in the extended position. Then repeat on the same side until fatigue in the muscles sets in.

Step Four: Repeat on your other side.

RIB CAGE EXERCISE 6:
Mounted Rib Cage 360s

Mounted Rib Cage 360s promote the mobility of your rib cage as well as improve awareness of its alignment with your pelvis.

Step One: Ask your mount for a walk.

Step Two: "Lift" the rib cage and set it down an inch or so directly to the right of your center. Do this by first bringing the ribs directly upward (vertically). While holding them "up," move them sideways before "setting them" down. Don't poke the lower ribs outward or slump them under when you do this. Instead, keep them neutral but shifted over to the right.

Step Three: Notice how this shift in the rib cage automatically invites you to step into your right leg. It's great to pull this strategy out of your toolbox when you need a weight aid.

Step Four: Lift the rib cage and bring it back to neutral, sitting squarely over your pelvis.

Step Five: Repeat these steps, but this time lift and set the rib cage down to your left. Note the effect this shift has on your left seat bone, leg, and foot. Return the rib cage to its centered, neutral position.

Step Six: Lift the rib cage again, now setting it down to your front. Feel what this action does to your seat and the horse's forehand. Return to neutral.

Step Seven: Next, lift and set your rib cage down somewhat rearward of the neutral position. Feel how this rocks you back on your coccyx and off your pubic bone, destabilizing the pelvis. You have pulled yourself out of alignment and behind the vertical. *Oops!*

Step Eight: Finally, try moving the rib cage in a circular fashion 360 degrees around. Go both clockwise and counterclockwise. Once you master this at the walk, you can try it at the trot and canter.

chapter takeaway

The rib cage connects to both the sternum and spine. It should be both stable and supple. If the rib cage is held in tension, you are putting extra strain on your lower back. Allowing your ribs to move with slight rotations from side to side is beneficial to your movements both in and out of the saddle.

CHAPTER FIFTEEN
THE RIDER'S NECK AND HEAD

"The head should be centered. Hang by your head from a star, as you walk, and feel the release of bodily stress."
— Mabel Elsworth Todd in *The Thinking Body* (The Gestalt Journal Press, 2008)

THE NECK CONNECTS

The rider's neck supports the weight of her head and plays a critical role in suspending the collarbones, shoulder blades, and arms. A forward head posture pulls the neck forward with it. Frequently, the upper back follows, falling into a rounded shape. As the neck collapses, it may cause a host of problems, including headaches, shoulder pain, and spinal compression.

To find a healthy position for your neck, you need to lengthen it.

Try this: Pretend there is a bungee cord coming out of the vertebra just above *your* withers (fig. 15.1). Note that I said *your* and I am referring to the *human withers* (where your neck attaches to your trunk), not the withers of your horse! Hook the other end of the imaginary bungee cord to a tie ring on a wall behind you. The height of the tie ring should be roughly at your eyebrow level. Sense how your neck would be pulled diagonally upward and backward by the tension of the cord. I prefer this image rather than the common visual of tying a balloon and string to the top of your head. The bungee cord image positions both head and neck well, and in positive tension with the trunk. The balloon image simply pops the head upward without correcting any erroneous alignment of the neck and head.

15.1 Pretend there is a bungee cord connected between the back of your neck and a hook on the wall behind you set at about eyebrow height. Feel the cord pull the base of your neck diagonally upward and rearward. This will position both your head and neck well.

THE HEAD ALIGNS WITH THE SPINE

The human head rests upon the spine at the top cervical vertebrae (C-1). It weighs an impressive amount, typically 10 to 13 pounds. Consider that the C-1 weighs but a fraction of that amount! Imagine a heavy medicine ball sitting on the tip of your pinky—or a seal balancing a bowling ball on the tip of his nose. These images depict a challenge similar to the one C-1 has of attempting to balance your head. Understanding this relationship sheds light on how critically important it is for the rest of the spine to transfer those compressive forces.

Your head and neck have the vital role of delivering oxygen to your brain via the blood in your arteries. Any diminished flow will negatively impact brain function. But modern life invites us to frequently carry our heads in a forward position, while driving, texting, or working on the computer, for example. Instead of being well supported by the cervical vertebrae, our heads are often carried in front of the cervical base. C-1 and its attached ligaments have no opportunity to buttress the skull when it is in that position. Even worse, as the head droops and the upper spine bends, C-1 can be carried forward and displaced. *Ouch!* Unfortunately, many people are unaware of moments when their head comes in front of their spine.

Here is a way to check your head and neck alignment without using a mirror. If your head is correctly aligned with your spine, you will feel:

1 An automatic movement in between the shoulder blades as the scapulae gently squeeze toward each other.

2 A small pull or positive tension in the sternum as it lifts with each inhale.

3 A gentle pull (like a relaxed awakening) of the lower jaw.

What are the implications of head position for the rider? Well, when your head is carried over your spine and your neck is lengthened, your pelvis can now follow the movements of your horse properly. It also shores up your self-carriage (see p. 81). But if you look downward with a dropped head, it prompts your horse to weight and travel on his forehand. I often remind my riders that their horse is the expert at using four feet—we don't need to look down to micromanage that! A rider's dropped head also has the effect of causing her hands to be harsh and heavy. *Ugh!*

Some riders tilt their head to one side, rather than jutting it forward. For these riders, it is helpful to remember that both your chin and the

The Rider's Jaw

The human jawbone *(mandible)* is horseshoe-shaped and attaches to the skull at the *temporal bones* (near the ears). You can maneuver your jaw by opening it, closing it, sliding it left and right, poking it forward, or retracting it backward. The powerful *masseter muscle* of the jaw is used for chewing. To feel the masseter working, move several fingers up and down the back edges of your cheeks as you open and close your mouth. When you are tense, the masseter clenches, not only inhibiting jaw movement, but also your breathing, body movements, and proper spinal alignment. Clenching the masseter encourages tension and misalignment in your riding.

Here are a few ways to keep your jaw relaxed and happy:

- Yawn! Yawning helps you relax your jaw muscles. Horses are masterful at relaxing their jaw muscles through the use of yawning!

- Tilt your head back to look up at the sky or ceiling. As you do this, allow your lower jaw to open softly and naturally. Gently move the jaw forward and rearward a few times, then slide it left and right. As you return your head to a neutral position, allow your lower jaw to close on its own accord. Don't deliberately shut your mouth.

- Release your jaw muscles very slowly, gently opening your lower jaw to a slow count of 20 to 25. Rest a few seconds in the fully open position, making sure the jaw muscles continue to stay relaxed. Then close your jaw for a count of seven to eight.

- You are about to give the floor of your mouth a massage! The *mylohyoid muscle* is contained by the bottom of your jaw and functions like a hammock. Put a few fingers on the bottom or back edge of your jaw on the right side, sliding them forward toward your chin. The spongy mass you feel at first is a salivary gland; keep aiming forward with your fingers and you will meet some firmer tissue. This is the "floor" of your mouth. Gently massage there on the right side, keeping your jaw relaxed and moving it slowly and softly forward, rearward, left, and right. Release your hand and notice how relaxed your entire right side feels. Repeat on the left side. The myohyoid muscle has similarities to the pelvic floor muscles as well as the diaphragm, and if you exhale while gently sucking the floor of your mouth upward toward the "roof," your deep core myofascia will invite a horse's back to come up. Remember to relax, and allow the floor of your mouth to descend on each inhale.

point midway between your eyebrows should line up with your horse's mane. If riding with a tilted head is problematic for you, it is worthwhile getting a comprehensive eye exam by a qualified eye doctor. Mention your tilted head position when you make your appointment. In some cases, the doctor will want to check you for a prismatic or other correction.

Finding correct alignment is largely about centering your head. You may need the assistance of a ground person to let you know when your head is correctly centered. Our perception of straightness is often altered by our habits.

Neck and head exercises can help restore proper alignment and functioning. However, please check with your health care provider before you attempt the following to be sure they will be safe for you. As always, if you feel pain, stop the exercise.

NECK/HEAD EXERCISE 1:
Bobbleheads

You are about to try the same movement as the bobbleheads that sit on vehicle dashboards. This exercise is a super way to engage and strengthen the stability muscles that keep your head and neck strong and well.

Step One: Place your head directly over your spine. Consult an observer to be sure it is positioned well.

Step Two: Now, bobble away! Bobbleheads consists of tiny but quick movements of your head upward and downward. Keep your jaw and tongue relaxed.

Step Three: While continuing the bobblehead movements, turn your head slowly left and right.

Step Four: Do this exercise out of different positions (standing, kneeling, sitting, crawling, or mounted, for example). Bobbleheads can be done either while standing still or moving about.

NECK/HEAD EXERCISE 2:
Duct Tape Roll Up

To practice this exercise, you need a roll of duct tape with only 1/4 to 1/3 of the tape remaining. Don't worry, we won't be pulling the tape off, so you should be able to use your "nearly-used-up" duct tape roll, over and over.

Step One: Put a partially used up roll of duct tape with the rounded outer side under your chin and drop your head down to your chest.

Step Two: Slowly roll the duct tape up against your chest until your head is well back over your spine.

Step Three: Roll it back down again and repeat. Do this exercise to fatigue, then remove the duct tape and yawn.

NECK/HEAD EXERCISE 3:
Turning Head Hovers

Challenge yourself with this neck strengthening exercise! Be careful to gradually build up the intensity and duration.

Step One: Lie down on your back.

Step Two: While keeping your face parallel to the sky or ceiling, raise your head directly upward about 1/2 to 3/4 of an inch. Imagine there is a dinner plate balanced on your face that you don't want to fall off.

Step Three: While holding this head-hover position, slowly turn your head left and right. Pause a few seconds when you reach the fully turned position.

Step Four: Now turn into a side-lying position—arms extended in front of you or overhead, with your legs stacked. Hover your head over the mat as described in Step Two, being sure your head is centered and not tilted. Go to fatigue.

Step Five: Repeat Step Four on the other side.

NECK/HEAD EXERCISE 4:
Head Planks

Practicing Head Planks has a big payoff for the head, neck, and core. This exercise will help you achieve strong, steady alignment in the saddle. Be sure to try your Head Planks facing forward and backward, as well as left and right.

Step One: While standing a foot or two away from a wall, place a piece of foam on your forehead and lean into it. Hold your body in a plank-like position.

Step Two: Drop your arms and hands to your sides. Check to make sure your head is still aligned with your spine (fig. 15.2).

15.2 Head Planks

15.3 Barbell Head Balances

Step Three: You want to go to fatigue, but do all four positions—front, back, left, and right—in equal amounts. I recommend starting with about 10 seconds (or less) in each position.

NECK/HEAD EXERCISE 5:
Barbell Head Balances

Yes, you will need a barbell to practice this next exercise—but you can make one out of a dowel, ankle weights, and duct tape. You will also need a piece of foam to protect your head. Barbell Head Balances help you position and stabilize your head when you ride.

Step One: On the ground, place a piece of foam on your head in a front-back orientation, then align your barbell on top of it.

Step Two: Balance under the barbell as you walk, turn, circle, "longe," do hill work, sideways work, "leg-yield," or "pirouette."

Step Three: Reset the barbell in a left-right orientation, and try the exercise again.

15.4 Marble Heads

NECK/HEAD EXERCISE 6:
Marble Heads

For this exercise, you will need a tray with sides an inch or higher, a piece of foam, and some marbles or small bouncy balls. Have fun doing all the moves mentioned in the Barbell Head Balances (p. 153)—plus, add some quick stops and starts in all directions. This exercise is fabulous for developing stability in the saddle because it trains your acceleration/deceleration muscles at the same time it trains your spinal stabilizers.

Step One: Half fill a tray with assorted small objects with some weight to them—marbles and bouncy balls work well. Hold the tray on top of your head (fig. 15.4). A piece of foam should be placed between the tray and the head for your comfort. This exercise can get vigorous and be fast-paced.

Step Two: Move in all directions, at varying speeds, as you balance under this wildly moving headpiece. While you start with the tray centered on your head, it will likely shift with your exertion. Re-center the tray at will.

NECK/HEAD EXERCISE 7:
Head Hangers

In the Head Hangers exercise, you get a sense of what it's like to balance under someone who has a *well-aligned* head versus someone with a *forward* head posture. It's a lot tougher to balance under a forward head posture, even with a light

15.5 Head Hangers

Bit of Advice:
Tongue and Jaw Placement

Your tongue and jaw placements can influence how you subconsciously hold your body. This in turn can influence your horse's body position. Try this:

If you want to turn right or leg-yield toward the right, place your tongue either on the right side of your cheek or just inside your top molars on the right side of your mouth. Alternatively, slide your lower jaw off to the right. This will encourage your horse to turn right or leg-yield toward the right.

Repeat for the left side.

Also be aware that putting your tongue on the roof of your mouth just behind your two front teeth will help give you good focus and concentration. Resting your tongue on the floor of your mouth will help relax you.

load. But the Head Hangers exercise gives you a hint of what our horses contend with when their rider is not in alignment.

Step One: Arrange two foam balls on wire hangers; these will serve as the "heads" in this exercise. Bend one of the "heads" forward as if to represent a forward head position; the other head should be placed more centrally to represent a head well-aligned over the spine. Hold both hangers in front of you at the height of your head or higher (fig. 15.5).

Step Two: Move in all directions as you try to balance under the objects. If you were a horse, which rider would you choose to carry?

> **chapter takeaway** ✓
>
> **A human head is heavy, and it needs the support of your spine directly under it. The neck also plays a critical role in suspending the collarbones, shoulder blades, and arms. A forward head posture can significantly interfere with your riding, because it pulls your neck and upper back along with it, thus causing the spine to fall out of alignment. This in turn weights the horse's forehand.**

PART 2

CHAPTER SIXTEEN

SHOULDERS, ARMS, AND HANDS

THE SHOULDER COMPLEX

Our shoulders are extremely mobile and struggle for stability. Instead, they tend toward *hypermobility* as the shoulder muscles, scapulae (*shoulder blades*), and connective tissue attempt to stabilize them in their sockets. Contrast that to our hips, which have the benefit of being stabilized by the large bones of the pelvis.

The muscles surrounding the scapula and shoulder that provide the area with some stability are collectively known as the *rotator cuff*. These muscles are susceptible to imbalances, injury, and pain. Shoulders are further challenged by our daily activities, which tend to recruit two large and powerful muscles—the *pectoralis major* (chest) and the *latissimus dorsi* (sides of the back). The "lats" hook from your back through your armpits and onto your upper arms. When your arms are at your sides, the lats are in their shortest position. When your arms are stretched overhead, the lats are lengthened. If you consider how often you reach overhead as compared to

16.1 The shoulder girdle is "hung" like a yoke along the top of the thoracic area. The horizontal wooden portion of the yoke represents the collarbones. The shoulder complex is comprised of *collarbones, scapulae (shoulder blades)*, and *tops of the arm bones* (humerus).

how often your arms are at your sides, it is not surprising that the lats are apt to get short and tight, pulling the shoulders forward and down.

The *shoulder complex* (collarbones, shoulder blades, and tops of the arm bones) hangs from suspensory attachments to the head and neck. If you visualize a strong attachment between the *shoulder girdle* and the head and neck, you will position this area naturally and properly (fig. 16.1). Although the shoulder girdle eventually connects to the spine through the sternum and rib cage, there is no solid spine connection. Note that the shoulder blades can rest lightly on the rib cage, but they don't sit or sink upon the ribs. It is important to establish this "hanging" notion of the shoulder blades.

If you deliberately hold your shoulders back the "time-honored way"—rolling your shoulders rearward as you stick your chest out in front of you—it sets off a cascade of negative effects on your position in the saddle (figs. 16.2 A–C). First, you throw yourself out of alignment by positioning your shoulders behind your ears. This action also increases your lower back curvature, putting pressure on your spine and sacrum and dissolving their stability and shock-absorbing qualities. It also tends to slide your legs out of position, jeopardizing your balance. *Yikes!* So, what to do? You can start by reviewing the last chapter (see p. 147), in which I explain proper neck and head position. But as a quick reminder, when your head is directly over your lengthened neck, you will feel the shoulder blades automatically, softly squeeze together—that is your litmus test for proper shoulder placement. Note this scapular squeeze is *not* a deliberate action.

JOBS FOR ARMS AND HANDS

Your arms should connect to your horse's mouth such that you can feel in a sensitive, subtle fashion his mood, attention, acceptance, level of vibrancy, and his degree of love for what he is doing. Riders should strive to feel these qualities energetically, rather than a tactile fashion. When you are "plugged into" good alignment and are connected to your horse's mouth with sensitivity, you can read his every move before he makes it, and he can read yours. Keeping your elbows soft and elastic is key to allowing this action.

If you start with a neutral pelvis, neutral spine, lengthened neck, and properly aligned head, you will set the stage for excellent hands. Good hands are always supported by an elastic, stable back. If I could pick a one-word description of desirable hands for riding, I would select the word *receiving*. The arms and hands *receive* energy from the horse; using the hands in any way that blocks the energy flow from the horse has huge—and potentially disastrous—consequences. If there is a lax, "fuzzy" connection, both you and your horse will wonder if the other one is there. If there is a super-tight connection, both you and your horse will be stiff and tense from

16.2 A–C This rider displays a droopy posture, and her shoulder complex is not "hung" from her head and neck (A). She is excessively weighting her horse's forehand. If you need any proof of the horse's thoughts, just look at his expression! When the rider overcorrects and "throws" her shoulders back, bringing them behind her ears, she is unstable in her balance, and her spine will suffer—not to mention the ill effects on her horse's back (B). Correct alignment of the shoulder girdle is accomplished when the head and neck gently move rearward, drawing the shoulder blades rearward as well (C).

the input overload. Sally Swift, author of *Centered Riding* and a master of riding-related imagery, suggested the rider holds the reins like two baby birds you want to keep gently contained in your hands. This image has helped many riders to establish clear, friendly, and inviting communication with their horses. This positive connection allows the horse to understand your rein aids, and you will be able to understand his reactions.

> ## The Elbow's Role
>
> Our elbows have the critical role of connecting the horse's mouth to our seat and back. The rider's elbows should be elastic. I often ask my riders to envision the reins as if they attach directly to the elbows. This image helps riders stay fluid in their arms and allows a more subtle feel of the horse's mouth and energy.
>
> It can be a bit of a challenge to release tension from elbows. Modern life requires the use of the biceps muscles on the *front* of our upper arms. But our triceps (located on the *back* of the upper arm) should match the strength of the biceps. An easy and effective way to weave some triceps work into your daily routine is to deliberately swing your arms behind you more when you walk.

To find a desirable level of grip strength on the reins, visualize your arms as short lengths of garden hoses, with a spray nozzle held in each hand. If you grip the nozzles too softly, you will only get a few drips of water from the nozzle. If you have a superhero grip on them, you will get a strong blast of water. But when you have a middle-of-the-road, "educated," grip on them, you can get a steady flow at your desired level of water pressure any time. Your horse will feel the most secure with the educated grip—and he will appreciate it!

For riders who struggle with hand issues, I employ a variety of techniques. I have used Braille boards to increase the sensitivity of their fingers by teaching students to use each of their 10 fingers to read the boards. I've also had riders hold water balloons in their hands along with the reins, pretending the balloons are Sally Swift's imaginary baby birds. Some riders have found improvement by rolling small bouncy balls over the palm and back side of each hand to restore and freshen the fascia.

You can give your shoulders, arms, and hands a natural workout by hanging from a beam or tree branch a few times a day. Work up to being able to swing while hanging! Or try some of the following exercises instead.

16.3 Overhead Rope Pull

SHOULDER/ARM/HAND EXERCISE 1:
Overhead Rope Pull

The Overhead Rope Pull is fabulous for exercising the upper torso. It also serves as a useful warm-up or cool-down exercise for riders. With some creativity, Overhead Rope Pull can be done anywhere. For instance, you can loop a battle rope or standard rope over a tree branch.

Step One: Toss the end of a 40- to 50-foot rope over a tree branch and hold one end.

Step Two: Ask a helper to hold the other end of the rope and back up until she can feel some tension. At that point, she should pull on the rope with moderate force.

Step Three: While keeping your arms overhead, reel your helper in closer to you, using a hand-over-hand motion (fig. 16.3). This action will warm your back and shoulders up nicely prior to riding.

SHOULDER/ARM/HAND EXERCISE 2:
Kitchen Counter Stretch

As the name implies, Kitchen Counter Stretch is easy to practice at home—but lots of other solid surfaces between waist and chest height will also work. This exercise is a good way to lengthen tight muscles in the chest, shoulder, and back. It can be done either as a *resistance stretch* (with steady pressure), or you can do tiny bounces for a *ballistic* effect.

Step One: Place your hands on a counter or other solid surface (like a jump rail!), then back up until your arms straighten.

Step Two: On an exhale, hinge at the hips, dropping and releasing the upper torso.

Step Three: Slowly turn your head to each side, gazing off toward the horizon (fig. 16.4).

SHOULDER/ARM/HAND EXERCISE 3:
Scap Pushes

Scap Pushes teach the shoulder blades how to work properly with the rib cage. This harmony translates into good self-carriage of the rider's upper torso in the saddle.

Step One: Hip hinge and place your hands flat on a solid surface like a chair (fig. 16.5 A). Keep the knees slightly bent. Choose a height to lean on that feels comfortable to you.

16.4 Kitchen Counter Stretch

16.5 A & B Scap Pushes start (A) and end (B).

SIXTEEN: SHOULDERS, ARMS, AND HANDS | 163

Step Two: While keeping your arms straight, push down into the chair until you feel your torso rise higher toward the ceiling (fig. 16.5 B).

Step Three: Sink the torso back to the height of Step One and repeat the exercise to fatigue.

SHOULDER/ARM/HAND EXERCISE 4:
Trace a Horseshoe

For this movement, you will be using imagery to trace a horseshoe shape with one hand. Go slowly and keep your arm as straight as possible. Keep the range of motion within your safe and comfortable limits.

Step One: Lie on your back, holding an imaginary piece of chalk in one hand. Position that hand near the hip on the same side.

Step Two: While keeping your arm as straight as possible, draw a large horseshoe shape starting at the hip, extending overhead, and finishing at the hip on the other side (fig. 16.6). You will reach a point where you have to turn your hand over. Go slowly.

Step Three: Pause when you reach the end of the horseshoe, then trace the imaginary chalk back along the same path to the original hip position.

Step Four: Repeat this exercise with one hand to fatigue. Do the same number of tracings with your other hand.

SHOULDER/ARM/HAND EXERCISE 5:
Yo-Yo 'n Hoop

Yo-Yo 'n Hoop is a challenge that is as good for your hands as it is for your shoulders. The coordination you develop with this exercise will help you coordinate your aids when you ride. Have fun with it!

16.6 Trace a Horseshoe

Step One: Swing a hoop in a circle around your forearm.

Step Two: With your other hand, start the yo-yo movement (fig. 16.7). The "hoop arm" needs to stay fairly stiff, but the hand on the yo-yo needs to be relaxed and should move with rhythmic fluidity. It's like patting your head while rubbing your stomach—only harder!

Step Three: Time the number of seconds (or minutes) you can keep both these motions going simultaneously—then try to beat your own record.

Step Four: Repeat on the other side of your body.

16.7 Yo-Yo 'n Hoop

chapter takeaway

The shoulder girdle is "hung" like a yoke along the top of the thorax and is largely suspended from the head and neck. If you lengthen through the back of your neck to keep your head well-positioned, your shoulders and arms will come to a relaxed, correct, natural posture. Keep your elbows elastic, and remember to grip the reins as if they were baby birds (thank you, Sally Swift!) or water balloons.

CHAPTER SEVENTEEN

FEET, ANKLES, AND LEGS

TREAT YOUR FEET WELL

Our feet are involved with balance, support, locomotion, and grounding. But also consider that our feet teach us how to move by functioning as a sensory organ and sending messages to the brain about our balance as well as our position in space. We are programmed to detect differences in ground surfaces and can adjust our stride accordingly. We are also programmed to build strong yet supple feet through varied movements. Let's take a closer look.

The foot contains three parts. The *forefoot* has toes, which help us grip and balance when necessary. The *midfoot* has metatarsal bones, which help make the arch of the foot, providing us with support and stability. The *rearfoot* contains the *heel bone*, the *talus bone* (which is like a shock absorber), and the *tarsus bones* (which transfer our weight to other parts of the foot as needed). There is also a band of connective tissue that runs from the heelbone to the toes called the *plantar fascia*. Anyone who has experienced *plantar fasciitis* is painfully aware of this tissue on the bottom of our feet. When you have plantar fasciitis, this connective tissue becomes inflamed, typically due to high impact activities, over-stretching, underuse of certain muscles, or heel spurs (a calcification of the heel bone).

Unfortunately, when we stand or walk, we weight the forefoot. This tightens your calf and sometimes hamstring muscles, even to the point of cramping. So try this: Stand barefoot and make three points of contact with the ground: your heel, your big toe pad, and your pinky toe pad. You should feel like there is a triangle of support on those areas of your feet as they support your body weight.

It's important that the body's weight is carried over the center of each heel bone in an equal fashion, putting your ankles under your pelvis. The forefoot, but not the toes, should press into the ground. But remember, the forefoot needs to press without supporting your body weight. The majority of your body weight should be supported by your heels. Only when

> "While you have about 200 bones in your entire body, 25 percent of them reside from the ankle down. The same goes for your muscles—a quarter of all the muscles and motor nerves in your body are dedicated to your feet. Despite all of those moveable parts, I'll bet you've never been told this part of your body needs movement to keep healthy."
>
> —Katy Bowman in *Move Your DNA* (Propriometrics Press, 2017)

you have achieved this balance between the heels and the forefoot can you come into proper alignment and utilize ground reaction forces.

If you are wearing anything but a zero- or negative-heeled, thin-soled, minimalist shoe, both your alignment and proprioception will be compromised. The muscles of the feet take a long time to "wake up" and strengthen. If you are considering purchasing a zero-heeled, minimalist-type of shoe, build up to wearing it gradually, starting with only 15 minutes a day. In addition to improved balance and proprioception, this type of shoe boosts your arch, creating muscles and waking up your deep core myofascia, and this benefits your riding.

Walk on a variety of irregular surfaces such as cobblestone mats, pea gravel, or river stones. Walking or running on trails, dirt roads, or in other natural environments will help support your efforts. This type of training helps your riding as you will likely make broad gains in your balance and proprioception.

Our toes are quite eager to grip. When you curl your toes under in your boots or press them into the ground, they grip and become good at it. When done to excess, this motion creates tension, and the energy going from the feet into the calves gets blocked. However, lifting the toes activates your movement muscles, and this action tends to compromise your postural muscles and balance. Those of you who lift your toes to the tops of your riding boots have lost both your grounding and your stability. Your foundation is wiped out and your balance muscles go to sleep. It's only when your toes are held at ease in a neutral fashion that you activate your foot stabilizers and postural muscles. This is the ideal position to hold your toes in when you ride. After you dismount, it is good for your toes to move individually. Find a safe place where you can remove your riding boot, and pull outward, wiggle, lift, or circle each toe by itself. Guide each toe with your fingers at first. Work up to being able to move them by themselves, hands-free.

Your feet have arched areas to support your body weight. The arches run longitudinally, laterally, diagonally, and transversely. Note that your toes are not part of the arch system. The arches of the feet are not structures—they are formed due to the way the muscles of the feet and legs shape your bones. To create a healthy arch, you need to devote time to strengthening, stabilizing, suppling, and improving the mobility of each foot. Poor arches can be too high (hollow) or too low (flat). To determine whether you have good, functional arches, try this: Stand barefoot and ask a helper to slide a finger under the inner edge of each foot, halfway between each heel and toe. There should be enough space under each foot for her to slide her finger inward almost an inch (up to the crease of her first finger joint) before touching the bottom of your foot. If her finger slides in deeper than that, you have high arches and hollow feet. If her finger can barely slide in, you have collapsed arches and flat feet. Why does this matter to a rider? Any faulty arch pattern will result in faulty posture and movement patterns. You not only struggle for your position, you put the muscles, tendons, ligaments, and joints further up the legs at risk for injury as they struggle to do the work of the arches. Spine, hip, or knee pain, anyone?

So, what to do if you have learned your arches are too high or too low? To make healthy arches on both feet, try this: While barefoot, stand on the balls of your feet, lifting your heels about half of their maximum height. Keep your toes relaxed and neutral. As you bring your heels to the floor, tension and move them slightly toward each other. You will create a bit of a "kidney bean" or "horseshoe shape" to your feet, with the open ends of the horseshoes on the inside edges of your feet (fig. 17.1). Here are some other ways to feel your newfound arches.

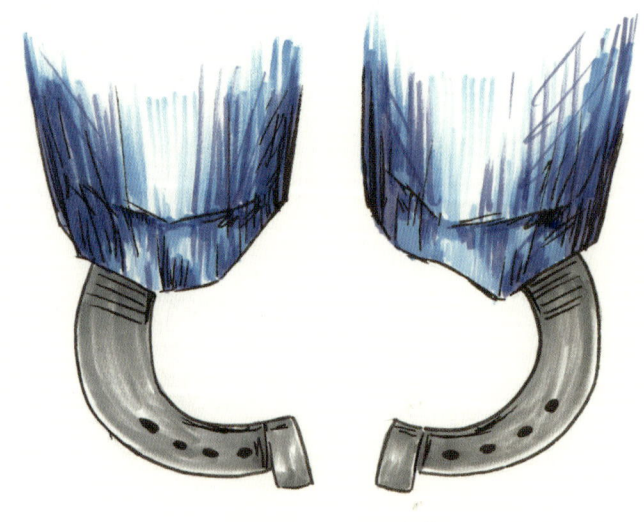

17.1 To create the proper arch formation of your feet, imagine you are wearing horseshoes with the open edge oriented toward the inner edges of your feet.

- Have one foot "flick" imaginary sand at the other foot.

- Pretend there is a mini vacuum at the bottom of each calf, suctioning up the arches.

- Sit on the edge of a hard-backed chair with your feet wrapped around the outsides of the legs of the chair. Then tension (don't move) the feet toward each other.

Your pelvis and feet work closely together, because the part of your foot over which the pelvis is held receives your body weight. Remember, it's the center of the heel bone that receives and supports our weight the best. To help you engage the self-carriage muscles necessary to encourage this type of positioning, think of your pelvis as a horse wagon. Hold your trunk as if you were sitting vertically in the wagon. Pretend the wheels of the wagon are in your feet (fig. 17.2). It's very important to keep the wheels under the cart! You can't put the wheels in front of or behind the cart and expect everything to move properly. However, as already discussed, many people stand and walk with their hips pushed forward and their pelvis in front of their ankles. By doing this, you are hyperextending your lower back without realizing it. That posture in humans is called *swayback*, and you may remember that

17.2 Imagine you are sitting on a vertical plumb line in a small horse wagon located in your pelvis. The wagon's wheels are in your feet (as shown). Align yourself such that the wheels stay directly underneath the cart.

I call it the "trainer's stance" due to the frequency with which I have seen trainers stand and move this way (see p. 77).

Treating the feet well should be of prime importance to riders, due to the foot's relationship to the stirrup. It's the touching, not the

SEVENTEEN: FEET, ANKLES, AND LEGS | 169

pushing down or bracing, of the foot to the stirrup, that stimulates the proprioceptors of the feet. These proprioceptors give your balancing and stabilizing muscles good information about what they have to do to keep you centered and upright. Here are some additional ways to take care of your feet:

- Dry brushing with a good quality skin brush (see p. 89).

- Soaking them in dead sea salt or Epsom salts.

- Whirlpool foot basin treatments.

- Fascial foot rollers or golf ball rolling (see p. 106).

- Ayurvedic reflexology.

- Wearing properly fitting footwear when you are unable to go barefoot.

- Walking barefoot over natural terrain.

THE RIDER'S LEGS

The position of the legs is a direct result of the position of the pelvis. If you are going to correct your leg position (or someone else's), always adjust the pelvis first. Legs get "grippy" because of weak, stiff, or inflexible muscles in the pelvis and core. Those compromised muscles typically result in one or more of the following:

- Leaning (sideways, forward, or back).

- A collapsed or protruded rib cage.

- Pushing or bracing into the stirrups.

- A forward head/neck posture.

Legs also get grippy due to tension or fear. When the legs grip, you can't use your seat independently of your legs. This is not desirable! The

Supple Your Ankles

To ride well, you need strong but supple ankles. Your feet and ankles should not "lock into position"; instead, allow them to make subtle adjustments when you ride, just as they would if you were walking on uneven terrain. Consider that the foot is horizontally oriented and the legs vertically oriented. It's the job of the ankles to make the transition in orientation. This is best achieved when you are aligned properly (ear-shoulder-hip-ankle), and when there is a good upward pull from the arches of your feet into your pelvis. It is important to examine the role of the legs in achieving this.

best way to avoid using your legs as grippers is to work on developing a stable spine with fluid hips. (We will explore this concept further in the next chapter—see p. 175.)

Each leg has one bone in the thigh (*femur*) and two in the lower leg (*tibia* and *fibula*). The femur is the body's longest bone. It has a round head that fits into a notched-out area of the pelvis to form the hip joint. The femur's head and neck angles inward, placing our hip joints over our seat bones. There are also two noticeable protuberances of the femurs—the *greater* and *lesser trochanters*, to which many critical riding muscles are attached.

The *calves* are an integral part of your grounding system. The *tibia* (shin bone) is the most vertical bone of your body when you are standing in proper alignment. And it's the tibia that transfers the weight of your body to the ankle and foot. Our calves tend to get quite tight due to wearing shoes that have positive heels (even slight ones), and this tension is exacerbated by walking or running on hard, flat surfaces. Energy then gets blocked and the ankles become stiff.

Here are exercises to help you counteract the deleterious effect of wearing shoes as well as other modern lifestyle conveniences.

Posting and the Pelvis

To create a rhythmic rising to the trot, the rider should have a stabilized, neutral pelvis. So often, a rider unknowingly tucks and tilts the pelvis when posting. When a rider's thighs drift forward at the top of a rise, the pelvis (and attached spine) slips out of neutral. This misalignment produces a "hip thrust" at the top of the rise, and the rider is unable to access her core to ensure a gentle return to the saddle. Her horse's back becomes a trampoline. The rider is better off thinking of her lower torso as a fence post, with no movement at the waist to drive a tucking or tilting pelvis. Many riders cannot feel when their alignment is correct, so a trained ground person is helpful with this issue.

Note that the instruction to "post higher" or "post lower" does not fix the key issue of keeping the pelvis and spine in a neutral arrangement. For riders working on finding this neutrality, I suggest trying the Slomo exercise (see p. 174). "Slomo" stands for "slow motion in your posting," and this ground exercise transfers well to the saddle. It teaches the rider to post with self-carriage, which is the hallmark of good posting.

FEET/ANKLES/LEG EXERCISE 1:
Heel Walk

I like to give this exercise to my super-busy clients because it's easy to weave into your day. Practicing Heel Walk will help you use your heels to support your body weight. When your body weight is supported by the center of your heel bones, your balance improves and your feet come under your seat. Heel Walk improves your ability to feel and find a good leg position when you ride.

Step One: Stand barefoot with your feet hip-width apart.

Step Two: Keep your toes neutral (neither curled nor lifted) as you bring your weight to your heels, allowing your forefeet to rise up off the ground.

Step Three: Begin to walk on your heels, pausing on each heel for a breath or two. Work up to taking 10 steps forward, 10 backward, 10 steps to the left, and 10 to the right. Continue to pause for a breath or two on each heel.

Step Four: Challenge yourself by Heel Walking in a leg-yielding pattern…then leg-yield backward!

FEET/ANKLES/LEG EXERCISE 2:
Toe Spreading

This move will give each of your toes some "breathing space," and it will help counteract the negative aspects of footwear.

Step One: Line up the outside edges of each foot with a straight line on the floor, carpet, or your mat.

Step Two: While keeping your toes on the floor, spread them away from each other, creating space between each one. Take a few slow breaths.

Step Three: Bring your toes back to neutral, and repeat to fatigue.

Step Four: Now try this exercise one foot at a time. When that feels easy, lift the nonworking leg up and balance on the working leg as you spread those toes.

FOOT/ANKLES/LEG EXERCISE 3:
Foot Twists

Creating a good arch requires a "twist" in the foot. This exercise will train the feet to twist properly, which is critical because your arch-forming muscles are part of your deep core myofascia.

Pulling upward through your arch muscles when you ride helps you access your deep core, and it encourages your horse's back to lift.

Step One: Sit in a chair or on a hay bale (or two), and firmly hold your right heel against your left thigh (in a "figure 4" fashion).

Step Two: Use your right hand to wiggle or twist your right forefoot so the big and pinky toes alternate being on top.

Step Three: Now hold the right forefoot with your right hand and wiggle and twist the right heel in a similar manner.

Step Four: Hold the right forefoot in your right hand; at the same time, hold your right heel with your left hand. First, try twisting your forefoot and heel in *different* directions; then twist them in the *same* direction.

Step Five: Repeat this exercise using your left foot.

FEET/ANKLES/LEG EXERCISE 4:
Side Slides

Practicing Side Slides, which are basically a side shuffle, will strengthen the *lumbricals*, some of the small foot stabilizing muscles. Side Slides are super training for balance, coordination, and proprioception. Plus, they're fun to do!

Step One: Stand barefoot in an area where you have enough space to move sideways at least 10 steps.

Step Two: Point the toes of both feet to the right, keeping the soles of the feet flat.

Step Three: Shift your weight to the balls of your feet as you pivot on your forefeet. Lift the heels slightly as you swing them both to the right and set them down.

Step Four: Sink into the heels and pivot on them as you lift the forefeet. Slide both of your forefeet to the right and set them down. Notice that you are moving sideways to the right.

Step Five: Repeat to fatigue, then do the exercise toward the left.

Step Six: When you become balanced and skilled at this, try it on a single leg. Bend the non-stance leg back behind you in a hamstring curl—you will feel like you are kicking yourself in the bottom with one leg. Make sure you stay in complete control of your body weight, as well as your speed and direction.

FEET/ANKLES/LEG EXERCISES 5:
Slomos

"Slomos," or unmounted slow motion posting, will help you position your pelvis during posting trot.

Step One: Kneel on a padded or soft surface. Sit on your feet with the tops of your toes flat on the floor.

Step Two: Without bending at the waist, take about seven seconds to rise up to a full kneeling position.

Step Three: Hold your torso as one solid fence post, and slowly sit back down on your heels. Work up to taking about 25 seconds to descend. Breathe and go slowly! Be sure to support your body weight with your core.

Step Four: Repeat this exercise to fatigue.

FEET/ANKLES/LEG EXERCISE 6:
Calf Lengthening

Calf Lengthenings help you release tight calves and lead to better placement of your feet in the stirrups. To practice this exercise, you will need a rolled-up towel. I recommend doing it twice a day.

Step One: Place your left forefoot on a rolled-up, full-sized towel. Keep your foot straight and place the left heel on the floor. Keep your knees straight but not hyperextended.

Step Two: Step ahead with your right foot and place it on the floor just in front of the towel. Be sure the toes on both feet are pointing straight forward.

Step Three: Keep your pelvis over your left foot. Do not allow your hips to drift forward.

Step Four: You should feel a good stretch in the left calf.

---

chapter takeaway

Our feet are involved in balance, support, locomotion, grounding, and sensing our environment. But modern lifestyles and wearing positive-heeled shoes have not given our foot stabilizers a chance to do their job. Reviving these important muscles can be achieved by barefoot walking on a variety of slopes and irregular surfaces, a practice which is also great for our legs and hips.

CHAPTER EIGHTEEN
FLUID HIPS, STABLE SPINE

FLUIDITY OF THE HIPS

The hips house our massive, powerful crouch/spring/walk/run muscles—well, they *should* be massive and powerful! But too often, riders struggle with weak, stiff hips. Why does this happen? Some common causes include:

- Sitting

- Driving

- Standing or squatting with your knees collapsed inward

- Lack of varied movements

- Wearing footwear with a positive (elevated) heel

- Weak, inflexible hip extensors (glutes, hamstrings)

- Pelvis not held in a neutral position

- Stress

- Isolated rather than full-body exercises

- Chronic slouched position

- What I call "trainer's stance" (hips sway forward in front of ankles when standing—see p. 77).

Each hip has a ball-and-socket joint located fairly deeply in the lower trunk, approximately over the seat bones. The hips transfer leg power *upward* to the pelvis but also diffuse compressive forces coming *downward* from the spine. When hips are healthy and functioning properly, they have good mobility in many directions. Healthy hips can describe a circle, but don't have the full mobility our shoulders do. In chapter 13 (see p. 126), I included a couple of exercises beneficial to the hips: Buttwalking (see p. 134) and the Lizard Crawl (see p. 135). To enhance the benefits of those exercises, try them in a leg-yielding pattern. (You will find more suggestions later in this chapter.)

When you ride, your hips don't rotate the way your rib cage does. The rider's hips should stay fluid and parallel to her horse's hips. Envisioning water wheels for hips can help a rider better follow the motion of her horse (fig. 18.1). Notice in that the water wheels can turn forward (with a hip action similar to that when pedaling a bike) or backward. When you ride, you are seeking the same forward turn of the hips, because this motion encourages the forward movement of your horse.

Try this: Sit on the ground with your legs stretched out before you in a Buttwalking posture (see p. 134). Start turning the water wheels

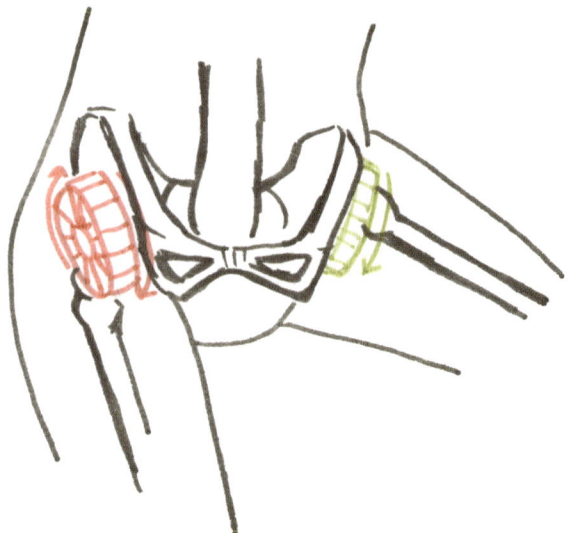

18.1 It is helpful to imagine your hips as water wheels that can turn powerfully but easily. When you ride, they encourage forward movement when they turn in a forward direction (similar to pedaling a bicycle). For rein-backs, they turn rearward.

Bit of Advice: Hip Rotators

The hip rotators tend to tighten up and resist our efforts to stretch. It's helpful to roll out the fascia at the lower and outer edges on the backsides of your pelvic halves. You can use a fascial ball, tennis ball, or lacrosse ball placed on a wall to accomplish this (fig. 18.2). Listen to your body—it will tell you when you've done enough. Try to roll this area out every other day.

18.2 Hip Fascia Roll Out

rearward, and notice how you are Buttwalking backward. Pause, then allow the circular forward motion of the water wheels, and notice how you automatically Buttwalk in a forward direction. It's important when you are riding that you fluidly follow your horse's movements. Do not deliberately push and shove the water wheels in any direction. Many riders continually back-pedal the water wheels in their hips—but consider that neither your hips nor your horse's hips circle backward for forward movement! They both circle *forward*.

When your hips are fluid and agile, you can move easily and freely in a supple, coordinated, vibrant fashion. But whether on or off your horse, to be functional, you need to control your bodyweight as your hips move around, which requires a stable spine. In the next section, you will learn how hip agility and spine stability work together.

STABILITY OF THE SPINE

Although some of the bony projections on the spine can be felt superficially, the central spine is quite deep. A spine with proper curves is a stable spine with good shock-absorbing qualities (fig. 18.3). The spine works in a ripple-like fashion, where the forces of tension (*pulling*) balance out the compressive (*pushing*) forces. This happens most readily when your spine is *neutral and*

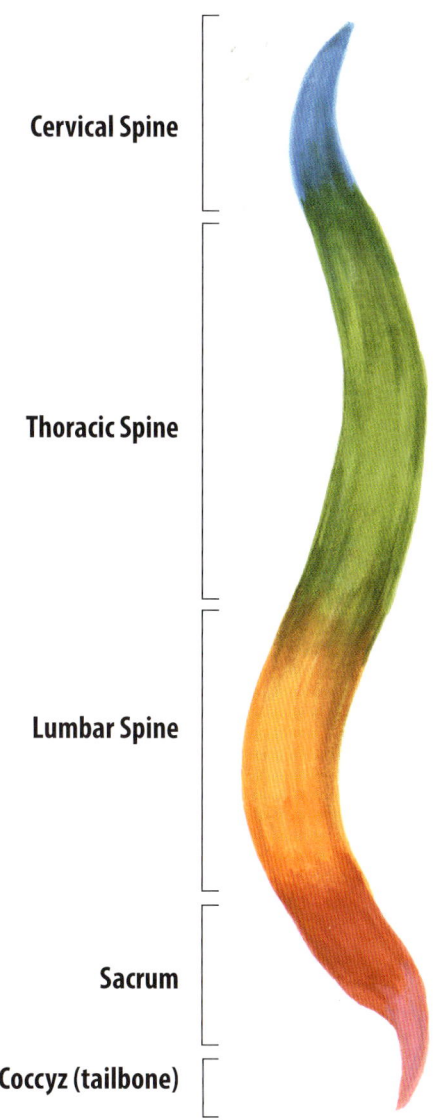

18.3 Here, the artist portrays the natural curvatures and sections of the spine. Notice how the curves alternate between *posterior convexity* (*kyphosis* of the thoracic and sacral/coccygeal spine) and *anterior convexity* (*lordosis* of the cervical and lumbar spine).

lengthened (as compared to flexed/bent forward or extended/bent backward).

Your back has the following five sections:

- Cervical (neck)

- Thoracic (upper torso)

- Lumbar (waist area)

- Sacral (pelvis area)

- Coccygeal (tailbone area)

Bit of Advice: Finding Neutral Spine

To find the feel for a neutral spine, get in "dressage position" by standing in an ear-shoulder-hip-ankle alignment, with a slight bend in your knees (ask an observer to make sure you are correctly aligned). Face a wall and hold your arms and hands as if they were holding reins. Push the hands energetically into the wall while continuing to stay in good alignment. Keep your front line soft, and do not lean toward the wall with your body. If you do this exercise correctly, you will feel the muscles around your center activate, and your sternum will automatically rise. The push forward you feel from this action is coming from your core. The power you are able to generate during this move directly depends on the extent to which your spine is in its neutral position.

The four opposing curves of the spine give it the strength to carry your body weight but still move in a supple fashion. However, it's the *lumbar* section that specializes in stabilizing the trunk. The lumbar area is quick to become unstable if you pull the chest up or jut the lower front edge of the rib cage forward and upward. Ironically, riders often make these postural adjustments in an effort to achieve "good posture," but instead they crowd the *thoracic* and *cervical* vertebrae. This action then causes the lumbar vertebrae to stretch into a sag, thus becoming unstable. Further, when the spine is not held in its neutral curves and aligned with the body's central axis, your nervous system cannot function optimally.

Here are some other ways we destabilize the spine:

- Swaying the hips forward (the "trainer's stance" described earlier—see p. 77).

- Side-bending while twisting.

- Tucking the "tail" under (posterior pelvic tilt).

- Tilted head posture.

- Forward head/neck posture.

- Hyperextending the lower back.

- Bending/lifting without a neutral spine.

And here are some ways to keep the spine well-stabilized:

- Improve the tonicity of the myofascia surrounding the spine.

- Incorporate many varied full-body movements throughout the day.

- Maintain the spine with its natural curves while sitting, standing, moving, and loading.

- Practice grounding and centering.

- Specific training in anti-rotation, anti-flexion, anti-extension, and acceleration/deceleration using full body movements.

"Brace the Back" vs. "Stabilize the Spine"

I avoid using the phrase "brace your back" with riders, because a typical response is to recruit the abdominal or the vertically oriented long back muscles to achieve this posture. But these are not the muscles that stabilize you on the back of a moving horse. The true stability muscles are located super-close to the spine; they are smaller and specialize in preventing unwanted movement. Therefore, I instead use the phrase "stabilize your spine;" it feels like the sides of your body are pulling toward the spine in the area behind your waist. Other muscles supporting this action include the lower rib cage muscles (the rib anchor explained in chapter 14, p. 139) as well as the muscles along the sides of the pelvis and legs (review the sandpaper exercise of chapter 3—see p. 26).

When a rider first starts working on stabilizing her spine, it can look a bit robotic. As you practice, remember these two important details:

1 Positive tension means holding no more tension than what is needed to stabilize.

2 The hips must continue to be as fluidly moving as water wheels (p. 130).

Another comparison that may be helpful is this: consider the action of a yo-yo. It will only rebound if there is a certain amount of *positive tension* in the string (like your spine), coupled with the fluidity of your arm/shoulder movements (like your hips). If the string is too tight, the yo-yo (rider) bounces uncomfortably. If it's too loose, the yo-yo wobbles and veers off uncontrollably. I often give out yo-yos in my lessons so riders can feel this firsthand!

- Develop core endurance by using a repeating pattern of short isometric holds in positions requiring stabilization, followed by a short rest. (This type of hold was explained in detail on p. 107.)

Keeping a stable spine, along with hip fluidity, has big implications for riders. If you are astride a horse, you need to make continual, soft, smooth, subtle adjustments to your body. Achieving stability is not about making no movement; it's about making well-controlled-but-no-extraneous movement. *Stability is dynamic*. In his classic text *Reflections on Riding and Jumping* (Trafalgar Square Books, 1997), Olympic show jumper William Steinkraus referred to good riding as "a function of balance and controlled relaxation."

Here are a series of whole-body exercises to supple your hips and improve the stability of your spine.

FLUID HIPS/STABLE SPINE EXERCISE 1:

Ride Your Noodle

For this exercise, you will need a pool or pond, and a pool noodle.

Step One: Warm up with a few laps around the pool in both directions at a moderate pace. You don't want it to feel easy…but you don't want it to feel difficult. Once you are wet, "mount" your pool noodle.

Step Two: If possible, lift both arms above the surface of the water. (If this is not possible, keep both arms—or one—on the water surface.) Start vigorously circling your legs as if forward pedaling on a bicycle. Keep your spine vertical.

Step Three: My clients love doing their dressage tests or a mock jumping course on their noodles, all the while keeping their hands above the water's surface. Try it!

Step Four: Now, practice rein-back by backward pedaling.

Step Five: Avoid propelling yourself by momentum by resisting all temptations to lean. Instead, stay vertical and spin those bicycle pedals!

FLUID HIPS/STABLE SPINE EXERCISE 2:
Scorpion Seat

Scorpion Seat will challenge your core stability at the same time it addresses good mobility of the hips.

Step One: Kneel on a mat or another comfortable surface with knees under your hips.

Step Two: Hip hinge (bend at the hips) and fold both legs to the right as you sit down gently and with control (fig. 18.4).

Step Three: Without using your hands, come back to kneeling.

Step Four: Repeat the hip hinge of Step Two, but fold both legs to the left.

Step Five: Repeat Step Three. Cycle from left side to right side until you reach fatigue.

18.4 Scorpion Seat

18.5 Hip Extension Release

FLUID HIPS/STABLE SPINE
EXERCISE 3:
Hip Extension Release

Even the "desk jockeys" will be able to do this one! The Hip Extension Release helps lengthen your hip flexors and release your hip extensors. This is a critical aspect of being fluid with your hips and dropping your knees when you ride.

Step One: Sit toward the front edge of a sturdy chair and stretch your legs out straight (fig. 18.5).

Step Two: Lean your upper torso toward the back of the chair such that your body makes a straight line from your head to your feet.

Step Three: Keep your rib cage well anchored at the bottom.

Step Four: Knit the back of your waist by engaging the horizontal muscles there. This action will pull your sides toward your spine to stabilize your lumbar vertebrae.

Step Five: While being mindful to keep your ribs anchored (see p. 139), raise your arms overhead. Stop when your lowest ribs start to poke forward and upward.

FLUID HIPS/STABLE SPINE EXERCISE 4:
Heel Skating

Get more "glute action" into your walk by incorporating Heel Skating in your daily routine. Wear your riding helmet, as Heel Skating may alter your center of gravity. When you practice varying unmounted positions and movements while wearing your helmet, you give your centering muscles experience and facilitate centering and balancing when you are mounted.

Step One: Begin by lifting your forefeet and balancing your body weight on your heels.

Step Two: Glide off with alternating feet, as you might do if ice skating (fig. 18.6).

Step Three: Be sure to do some backward "heel skating" too.

18.6 Heel Skating

FLUID HIPS/STABLE SPINE EXERCISE 5:
One Stirrup Work

Dropping only one stirrup gives your core musculature experience with one-sided stabilization. Remember, there should be *no* gripping your legs to maintain your balance.

Step One: Drop a stirrup and walk in both directions of the arena. Include various figures such as serpentines and spiraling in and out.

Step Two: Do some transitions to halt and back to walk again.

Step Three: With your trainer's permission for reasons of safety, try this exercise at the trot—sitting, posting, or in jumping position.

FLUID HIPS/STABLE SPINE EXERCISE 6:
"T" Arm Cavalletti/Jumping

Your core needs to learn how to automatically kick in when it's needed, including responding to the appropriate degree. You will get instant feedback if your core is not stabilized—for example flopping around, side-bending, bouncing, or twisting. Your horse may also register his displeasure! The "T"-arm formation can be used at any gait but here is shown for a rider who is jumping.

Step One: First, practice holding "T" arms on the flat (arms held out at about shoulder height), in a controlled setting, and under the supervision of a trainer.

Step Two: If this practice goes well, and your trainer feels it is a safe exercise for you and your horse, proceed to holding "T" arms while doing some jumping gymnastics (fig. 18.7).

18.7 "T" Arm Cavalletti/Jumping

FLUID HIPS/STABLE SPINE EXERCISE 7:
Stability Hug

The Stability Hug helps the rider to assess how stable her spine is by pivoting at her hips to move her trunk. Remember: A stable spine maintains its natural curves. The Stability Hug is a fun movement that your horse is likely to enjoy too!

Step One: Ask a helper to hold your horse at the halt.

Step Two: Bend at the hips and give your horse a big hug around his neck. Stay down! Keep your torso resting on your horse's neck.

Step Three: Extend your arms into a "T" formation (fig. 18.8).

18.8 Stability Hug

Step Four: While keeping your natural spinal curves, sit upright again by unfolding from the hips. Don't use your arms, and don't allow your legs to slide back. Use your core stabilizers instead.

Step Five: Repeat to fatigue.

> **chapter takeaway**
>
> Varied full-body movements that challenge the spinal stabilizers as well as hip mobility are beneficial for the equestrian. Such movements train these important sets of muscles to hold when needed, move when needed, and release when not needed. Balance, stability, safety, mobility, and fluidity are all enhanced.

CHAPTER NINETEEN

NOURISHMENT: OUTER AND INNER FITNESS

OUTER FITNESS

Your level of physical fitness can be affected by either too much or not enough exercise. But remember that exercise, even a daily workout, represents only a small percentage of the total movement you make throughout each day—and all that movement adds up! Exercise cannot replace all of the hours you spend bending, reaching, climbing stairs, walking to your car or the bus stop, pushing the grocery cart, cleaning the house, or completing any other routine daily task. However, exercise can *supplement* your daily movements to increase your level of fitness. Do the amount and type of exercise that makes you feel stronger (fig. 19.1). Avoid what weakens you.

Here are some tips to make your workout routine successful:

- Center your warm-up around getting the blood and fluids flowing, as well as loosening up the joints.

19.1 If riding and caring for horses makes you feel pumped, then go for it! Chores such as grooming, tacking up, feeding, and riding your horse are all full-body movements that will support your fitness and functioning.

- Make it fun! If you perceive your exercise routine as "play," you will look forward to your workouts. Enjoyable movement becomes easily and smoothly etched into your neuromuscular system—unlike the drudgery of repetitive exercise.

19.2 Mixing fun and fitness together in a lovely Vermont winter.

- Focus on eating nutrient-dense whole food. Eat when you are hungry, particularly after a workout. It will help to recharge and refuel you.

- Stay hydrated.

- Vary your movements, workouts, and the surfaces you sit on, stand on, walk on, or hang from. Mix it up!

- Avoid snug, body-controlling garments. This type of clothing turns off your natural core musculature and has a negative impact on breathing and digestion.

- When you have to sit for an extended period, don't just sit there—wiggle, squirm, and shake!

- Find a coach who is as knowledgeable about riding as they are about fascial fitness, posture, and movement patterns.

- Allow proper time for winding down before bedtime and s-l-e-e-p!

- Limit resistance and high-intensity training to only two or three days a week, and never practice these forms of exercise for two days in a row. Factor in recovery time.

- Your *outer* fitness and world will only come into order when your *internal* fitness and world have done so. (We explore this beginning on p. 188.)

- Be creative about how to sneak fun, full-body movements into your day (fig. 19.2).

INNER FITNESS

Remember the *Bubbling Spring* acupressure point at the base of the ball of the foot? We learned how pressing on this point for a minute stimulates the kidneys and rejuvenates the spirit in chapter 9 (see p. 92). The point is just where the stirrup lies on a rider's foot. No wonder the feeling of being "in the irons" is so delightful! Tapping this area is also a great grounding and "inner warm-up" exercise for the rider (fig 19.3).

For me, one of the most peaceful sounds in the world is that of horses munching hay. The sound of munching is so vivid to me I can pull it out of my back pocket anywhere, anytime—and I do just that! When I imagine the sound of munching, I feel deeply nourished in place, and this feeling in turn prompts me to take a pause in working toward my goals. Instead, I work on my attitude and my gratitude to others. This redirection of my thought process and my energy serves as a second source of nourishment—*inner nourishment*.

Inner nourishment has to do with how well you feel satiated with support and encouragement. It includes the messages you tell yourself. When you "clear out the waste," such as self-doubt, jealousy, and blame, you create space for peace and wisdom to enter. Do you support your efforts with positive affirmations?

19.3 Earlier in the book I told you about the *Bubbling Spring* acupressure point (see p. 92). This rider shows us again where to tap to support your inner fitness.

Or do you berate yourself with your own verbal assaults?

There is an indescribable poetic attraction between horses and humans. Fellow horse lovers understand this and typically bond together. But as amazing, fun, and supportive as the horse world is, it can also be frustrating, critical, and disconnecting. I've heard too many riders berating and blaming themselves for what they feel was a "bad ride." I might hear them say, "I am stupid," "I am slow," "I am crooked," "I am clumsy," or a host of other negative attributes. And yet, the perfect match for the keyhole of success is *self-acceptance*. There is no such thing as a perfect body shape, a perfect brain, or a perfect rider. We tend to accept horses of all body shapes and sizes, with different types of strengths, and with varying roles in their social relationships. But too often, a rider abandons rather than supports herself. And learning to support yourself is really about increasing your inner nourishment.

To nourish yourself, seek out the things, people, animals, and places that are your touchstones. Do what strengthens you. Release what weakens you. Riding is a challenging sport! You can't just yank a body into alignment and expect it to stay there. Every body has its own neutral arrangement, where it is naturally balanced and poised without tugging it into place. Your personal ideal position is never going to be the same as the textbook ideal—and that's okay. If you look at famous, successful riders from throughout time, no two of them position themselves the same way. Individuality is one of the beautiful qualities of being human. Accept and embrace yourself without apology. We are all amazing in our unique way.

> **chapter takeaway**
>
> **Your *outer fitness* will only come into order when your *inner fitness* has done so as well. Accept yourself, including your past failures. Choose to nourish and embrace the true self you are becoming.**

CHAPTER TWENTY

TEACHING HUMANS AND HORSES

SENSE, FEEL, DISCOVER

You are the expert in your own life. Believe in yourself! To move forward with your riding, you need to make your own discoveries. Trainers can be vastly helpful, but the pearls of their wisdom do not flow out of their mouths and into the gaps of your mind, the weak links in your body, or the glitches of your nervous system. *The most important pearls of wisdom about you are found within you.* Your body-mind has an intelligence all its own. It devotes itself solely to you when you believe in yourself. Its answers are powerful, accurate, and visceral. To cultivate your body-mind intelligence, I encourage you to embrace a little bit of knowledge from each trainer or clinician with whom you have ridden. And like a bee who collects the sweet essence of each flower visited, extract the takeaway messages from each mentor that seem to speak to you and your horse.

As a strategy to make progress, riders are apt to look outside of themselves. They select an elite rider or two to emulate, and hope their trainer will "fix" their position or riding challenges. Please use this approach with caution, because no two body-minds are ever the same. You may be long through the waist and torso, and perhaps your mentor has a similar physical profile. But her strategies are not necessarily going to be the keys to your success—even if you ride the same horse. Presumably, she spent years working on finding her body's best position and balance. Consider that her daily movements and postures, the rhythm of her breathing, the way her organs slide around during breathing, her ability to integrate the left and right brain hemispheres, her old injuries, her ability to feel, her insights, and her ability to imagine and visualize all combine to give her a full profile that is solidly different from yours. If you force yourself into an approximation of your trainer or your favorite elite rider's position, you will not find your own body's balance or your supple position. Instead, you will generate unwanted tension. Most trainers understand they cannot create other elite riders by using the same strategies they employed to sculpt themselves into success.

I've spent a lifetime teaching people of all ages and abilities about horses and riding. Here are a few things I learned about teaching along the way:

- As a trainer, I don't need to have all the answers. I simply need to ask the right questions.

- Believe in and nourish the "Little Engine That Could" that dwells within each and every rider—recognize the talents and gifts you possess that enable you to fulfill your potential as a human being.

- The best I can do for my students is give them a virtual leg up through my modeling and teaching. Then I must allow them to ride off independently, to discover on their own what I was hoping to teach them.

- Although I cannot fix all a rider's challenges, I can help her learn to sense, feel, and discover what is working as well as what is *not* working. Then I can facilitate her journey onward.

- It's the horses that often point to the solution for any given challenge. Listen carefully, and embrace their wisdom.

- If I cannot help a rider learn how to feel her horse's movements, her body's balance and position, her timing, her coordination, her need to self-correct, and her suppleness, then I give her nothing of lasting value—and she will always be dependent on me. This is *not* the goal!

- There is a massive amount of input—both internal and external—involved when riding a horse (fig. 20.1). As a trainer, it's my responsibility to not add to the overload. It is best for me to introduce one new way or change at a time, and give the rider a chance to work on it before I offer comments. I need to continually remind myself, "Don't talk so much!"

THE ART OF SELF-CORRECTION

Just like many other sports and disciplines, riding well is *not* about achieving perfection. It's about *self-correction*. Much of the time, self-correction involves taking away extraneous elements rather than adding in extra things. Approaching self-correction in this way means a rider is sculpted instead of painted into her posture. It's the slow, steady, subtle sculpting that gives positive, lasting results. When you self-correct, it pays to think in soft terms such as "weave," "knit," or "draw," instead of harsher terms such as "push," "pull," or "force." Be careful not to bully your body into position! Instead, let your position grow from the subtlety of your intention to align your center of gravity with your horse's center of gravity.

20.1 There is already so much input to a rider's brain that hearing "eyes up, weight your right seat bone, chin over the mane, straighten your "C"-curve, watch the timing of your aids, r-e-l-a-x," all in the space of a few minutes, is *beyond* overload! When teaching, work on just one thing at a time, and allow the rider to process and play with a new tool, image, or awareness for a while before you offer your suggestions.

There is a constant flow and fluidity between the conscious and subconscious minds, representing the connection between *expressing* ourselves and *listening* to ourselves. This connection can result in a gentle form of self-correction to better support who you are. Creativity and correction then grow out of your subconscious and into more conscious movements. This is the reason why visualizing and imagery are so beneficial to your riding. These tools enable you to connect to your horse at a deeper level. Consider the circulating energy between horse and rider (fig. 20.2). When the rider is well-aligned, the energy of both horse and rider co-mingles at the points of contact (seat bones and legs). Correct alignment is learned and achieved only through

20.2 When horse and rider are aligned well and in tune with each other, they become involved in a vibrant energetic exchange. But alignment is dynamic and requires lots of gentle, subtle self-correction on the rider's part.

Questions Underlying Self-Correction

Here are a few questions to ask yourself to help establish a better connection with your horse through the art of self-correction:

• *Am I feeling tension anywhere in my body?*
If so, engage the muscles in that area of the body for a few seconds, as if you were making a hard fist. On an exhale, soften the area as you sigh. Take a few deep breaths and direct the energy of the inhale toward the spot you just released.

• *Am I supporting my body weight in good self-carriage?*
If not, gently adjust it without harshness or judgment. No one has correct posture all the time.

• *Am I breathing deeply and rhythmically?*
If not, imagine your diaphragm gently pulling downward on an inhale as you create space for fresh air in your lungs.

• *Do I feel lively and energized?*
If not, imagine oxygen molecules going for a ride as if they were on a mini rollercoaster in your bloodstream. Bring new life and laughter to your droopy, "sleepy" cells.

• *Do I feel centered and grounded?*
If not, imagine your spine is the central trunk of a tree, and its roots are growing downward from your feet deep into the earth's inner core.

• *Do I know the type of unmounted work that can help support my self-correction?*
If not, turn to the Appendix of this book for the Equestrian Training Pyramid (see p. 263). It details the aspects a rider is encouraged to include in her unmounted training.

• *Have I forgiven myself for the mistakes I made (horse-related or otherwise) this morning, yesterday, a year ago, or many years ago?*
If not, breathe compassion into your heart. Compassion for others starts with a solid foundation of self-compassion. You are doing the best you can at any given moment. Treasure and celebrate this effort.

conscious effort. But the energy flows subconsciously, through energetic channels known as *meridians*. This energy gives a sense of vibrancy to your riding.

THE RIDER'S TEAM

It takes many hands and minds to support a horse-rider team. Dozens of people may be involved, from the trainer, barn owner, and farm or stable manager to the vet, farrier, saddle fitter, road apple scooper, and so on. Each member of the team holds a flashlight in the darkened room of horse health, well-being, performance, and support, and each team member is important (figs. 20.3 A & B, 20.4 A & B, 20.5 A & B, and 20.6 A & B). I am hoping more equestrian ground coaches step up to the plate as team members. There is a need to train riders how to feel when they are correctly aligned, how to center and ground themselves, as well as how to embrace their passion in a visceral manner. I often see riders with large teams that offer wonderful support for their horses, and moral support for themselves. What I don't see often is a rider's support for herself. This is a tough sport. I encourage riders to be kind and gentle to themselves, rather than critical and disappointed in themselves. Be your own best friend!

20.3 A & B Dr. Amy Plavin is a veterinarian and horse owner. Here she rides Windy Hollow Modern Millie, a third-generation homebred Connemara mare. Dr. Plavin avidly supports the team concept by urging horse owners to consult with their veterinarian regarding their horse's care and well-being rather than relying on social media. Your vet will steer you toward a specialist or referral center as necessary. Dr. Plavin has the support of several team members who focus on her posture and movements, both while mounted and unmounted. As a result, she has become masterful at staying spot-on-the-vertical.

20.4 A & B "Doc" is well cared for and supported by his team members. Here, Lois Resseguie of Hanover, New Hampshire, walks with Doc under the watchful eye of Robert Oaks, farrier, and Austin Blake, farrier's assistant. Robert, Austin, and Lois will compare thoughts on Doc's gait, balance, and functioning prior to his trimming. Robert Oaks is a real team player. He recognizes that we need each other for assistance and support. Robert contacted me about scheduling workouts for his team members, because their work is extremely physically demanding. Being a farrier requires a lot of core stabilization to avoid injury and stay strong. Lois, Austin, Robert, and I have fun with group stabilization exercises.

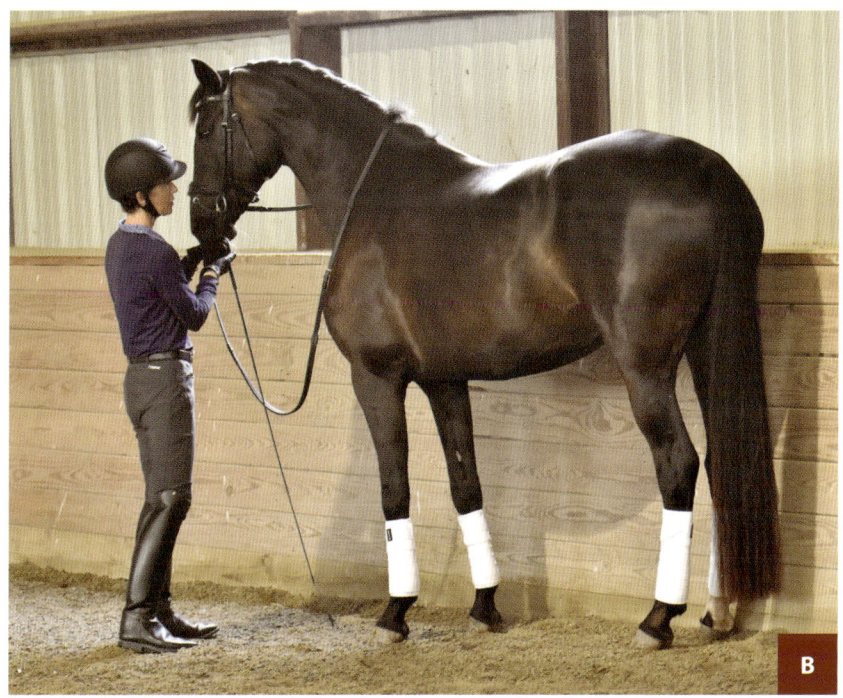

20.5 A & B In photo A, Grand Prix dressage rider and USDF-certified trainer and instructor Joy Congdon of Vermont displays her excellent alignment and strong core as she rides Swan's Red Storm, owned by Mary Ann Reich. Joy encourages her riders to participate in supplemental ground-based exercise programs in order to bring their best physical selves to their horses. She is doing some ground-based training with her mare Raffinesse FH in photo B.

20.6 A & B A barn or farm manager is a key person on a horse and rider's support team. Photo A shows Pat Read's skilled hands guiding young Finch. Pat is manager of Round Robin Farm in Tunbridge, Vermont. She works with a large team of family members and others to ensure everyone's needs are met. Even turning a horse out becomes a family "team" affair as Pat is often joined by her grandson Bodhi Benoit, daughter Bekki Read, and canine co-pilots Elsie and Eve. Lucky Arwen gets this team support from the barn all the way up the hill to his paddock in photo B.

chapter takeaway

Your trainer can give you guidance and pose questions, but ultimately, *you are the expert in your own life*. The answers lie in your own body-mind. Trust your inner wisdom and believe in yourself. Sense, feel, and discover!

PART 3

STABILIZING YOUR DEEP CORE

The seven chapters of Part 3 will help you better understand where your deep core is and how to activate it. You will be guided through a series of sounds and postures to "wake up" the deep core myofascia, bringing stability, and strength with suppleness, to your riding. You will therefore better be able to match the physical forces that bombard you and your horse as you ride. Your riding will become less mechanical, posed, and fixed; instead, it will be dynamic, vibrant, and expressive. These feelings will bring out your love for riding, and that's when you ride with passion!

CHAPTER TWENTY-ONE

RIDE FROM YOUR GUTS! (A VISCERAL APPROACH)

MUSCLES, BONES, OR ORGANS?

A look at our organs shows us that neither we nor our horses are perfectly symmetrical beings. For instance, the liver is situated on the right side of the body, whereas the stomach is on the left. Even the size of our lungs varies; the left lung is smaller than the right. All of this asymmetry presents a challenge to a rider who is invested in finding smooth symmetry. This asymmetry affects your position out of the saddle as much as it affects your riding posture, and its implications vary for each of us. I sometimes see a pattern where the left hip is carried a bit forward of the right hip, causing the right hip to drift off to the right as the rib cage leans to the left. But not everyone with a forward left hip has a right hip drift. It's all dependent on where your myofascia has been "hanging out" the majority of the day—and night!

To increase your *asymmetry awareness*, try the following exercise: Sit on a stool or at the front edge of a chair with your feet flat on the floor. Notice which knee naturally wants to go forward of the other knee. Ease the knee in front rearward to line up with the other knee, and notice if anything else about your posture automatically changes. Breathe deeply and slowly as you do this to allow your diaphragm to help shift your organs to a better-aligned position. Work to get your body more comfortable with being gently drawn into alignment, so as to not invite tension to the process. *Did you notice a change in how much each seat bone was weighted? Did the position of your rib cage automatically shift? What happened to your sternum?* Asking yourself these types of questions can help you develop body-mind awareness, which will assist you in your efforts to self-correct.

Repeat the exercise above, this time seeing if you can feel your viscera (organs) move around slightly in coordination with your subtle shifts in posture. Organs can move in a three-dimensional fashion, and it's important to give each organ enough space to move freely; this is one reason

21.1 Each of these riders has a different way of approaching her riding. The rider on the left rides from her muscles. She is tense, grippy, and not able to center herself well. The rider on the right rides from the framework of her bones. She is balanced and centered, but struggles a bit to connect deeply with her horse and feel his every move before he even makes it. She also has to work hard at improving her timing and coordination. The rider at the top *rides from her guts*! She brings the passion, joy, and energy of a victory gallop to every ride, exuding confidence and success because it springs forward from her deepest organs.

why breathing is so beneficial to the organs. Consider how your belly button moves downward with each inhale and upward with each exhale. It's not just your navel moving—your organs also move vertically, in a motion sort of like a tidal flow. Part of an athlete's training is learning how to give her organs a chance to move throughout their space in all directions.

One way to facilitate this motion is through rolling on the floor, both on the *vertical axis* (log-type rolling) as well as on the *horizontal axis* (hug-your-knees-to-chest- or rocking-horse-type rolling). Rolling is a wonderful way to improve circulation to your organs. Overall, it's important to maximize your internal organ space and movement because doing so will increase the range and power of your postures as you move around.

When you ride from your guts—the deep visceral aspect of your love for your horse and your sport—you are able to tap into the energy that stems from your center, which is where the organs are located (fig. 21.1). You effectively ride from the *inside out* rather than from *the outside in*. Let's explore this idea further.

Consider that your organs are your internal support system. Picture them as being three dimensional and weighted with fluid. The fluid nature of our guts is a big reason why I like to think of alignment in terms of stacking water balloons rather than building blocks. Envision moving your organs around by using deep, rhythmic breathing. Now imagine they are singing! Each organ is associated with its own vibrational frequency, and sounds have a vibrational nature (which we will explore in the next chapter—see p. 206).

Organs are also associated with various emotions. Consider the heart's association with caring and love, the kidneys' affiliation with energy and awareness, and the intestines being the digestive organs closest to your center of gravity when you are standing. Keep all of that in mind as we explore some ways to *activate your organs* to bring forth their energy to your riding. We will explore these ideas more later in this chapter.

RIDE WITH PASSION

When you take your trainer's suggestions under advisement, you are processing and then taking action from an external source. While there is value to this approach, many riders neglect to validate their own *internal trainer*. Your internal trainer is the wisdom and intuitive sense held in the cells and the recesses of your body-mind. When you function only from your external sources, you limit your perception of what a good rider should feel like, and you try to place yourself in that rigid definition. On the other hand, working from a visceral level is extremely validating. Doing so shows you had the answers to your dilemmas all along, and that you can trust and believe in yourself.

To ride from your internal trainer, you first need to bring your attention to your guts. According to Gerda Alexander in her book *Bones, Breath, and Gesture* (North Atlantic Books, 1995),

Bit of Advice: Acupressure for the Organs

There is an acupressure point four finger-widths above the wrist crease on the palm side of your hand. It lies between the two ropy tendons you can feel on the inner and outer edges of your wrist. Press on this spot with the opposite thumb to help bring balance to your internal organs. Applying pressure to this point also gives a calming influence to the rider, which is why it's great to do at horse shows!

21.2 A rider who slouches is restricting her organs' ability to function optimally, including her heart and lungs. Fluids cannot flow properly and freely throughout the body while it is in this position.

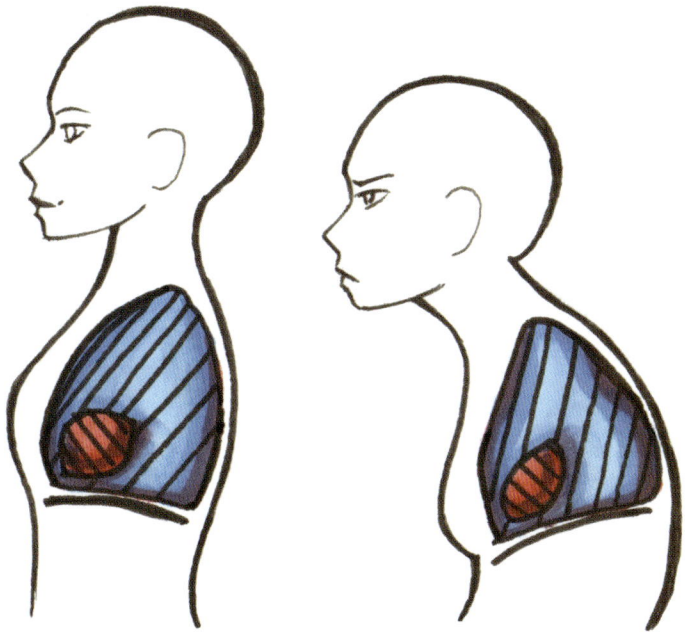

when you focus your attention on a body part, including an organ, the temperature of that area rises.

Envision your heart, stomach, spleen, liver, lungs, and kidneys. "Breathe into your organs," imagining your pelvic floor muscles and diaphragm moving downward on each inhale and upward on each exhale, as if they were a pair of eyebrows, rhythmically lowering and raising. However, you must keep the abdominal muscles soft and relaxed for the act of breathing to massage your organs and place them in good alignment. This imagery also helps your nervous system relax by serving as an invitation to "rest and digest."

Now direct your gaze to a specific organ you would like to activate, and tap over that area several times. Growl to wake them up! Make it a big bear growl, and put your hands over the area to create warmth. Finally, embrace the love, joy, and gratitude you have for your horse. If you are anywhere near your horse, direct that positive energy toward his heart by using your gaze.

Activate Your Organs

Slouchy posture in the saddle "crunches" the heart, lungs, and other organs and deprives them of the space they need to thrive (fig. 21.2). The rider's body's circulation of fluids will not be optimal. She will be unable to connect with her horse well, either physically or energetically. Although she could correct her position by quickly bolting herself upright and throwing her shoulders back to open her chest, doing so would be abrupt, artificial, and stiff, inviting her horse to be stiff as well. However, if she instead brings awareness to her organs, and visualizes them moving within their space as she takes slow, deep, rhythmic breaths, her body will

21.3 A & B The rider places one hand on her stomach to stimulate warmth as her other hand taps her lower belly for further organ activation (A). The payoff is a bold, artistic, confident rider (B)!

arrange itself (figs. 21.3 A & B). She will unfold and refresh like a droopy flower receiving its nourishment. The outcome of this approach is a graceful, coordinated, supple rider with positive tension (see p. 23), resulting in a beautiful alignment. She is revived and set free to ride with passion!

Bit of Advice: Belly Release

Many of us are in the habit of tensioning the belly inward as well as upward. But holding the belly in this way destabilizes the spine. A tense belly can lead to digestive issues, and it is even possible to squeeze the organs to foreign places, such that a hernia is created. Another possible unfortunate outcome is a pelvic floor problem, sometimes with organ prolapse. To avoid these types of issues, I suggest doing a *belly release* several times a day. Here are the steps:

Step One: Stand in good alignment with your legs straight, but not hyperextended at the knees.

Step Two: Keep your arms at your sides as you take an inhale.

Step Three: On the exhale, raise your arms over head as you stick out your tongue and roar powerfully like a lion!

Step Four: Bow (hip hinge) slightly on the pause between your inhale and exhale.

Step Five: On the next inhale, lower your arms as you allow your belly to fully release. Don't deliberately puff the belly out, just allow it to fully drop toward the floor. This may take several minutes or more.

Step Six: As you feel your belly release, notice any changes in your breathing.

Step Seven: As you do this exercise, take note of your emotions. (When I did this exercise for the first time, I pulled up a strong feeling of shame. Now I understand that my belly is the part of my body that stores shame.)

chapter takeaway

When you ride from your guts, you tap into the energy of your center, allowing you to *ride from the inside out*. Doing so brings passion and confidence to your riding, and fosters a deeper connection to your horse. Isn't that the unspoken goal?

CHAPTER TWENTY-TWO

Beneficial Sounds

THE BODY'S VIBRATIONAL ENERGY

As we explored in the last chapter, the activation and support of your organs affects your riding performance. In order to make a sound with your vocal cords, you also need to engage organic support. The degree with which you activate and enlist the support of your organs will determine the strength, passion, and quality of your voice. Notice the passion involved in a horse whinny (fig. 22.1).

When a sound is produced, all three of the body's diaphragms (*pelvic, respiratory*, and *vocal*) work together to create an internal pressure to protect and help stabilize the spine. A long sigh can also help relax the diaphragms. Through the action of the *glottis* (a space between the vocal cords), whispered speech can give good postural support.

Sounds are a form of *vibrational energy*, but even our thoughts and emotions create vibrational frequencies. The human *chakras* (energy centers) are said to vibrate with specific sound frequencies that we know as the music scale. Pay attention to the sounds your body makes. Listen to the beating of your heart, the creaking of your joints, your bones moving around, your stomach churning, and the sound of your breathing. You spontaneously moan when you are hurt and laugh when you are overcome with joy; you gasp when you are surprised. These are just a few examples of your body "talking," as the emotions of your organs express themselves in an expansive fashion.

Why does any of this matter to a rider? Because her horse is keenly aware of it all. There are times when your horse is more aware of your internal status than you are. Horses are creatures of energy and are particularly skilled at reading the energy of people, even subtle energy such as the energy of intent. This is why it's hard to trick a horse! But this awareness and energy works both ways. Pay attention to your horse's organic sounds. One of my riders bonds with her horse by emulating his rhythmic breathing, audibly exhaling in time with his exhalation. Try putting

PART 3

"The hooves of the horse! Oh! Witching and sweet is the music earth steals from the iron-shod feet."

— Poet and Horseman William Henry Ogilvie

your ear on your horse's side, and listen to his heart beating and the sounds his gut makes. I like to make this part of my tacking up routine, because it gives me a sense of his immediate world and where he resides physically and emotionally at that precise point in time. Checking in like this is a strong nonverbal message to your horse that you care about him, want an updated

22.1 This photo captures the essence of a horse's signature sound—the whinny. It's a sound with visible attributes as it springs from the horse's deep center and emanates outward in waves. You can see the organs shaking and jostling around as they push outward against the body wall. And if you are mounted when your horse whinnies, you absorb the energy and shake too!

The Specifics of Sound

The vibrations of your own voice have varying effects on your body and mind. Everyone has their own special signature sounds that work best for them, and this applies to horses as well. One of the horses I work with just loves the sound of mourning doves. When his owner makes a similar cooing sound, he sighs and calms down! I encourage you to try out the sounds listed here, and adopt the ones that produce the best results. You will need to repeat each sound about 20 times to give it a fair test before deciding which ones you like best. If you have a metronome handy, I like to pace my trial sounds at about 85 beats per minute. The following list offers some suggested sounds for you to try:

- **For grounding or lowering your center of gravity:**
    "Ooo" (as in groove)
    Guttural *"L"* (like you are swallowing the L)
    "Haaa!" (like you are fogging up a mirror)

- **For centering:**
    "Fffff" (as in forest)
    Neigh like a horse

- **For fluidity:**
    Extended vowel sounds (a, e, i, o, u)

- **For creativity:**
    Long *"o"* sound (as in *"flow"*)

- **For peace/calmness:**
    Long *"a"* sound (as in *"way"*)
    Sigh (*"Ahhhh!"*)

- **For posture support:**
    Singing, humming
    Whispered speech
    "Sh" sound (as in *"shoe"*)
    Long *"e"* sound (as in *"knee"*)
    Honk like a goose (fig. 22.2)
    Buzz like a bee
    Neigh like a horse

22.2 You may remember my earlier mention of one highly effective technique to counteract a sunken rib cage and sternum: honking like a goose (see p. 142)! It can't be a halfhearted honk, either. You must keep honking loudly until your throat clearly delivers a powerful punch sound.

- **For imagination/intuition:**

    "Mmm" sound (as in humming)

- **For organ activation:**

    A good belly laugh (*"Ha! Ha! Ha!"*)
    Strong *"th"* sound (as in *"think"*)
    Hiss like a cat
    Purr like a cat
    Neigh like a horse

- **For core activation:**

    Pretend to blow out a candle (*"Pffttt!"*)
    Clear your throat
    "Choo" sound (rhymes with shoe)
    Growl like a bear
    Buzz like a bee
    Neigh like a horse
    A loud grunt

- **For core stability:**

    "Fff" sound (as in *"Fee-fi-fo-fum"*)
    A loud grunt
    "Th" sound (as in *"thistle"*)

22.3 One way to get a visceral ride is to ride like an opera star who sings with passion!

sense of him, and truly "get" him.

Other sounds that influence animals include music and singing. Consider that there are dairy barns that play classical music for their cows because they have experienced better milk production from doing so! Humming and singing when you are mounted is beneficial to the use of your core and your ability to ride from your guts (fig. 22.3). Most horses enjoy being ridden to music, as many musical freestyles show with their vibrancy!

chapter takeaway

Strong sounds are powered from your center, your deep core, and your organs. Your voice can be used to support your posture and a host of attributes such as fluidity and creativity. But to lift your sternum, you really need to unabashedly honk like a goose!

CHAPTER TWENTY-THREE

WARM-UP AND COOL-DOWN FOR RIDERS

WHY WARM UP AND COOL DOWN?

You should aim to accomplish five things in your *warm-up*:

1 *Move!* You want to divert blood flow away from your organs and toward your skeletal muscles. When you are not exercising, blood "hangs out" in your organs, but it's needed in your muscles for your workout or ride. A proper warm-up will bring oxygen and nutrients to the working muscles, along with beneficial warmth. Warm muscles are better able to move through their range of motion, making them stronger and capable of enhanced performance. At the end of your warm-up (which typically takes about 10 minutes) you should feel ready for more vigorous activity.

2 *Flex and extend your joints as you move.* This will get the fluids flowing so your joints become lubricated. Getting the body's fluids moving sets the stage for a healthy workout, minimizing the risk of injury, pain, and stiffness. Your warm-up is also a great time to do an informal assessment to determine which joints may be stiff versus supple, tight versus loose, or "obedient" versus "cranky." Address any weak links in your warm-up.

3 *Begin to increase your body's core temperature.* You will know your warm-up is effective when you have to take off your outer layer, such as a sweatshirt.

4 *Increase your heart rate.* This is another indicator that the muscles are getting enough blood flow with oxygen and nutrient delivery. Your pulse rate and breathing will both increase.

5 *Sharpen up your neuromuscular system.* Your warm-up is a good time to establish communication between the nerves in your body and your brain. In this chapter, I've included crossover exercises to help facilitate communication between the left and right hemispheres of your brain. Remember that this coordination and communication between body and brain helps you give your horse clear aids in a timely fashion.

I suggest doing your warm-up before you tack up your horse, so long as you complete it within 45 minutes of your ride. Many of my riders pay diligent attention to the warm-up for their horses, but they neglect to do the same for themselves. This compromises their performance. If this sounds familiar, try envisioning your muscles as being gray and anemic looking. Do you really want to ride in that weak condition? If you choose to skip the warm-up, you are reducing your capacity to bring out the best rider in you, and the best athlete in your horse as well.

In contrast, the *cool-down* starts at the end of your ride, as your horse walks. This is a good chance to do exercises and stretches, preferably without stirrups so you can move and stretch freely if that is safe. Cleaning up the aisle and tidying up your storage area counts too. This type of puttering is important, because your body does not appreciate coming to a sudden stop at the end of a session. When you stop suddenly, you risk feeling faint, dizzy, nauseated, or fatigued. These are all warning signs that the blood that was in your muscles during your ride has not adequately returned to your heart and other organs.

Typically, only five to seven minutes of cool-down is needed, but follow your body's lead. If it needs more, this is a great time to do the myofascial exercises from chapter 10 (see p. 102). You should also consciously slow down your movements and thoughts as you make a mental note to get to bed on time. Remember, a good night's sleep is when your muscles repair, recover, and rebuild. During your cool-down, sip water and consider eating a small snack. I suggest choosing something healthy that will provide protein and a slow-release carbohydrate, such as a bit of nut butter on a whole-grain cracker.

The following set of exercises offers guidelines on what to include in your warm-up before riding. For your cool-down, choose any exercise(s) you find helpful.

WARM-UP/COOL-DOWN EXERCISE 1:
Arena Skipping

During the warm-up, it's important to do a bit of cardio first to help move blood and fluids around your body. Cardio will also bring some warmth to your skeletal muscles and increase your core temperature.

Step One: Go to your arena or another location of similar size. Pick a starting point and skip all the way around the arena one full lap. Be sure to swing your arms as you do this.

Step Two: When you are back at your starting point, skip backward one full time around. This will challenge and help re-set your neuromuscular system for enhanced coordination when you ride.

WARM-UP/COOL-DOWN EXERCISE 2:
Belly Button Vertical Breathing

In this important warm-up exercise, centering and grounding become automatic. Belly Button Vertical Breathing sets the stage for a strong ride.

Step One: Put one or both hands on your belly button and breathe slowly, deeply, and freely.

Step Two: Feel your belly button drop toward your feet on each inhale.

Step Three: Feel your belly button rise toward your rib cage on each exhale.

Step Four: Pause your breathing at the end of each inhale, and pause a bit longer at the end of each exhale.

WARM-UP/COOL-DOWN EXERCISE 3:
Full Body Shakes

Full Body Shakes get the blood flowing and link your nerves with your muscles so they are "speaking the same language."

Step One: Starting with your arms, do some short-range shaking with them (see p. 110).

Step Two: Next shake one leg.

Step Three: Shake the other leg.

Step Four: Shake your torso, visualizing your organs, and especially your diaphragm, shaking.

Step Five: Rest for a moment.

Step Six: Do some Bobbleheads (see p. 151)—shake like one of those dashboard ornaments! Be sure to turn your head left and right when you do this.

Step Seven: Finally, go for a full-body shake and "wake up" all your body's sleepy crevasses!

WARM-UP/COOL-DOWN EXERCISE 4:
Bouncy Ball Warm-Up

The Bouncy Ball Warm-Up highlights the connection of your arms and hands to the myofascia of your trunk.

Step One: Slowly roll a small high-bounce ball along the backs and palms of each hand, from your wrists to your fingertips. Do not roll the ball over any bony parts, and instead concentrate on the spaces between your fingers. As you do this, pretend you are squeezing water out of a sponge.

Step Two: Next, roll the bouncy ball slowly along each arm, from wrist to shoulder.

Step Three: The final step is to slowly roll the bouncy ball above and below each collarbone, then up and down your sternum.

WARM-UP/COOL-DOWN EXERCISE 5:
Throat Warm-Ups

When your jaw, tongue, and throat areas are tight or lack blood flow, your riding will be negatively impacted.

Step One: Hold your lower jaw in one hand and allow it to sink slowly to an open-mouthed position.

Step Two: Continue holding your lower jaw and use your hand to guide it slightly to the left and right. The hand is the leader here, not the jaw.

Step Three: Now close your jaw and clear your throat a few times.

Step Four: Finally, sing or make an animal sound. This is a great time to whinny like a horse!

WARM-UP/COOL-DOWN EXERCISE 6:
Heart Breathing

Heart Breathing will literally warm your heart and deepen the bond with your horse.

Step One: While in a standing position that feels centered, balanced, and grounded, think about all the ways you are grateful that you are about to share some time with your horse.

Step Two: With your next inhale, capture that gratitude and visualize sending it directly to your heart. As you do this, keep your gaze and attention on your heart by placing one or both hands over it. It can help to associate this energy with green or pink colored light.

Step Three: As you exhale, send the gratitude out with your breath. It might help to imagine you are exhaling through your *solar plexus*, which is the notch between the front of your ribs. This type of exhalation will help link the love and gratitude you hold for your horse with your gut instinct, strengthening your bond to him.

WARM-UP/COOL-DOWN EXERCISE 7: Grounding Stance and Walk

Grounding Stance is a standing pose that can also be "taken for a walk." Whether still or in motion, it promotes centering and grounding, and therefore is an asset to your riding! When practicing Grounding Stance, take advantage of *ground reaction forces* as you push downward. This action will help you feel connected to the earth and prepares your muscles for the positive tension they need after you mount up.

Step One: Stand with your feet hip-width apart and toes pointing straight ahead.

Step Two: Keep your legs straight and your spine neutral as you bend at the hips for a slight bow. Place your hands on your thighs and press downward toward the ground with your feet and hands. Sense how grounded you are.

23.1 Grounding Stance and Walk

Step Three: Keep your toes pointing forward as you take about 10 steps in this slightly hinged position (fig. 23.1).

Step Four: Stay in the same position and back up about 10 steps to reach your starting point.

WARM-UP/COOL-DOWN EXERCISE 8: Head Band Squat

Head Band Squat is a shortstop squat with an exercise band behind your neck. This exercise will elongate the back of your neck to help you create space in your spine. You will naturally sit taller!

23.2 Head Band Squat

Step One: Hold one end of an exercise band in each hand, and sink into a squat.

Step Two: Place the middle of the band behind your neck. Press your hands down onto your thighs (fig. 23.2).

Step Three: Keep your head in a neutral position and lift through the back of your neck to feel resistance from the band. Hold for five to seven seconds.

Step Four: Lower to the starting position, and repeat the exercise to fatigue.

WARM-UP/COOL-DOWN EXERCISE 9:
Head Wiggles

Head Wiggles is a great *brain crossover exercise* because it helps you pair what you *think* with what you *feel* when you ride.

Step One: Spread your fingers apart and place each hand on the opposite side of your head (fig. 23.3).

23.3 Head Wiggles

Step Two: Slowly make full eye circles, but don't move your head. Glance upward, look to the left, glance downward, and look to the right, moving only your eyes. Repeat three or four times, then make eye circles in the other direction four or five times.

WARM-UP/COOL-DOWN EXERCISE 10:
Trunk Circles

Our hip rotators get tight from sitting, driving, and simply not doing enough movement involving our hips. Trunk Circles help you feel this tightness, as well as feel its release. This exercise helps you achieve a stable spine with fluid hips—the hallmark of an effective rider.

Step One: Grasp a solid object (such as a tree) as you sit back in a figure "4" squat (fig. 23.4).

Step Two: While keeping your spine neutral (no bending or twisting in any direction), start making slow circles with your entire trunk, originating from your center, which is deep inside your core. Do five circles, then pause and circle in the other direction.

Step Three: Switch legs, and repeat each step.

WARM-UP/COOL DOWN EXERCISE 11:
Figure Eight Hip Circles

Practicing Figure Eight Hip Circles gives a different spin to the hips, because you are going to circle and control one pelvic half at a time. This action improves the fluidity of your hips, and it also helps you learn to use your body parts independently—an important skill for riders.

Step One: Stand with feet hip-width apart (fig. 23.5).

23.4 Trunk Circles

Step Four: Next, try moving the right pelvic half counterclockwise and the left one clockwise. Do the same number of figure eights in this direction.

Step Five: You can also try doing this exercise in a staggered stance (also known as *lunge position*).

WARM-UP/COOL DOWN EXERCISE 12:
Side Wall Circles

Side Wall Circles give your spine a chance to stabilize as you move your hips in varying directions. The success of your ride will depend on these actions.

23.5 Figure Eight Hip Circles

Step Two: Hold the left side of your pelvis still as you make a clockwise circle with the right pelvic half. After one full circle, stop the right pelvic half from moving.

Step Three: Now circle the left pelvic half in a counterclockwise fashion. Once again, stop after one full circle. You have just described a figure eight with your pelvis, first circling to the right, then the left. Repeat to fatigue, noting how many full figure eights you can make.

23.6 Side Wall Circles

Step One: Turn sideways to a wall and position yourself about 2 feet away from it.

Step Two: While leaning against the wall with your nearest hand or forearm, raise the opposite leg (fig. 23.6).

Step Three: Slowly start circling your top leg in large circles. Circle several times in one direction, then reverse the circle and match the number of times around.

Step Four: With your top leg fully raised, do "football kicks" both forward and backward. Keep your legs straight as you kick.

Step Five: Repeat this exercise on the other side of your body, trying to complete the same number of circles and kicks as you did on side one.

WARM-UP/COOL DOWN EXERCISE 13:
Pop-Up Walks

This exercise takes the Pop-Up Stance of chapter 13 (see p. 136) on a walk. It's a super way to activate your pelvic floor muscles before you ride.

Step One: Stand in an area where you can take at least 10 steps forward.

23.7 Pop-Up Walks

Step Two: Root down on the right foot strongly enough that it automatically pops up the entire left leg. Do not deliberately pick up the left leg! Allow the left leg to hover over the ground.

Step Three: Slowly swing your left leg forward into a small step and set it down.

Step Four: Deliberately press downward into the left foot and allow the right leg to automatically pop up to hover over the ground (fig. 23.7).

Step Five: Continue alternating these "pop-ups," and walk forward 10 to 15 steps. It may feel similar to ice skating.

Step Six: Repeat the exercise for backward walking, taking the same number of steps.

Step Seven: Finally, walk sideways (side-stepping) using the "pop-up" technique. Once again, try for 10 to 15 steps on the left side as well as on the right.

WARM-UP/COOL DOWN EXERCISE 14:
Overhead Wall Bird Dogs

Here's an exercise to get your diagonal connections communicating with your core stability muscles, preparing your body for giving aids and doing lateral work such as leg-yielding.

Step One: Stand a couple of feet away from a wall.

Step Two: Reach your hands high over your head, then place them on the wall shoulder-width apart (fig. 23.8).

23.8 Overhead Wall Bird Dogs

Step Three: Assume a well-aligned position. Focus on the core musculature of your mid-section as you simultaneously lift one arm and the opposite leg rearward. Hold them there for seven seconds.

Step Four: Switch to the opposite hand and leg and hold for seven seconds.

Step Five: Continue alternating to fatigue, but if this exercise gets easy, try shaking the free limbs in "bobble" fashion (see p. 151).

WARM-UP/COOL DOWN EXERCISE 15:
Positive Affirmations

It's time to warm up your positive thoughts and energy! State your intention for the day's ride in positive terms as if it is already true. Here are some examples:

- I am safe and at ease.
- I am fit and able.
- I am in tune with my horse.
- I give clear aids.
- I emanate confidence.
- I send love and courage to my horse.
- My body is supple and following.
- My movements are fluid.
- I am healthy and happy.
- I am healing.
- I am whole with my horse.
- I am expressing my authentic self.
- I am thriving in all aspects.
- All my attention is on my horse.
- I am positive and optimistic.
- I am happy with myself and my horse.
- I accept challenges with hope and determination.
- I ride with passion!

chapter takeaway

Warm-ups are vitally important to bring blood flow away from the organs and toward the skeletal muscles. When you ride, your muscles need the oxygen and nutrients delivered by the bloodstream, and the body's tissues also need to have waste carried away. A good warm-up supports this process. Cooling down gradually ensures that blood flow is steadily returned to the organs, where it is now needed for visceral functioning.

PART 3

CHAPTER TWENTY-FOUR

YOUR DEEP CORE

EXPLORING THE DEEP CORE

The space between your rib cage and pelvis is practically bone-free; only the small bones of the spine run through it. However, there are many heavy organs in this section, so without bones, how are they supported? This is where the muscles of your core kick in for stability and support—*when they are trained to do so*.

Core function and *control of the body by the core musculature* are both vital parts of movement efficiency, balance, and joint function, and are essential for reducing the risk of injury. The fitness industry has expanded its approach to training the core muscles, shifting from situps and crunches (which target the more superficial movement muscles) to doing planks and body weight exercises (which target the posture and holding muscles). But in reality, it is practicing a variety of full body exercises (both moving and isometric), executed in good alignment, that will best develop the core. I am a huge fan of this newer, varied, and more comprehensive approach, and have used it as the basis for this book.

24.1 This apple corer creates a small vertical slice of an apple that equates to a rider's deep core area. The deep core is the narrow area of musculature found nearest the spine.

The term *core* is pretty general and can be subject to personal definition. Sometimes, it is even described as "anything between the neck and the knees." In this book, I have chosen to highlight the *deep core* because it is of prime importance to riders. The deep core is a narrow slice of musculature found nearest the spine. It equates to the central, small, vertical slice you are left with after you use an apple corer (fig. 24.1).

Here are some examples of when you might feel your deep core in use:

- When you cough or sneeze.

- When you blow your nose.

- When you jump vertically and land softly.

- When you bite into a lemon and your face puckers.

- When you have the hiccups!

- When you gargle.

- When you vomit or have the dry heaves.

- When you whistle for horses in a distant field.

- When your trusty mount suddenly bounds over a deep stream.

- When you pant (yes, just like a dog on a hot day).

A strong core includes elements of all the following:

- The ability to stabilize the bones of the trunk.

- The ability to both rotate the torso or keep it still (anti-rotation), while always maintaining the neutral curves of the spine.

- The ability to maintain a neutral pelvis (slight "ducky tail"—see p. 18) when standing, sitting, walking, lying down, riding, or exercising.

- The ability to breathe deeply and correctly.

- The ability to control the body's elimination with neither too much nor too little tension in the pelvic floor muscles.

For the rider, controlled movements of the core are essential for staying in alignment and following the movements of her horse. If you have a weak or untrained core, you might inadvertently use your reins or stirrups to balance against the physical forces that act upon your body while in the saddle. This can result in the dreaded water skiing position I discussed in chapter 1 (see p. 7). But when you ride, you are responsible for keeping your body vertical, balanced, and connected. It's your deep core musculature that pulls your body parts to your center and anchors the floor of your seat. When not in use, these same muscles should be relaxed, only kicking in *when* they are needed and *to the exact extent* they are needed—no less and no more. Riding is more of a *postural sport* than ski racing or tennis, for two examples. Riding does not require intense deep core activation that holds firmly through a chunk of time. However, you do need enough core activation to hold your position and handle the physical forces that would otherwise destabilize you.

Holding your position in the saddle is best done *without bracing*. By *bracing*, I mean deliberately using your muscles in a flexed position to keep your body still. Bracing causes the rider to tighten and crunch inward, which is devastating to both you and your horse. It limits your mobility and your functioning, generates gobs of unwanted tension, and compresses your joints, including those of your spine. As you can see, a braced core is a compromised core. You may recall from chapter 11 (see p. 107) that muscles achieve the greatest function and elasticity when they are in a neutral position, neither flexed nor extended. The next two chapters will teach you how to "fire up" your *core stabilizers* so they are ready, willing, and able to work when needed, without your conscious effort.

It is important to consider the parts of your *deep core* that a rider might be concerned with. There is even deep core fascia in your feet! The deep core starts in your arches and connects to your inner calves, inner thigh muscles, and to the myofascia that connects your legs to your spine and pelvis. It then passes through the area containing your organs, to your diaphragm and through your thorax to your jaw and your tongue. The deep core is a central slice that includes the spine but encompasses more, such as the muscles and fascia that *surround* the spine. That whole section becomes a central slice—like an apple core. Of special interest to equestrians is that the deep core fascia includes the pelvic floor muscles that make up the floor of your seat. This chain of myofascia, running from feet to tongue, excels at transmitting energy up the front (anterior) of the spine. This energy is felt quite powerfully at the level of the pelvic floor (fig. 24.2). This energy is similar to a vortex

---

Pull In vs. Push Out

Quite a number of times, I have advised you to *not* suck in your gut or bring your belly button toward your spine in an effort to engage your core. This exercise will help you to better understand the reason why:

Step One: Whinny like a horse—nice and loud!

Step Two: Now suck in your gut. Hold your abdominal muscles in firmly and aim your belly button toward your spine.

Step Three: Continue to hold these muscles in while you whinny like a horse again. Try to be just as loud as you were the first time.

Step Four: Compare the intensity of the sounds you just made. Why was the sound barely audible and warped the second time around? Well, holding your belly button to your spine collapses the core and diminishes space for the organs.

How to "Zip" Your Core

When it comes to engaging the core, one image frequently offered is to imagine you have a zipper running from the pubic bone up to the collarbones; to keep your core tight, pretend you are zipping upward. This can be an effective visual, but be careful—you don't want to imagine this zipper as being located just under your skin. Instead, it should be imagined as being placed a bit in front of your spine (fig. 24.3). Notice the closed end is placed at the pubic bone, and the upper end runs along the length of the spine, just anterior (in front) of it. This is the way energy travels up the front of your spine when you ride. It then goes over the top of your head and down the back of your spine, which is also portrayed in the illustration. The back zipper is placed upside down because of the downward flow of energy there. Body parts that sink downward as you ride include the shoulder blades, the lower edge of the rib cage, and the sacrum.

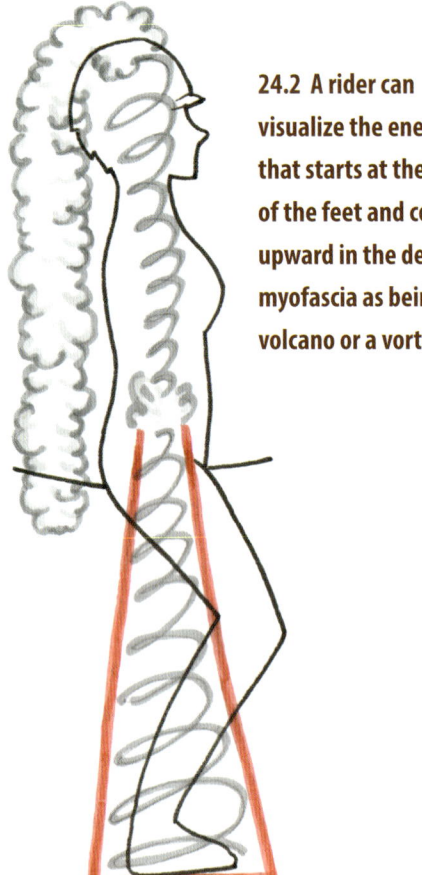

24.2 A rider can visualize the energy that starts at the arches of the feet and comes upward in the deep core myofascia as being like a volcano or a vortex.

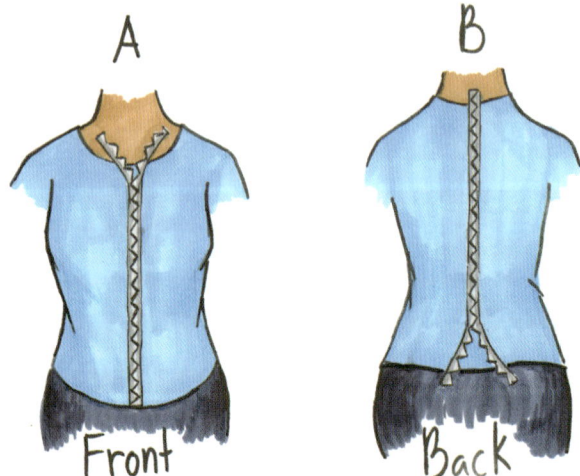

24.3 The *upward* pull of an imagined zipper placed just a tiny bit in front of your spine can help you get the sensation of upward energy flow when you ride. An upside-down zipper helps you get a feel for the *downward* energy flow just behind the spine.

as it powerfully spirals upward. It can also be visualized at the level of your sacrum as exploding ash from a volcano. This area is your center, just in front of the sacrum. When you embrace the vortex or volcano image, it has a powerful effect of recruiting your deep core and lowering your center of gravity. This enables you to be a stronger rider.

The following exercises will help you to activate your deep core so you will be ready to tackle the core stabilizing exercises of the next chapter.

24.4 Play an Instrument

CORE ACTIVATION EXERCISE 1:
Play an Instrument

Step One: Playing a wind instrument is great for your breathing, as you learned in chapter 4, and it is also a wonderful core activator. Even a harmonica will do (fig. 24.4)!

CORE ACTIVATION EXERCISE 2:
Scoop the Goop

Step One: Your tongue is connected to your deep core myofascia. "Scoop up" the soft tissue under your tongue (which I call the "goop") and gently bring it upward toward the roof of your mouth with a sucking motion upward as you exhale to activate your deep core. Do not do this forcefully.

Step Two: Release the goop downward on the inhale, because that is when all the diaphragm-ish muscles in your body descend.

CORE ACTIVATION EXERCISE 3:
Core Walk

Step One: Walk up and down hills in all kinds of ways (forward, backward, sideways, "leg-yield," "half-pass").

Step Two: As you do this, keep your hips back over your ankles, and reach up high with both arms. This alignment will recruit your diaphragm to help stabilize you and activate your deep core supports.

CORE ACTIVATION EXERCISE 4:
Deep Core Sounds

In chapters 13 and 22, we examined how the use of sound can be beneficial to the rider. Well, some sounds are especially good at waking up the deep core.

Step One: When spoken powerfully and with a deep voice "*liffft*" and "*grrufff*" will send energy soaring through your deep core!

Step Two: Try these same sounds when you are riding—they can also support the lifting of your horse's back.

CORE ACTIVATION EXERCISE 5:
Wall Push

Step One: Stand about 2 feet away from a wall. Make two fists as if you were holding reins, and bend your knees slightly, as if you were riding on the flat.

Step Two: Push your fists forward into the wall, without leaning your upper body forward. Keep your body weight supported over the center of your heels. Staying vertical will help you feel how the push forward comes from your deep core. This is a critical feel for both you and your horse.

Step Three: When you are riding, visualize the wall and remember the feeling of this exercise. Doing so will help you to isometrically push forward from your core instead of simply moving your hands forward.

CORE ACTIVATION EXERCISE 6:
Boot Flicks and Pulls

For the Boot Flicks and Pulls, you will need to wear a pair of close fitting rubber boots. Add thick socks in order to get a snug fit if you need to.

Step One: Take one foot and imagine you are "flicking" something substantial off your boot in the direction of your other foot—imaginary thick mud or heavy snow will do to activate your deep core nicely!

Step Two: When it comes time to remove your boots, use a boot puller or your other heel. When you feel suction in the boot you are removing, you are also using your deep core. Do this exercise on both sides.

CORE ACTIVATION EXERCISE 7:
Whole Body Scramble

You are about to get up off the floor and back down again by engaging your deep core—without using your hands for support.

Step One: Start in a face-down (prone) position and come to a full stand. Do this by rolling onto your back, bending your knees, and coming to a half-kneel position, with one leg kneeling on the floor and the other in front with the knee bent.

Step Two: Repeat this transition three times, starting with a different leg or using a different strategy each time.

Step Three: Repeat the exercise three *more* times, now starting and finishing from your *back* (supine).

Step Four: When the exercise gets easy, try it without touching down on either your hands or knees!

> **chapter takeaway**
>
> **Your deep core is a narrow slice of myofascia surrounding your spine. Stabilizing your core is largely about holding your spine in its neutral curves (see p. 177). This is the position that gives you the greatest strength and suppleness. It pays to train your core so that it is ready, willing, and able to work automatically, with no conscious effort on your part.**

CHAPTER TWENTY-FIVE

STABILITY EXERCISES FOR THE DEEP CORE

THE STABLE RIDER

Why is there such a big concern over strengthening and stabilizing your deep core? The core musculature prevents unwanted, risky movements, and keeps your body weight centered, despite any assaulting physical forces. For the rider, the core musculature prevents bending to one side, riding in front of or behind the motion, the drifting of body parts, and rotations, for a few examples. These important muscles also help lower your center of gravity. They keep you safely balanced astride your horse.

Exercises for the core are most effective when done from a relaxed, aligned base, meaning it's

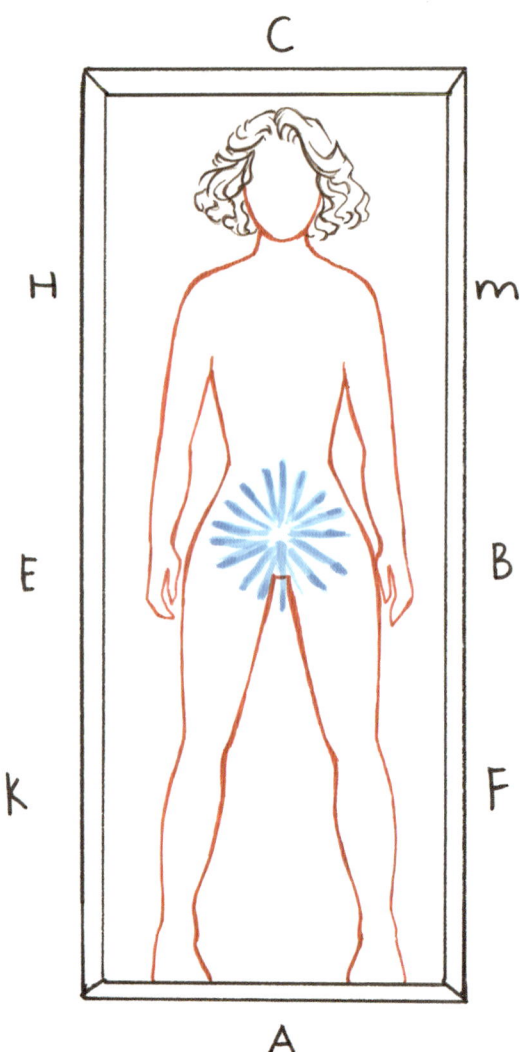

25.1 To get in touch with your *center*, imagine your body is a three-dimensional dressage arena. "X" is the center of the arena, and it also corresponds to the rider's center (the starburst). A rider should always be in touch with where "X" is in a ring, as well as where her center is in her body! In this image, the centerline of the arena aligns with the deep core myofascia in the rider's body.

> *"When the body parts are misaligned, balance is compromised and gravity is less friendly. The tussle is on. Such bodies seem to reject the agreement nature made; that is, accept the uncertainties inherent in the upright position and you will be graced with a marvelous facility for movement…. The bodies that say no to this are futilely seeking the impression of stability in their rigidity. They slump across the earth on insensitive legs and stand as locked as possible, pretending to a control that is illusory. Their shoulders hunch to the challenge, their heads jut forward. They are unyielding. Even the jaws clench."*
>
> —Denise McCluggage in *The Centered Skier* (Tempest Books, 1997)

---

critical to anchor the pelvis. The triangular floor of your seat should be solidly on the saddle, as described in chapter 13 (see p. 126). The key to core stability is how well the anchored pelvis relates to an anchored rib cage, lengthened neck, and neutral spine. Creating stability is about creating balance in varying positions and movements, but you can't create balance without a *center*. So this work hinges upon knowing where your center lies in all your postures and movements (fig. 25.1).

Stabilization exercises are important for riders because none of us have perfect proportions. A rider with a long torso or broad shoulders needs to do stability work to compensate for her higher center of gravity. A rider with stronger musculature on one side than the other can equally benefit. These are just a few ways in which our bodies may be asymmetrical or disproportionate; no matter your shape, size, or strength, all riders need to train their stability muscles to kick in automatically. In some of the photos in this chapter, you will notice the rider is wearing a helmet, even when she is not mounted. A helmet slightly displaces your center of gravity; it helps to train with a helmet on while on the ground so you can get in touch with how the helmet affects your balance and ability to stabilize in the saddle.

Let's take a further look at how to develop your core stability with the 12 components of core activation:

1 Maintain the spine's natural, neutral curves.

2 Keep the muscles in front of the body soft and following—remember, do not hold the belly inward!

3. Knit the back of the waist together using your horizontally oriented muscles.

4. Anchor your pelvis in its neutral position.

5. Anchor your lower rib cage toward your spine.

6. Lengthen through the back of your neck so your head is directly above your spine. Your face should then be parallel to an imaginary wall in front of you.

7. Use positive tension in the support muscles of your sides and legs.

8. Lift upward through the arches of your feet and inner thighs.

9. On each exhale, visualize the lifting of the diaphragm and pelvic floor muscles. Let them sink on each inhale. Keep your breathing slow and steady to use it as a fuel pump.

10. Imagine your guts pushing outward against your body wall. Use the *"fffff"* sound on your exhale to assist with this imagery.

11. Feel the vibrational energy travel up your front line, over the top part of your head, and down your back as your sacrum and center of gravity sink.

12. Give a grateful nod to the length and space you have just created in your body.

That's 12 steps. Do you see why *core activation* itself is a whole-body exercise? It's not reasonable to try to activate your core by memorizing and executing all the steps in sequence. *Whew!* It's best to train your body more reflexively, so it learns to stabilize you as needed without any conscious effort on your part. As you perform the destabilizing exercises presented later in this chapter, your focus will be on staying in alignment. Let your body figure out which muscles to move and which to hold. Trust in your body's innate wisdom!

Here are some exercises to increase your core stability.

Bit of Advice: The Quiet Core

Even with my eyes closed, I can tell if someone is engaging her core when she walks or runs. When her core is active, I hear a quiet *"step-step-step."* But when she throws her body weight around with no core engagement, I hear, *"Bam! Bam! Bam!"*

CORE STABILITY EXERCISE 1:
Warm-Up Logs

Warm-Up Logs help "fire up" your core so it will get maximum benefit from the other exercises in this section. Do not initiate movement from your arms, legs, or head. You have no option other than to direct the movement from your center. This exercise will help you find the center of your body when you ride.

Step One: Lie on your back on a comfortable surface where you have plenty of space to move. Reach your arms overhead.

Step Two: Without driving the movement from your arms, legs, or head, begin full-body "log rolling." Move from the center of your deep core (fig. 25.2).

Step Three: Repeat the exercise, now rolling in the other direction.

CORE STABILITY EXERCISE 2:
Dress-Ups

This exercise builds muscle strength and develops coordination, particularly around your body's intelligence regarding when to move and when to hold the pelvis and hips.

Step One: Put on your clothes, socks, and shoes, all without leaning on an object or surface.

Step Two: Now try to tie your shoes while balancing on the opposite leg!

25.2 Warm-Up Logs

CORE STABILITY EXERCISE 3:
One-Arm Shopping

No time to work out? No worries! Weave One-Arm Shopping into your next trip to the grocery store, ideally on a day you have a substantial list. Your core stability muscles work unilaterally in this exercise, helping to develop the spinal stabilizers you need when you ride. If you also incorporate some fast starts and stops as you push with one arm, you will build good front-to-back stability that will transfer to the saddle. This exercise is especially good if you find yourself falling forward or backward when your horse stops or starts abruptly while you're riding.

Step One: When your grocery shopping cart is about half loaded, begin pushing and pulling it with just one arm for the length of a whole aisle.

Step Two: On the next aisle, switch arms.

Step Three: Do this until the cart is loaded, but back off if you find yourself straining. Make sure you breathe rhythmically, slowly, and deeply, using whole-body breathing.

CORE STABILITY EXERCISE 4:
Unilateral Step-Ups

To practice Unilateral Step-Ups, you will need to find a curb or a ditch. For your safety, carefully check the path you will be walking before you begin. This move will help you balance and control your hip joints when you ride.

Step One: Stand sideways, close to the edge of a curb or ditch.

Step Two: Walk the length of it with one foot walking a higher path than the other.

Step Three: Go to fatigue, then walk backward.

Step Four: Finally, try the exercise with your riding helmet on. Notice the difference in your balance and centering with versus without your helmet.

CORE STABILITY EXERCISE 5:
Stability Breath Practice

After Stability Breath Practice, you will know how to recruit the proper breathing muscles to stabilize your spine when you ride. This is an important exercise for riders because the breathing muscles typically recruited can change the pelvis-rib cage orientation, thereby pulling you out of alignment. With a dowel and a helper, you will learn how to breathe and stay in alignment, both on and off your horse.

Step One: Get on your hands and knees, keeping your hands under your shoulders and your arms straight but not locked out at the elbows. Check that your hips are directly over your knees. Your face should be parallel to the floor.

Step Two: Ask a helper to put a 4-foot dowel along your back in a way that it touches the back of your head, runs between your shoulder blades, and contacts the back of your pelvis (fig. 25.3).

Step Three: Your helper should insert her flat hand under the dowel and on top of your lumbar area (at the back of your waist). If she can fit a whole fist, you *have too much of an arch*. Anchor those ribs! If she can't fit her flat hand in that space, you *don't have enough of an arch*. Make a slight "ducky tail" (see p. 18).

Step Four: Begin to breathe deeply and slowly. Keep all three points described in Step Two touching the dowel.

Step Five: Try varying the way you breathe, noticing which breathing pattern makes you lose contact with the dowel at each of the three locations. For example, if your pelvis tucks under every time you exhale, you will lose contact between the dowel and the back of your pelvis. You will have only two points of contact on the dowel—and that's an *unstable arrangement*.

Step Six: Reposition the dowel, and begin breathing with *good body alignment*. All three points should stay in contact with the dowel. Note the depth and rhythm of your breathing and the feel of specific muscles when all three points stay in contact with the dowel. *Three-point contact* is the style of breathing and the specific musculature to use during riding.

25.3 Stability Breath Practice

25.4 Ball Balancing Walk

25.5 Medicine Ball Tosses

CORE STABILITY EXERCISE 6:
Ball Balancing Walk

You will need a stability ball and some ankle weights for the Ball Balancing Walk. This exercise will significantly increase your self-corrections of posture and riding position. You will automatically get a feel of how your head, rib cage, and pelvis come into alignment, because the ball keeps you upright. The ankle weights give your upper back, neck, and head instantaneous self-carriage! Your spine will automatically stabilize underneath them.

Step One: Place 5- to 10-pound ankle weights on your head. Hold the stability ball at its largest point in diameter. Keep it close to your belly (fig. 25.4).

Step Two: Walk forward, backward, and sideways, feeling how the ball and head weights naturally draw you into alignment. When you ride, replicate this feeling.

CORE STABILITY EXERCISE 7:
Medicine Ball Tosses

Medicine Ball Tosses require an unstable surface. Gravel or irregular terrain both work well. Try this exercise with your helmet on. This will help to replicate the location of your center of gravity when you are mounted.

Step One: Get a fairly heavy object, such as an 8-pound medicine ball. Toss it to yourself, throwing up and down, left and right (fig. 25.5).

Step Two: Enlist help from a friend and play "medicine ball catch." Either way, this exercise will stir up the core power needed to support you when your horse moves unpredictably—such as when he shies.

CORE STABILITY EXERCISE 8:
Hanging Froggy Lifts

To practice Hanging Froggy Lifts, find a safe tree limb or bar to hang from. You will also need a soft core ball, starting with one weighing about 2 pounds and working up to a 5-pound ball over time. This great movement will strengthen your spine's connection to your legs, thereby stabilizing you in the saddle and helping you to access your core when you ride.

Step One: Put your riding helmet on and find a safe tree limb or bar. Test for its sturdiness by hanging from it briefly.

Step Two: Ask a helper to place a soft core ball or another suitable object between your feet.

25.6 Hanging Froggy Lifts

Step Three: Perform Froggy Lifts by keeping your knees wide and drawing the ball closer to your torso before slowly lengthening your legs again (fig. 25.6).

Step Four: Repeat to fatigue. Release to the ground and rest for a minute, then try a second set.

CORE STABILITY EXERCISE 9:
Stir the Pot

Stir the Pot is a superior exercise for core stability training. You will develop anti-rotation, anti-extension, and anti-flexion muscles. In other words, your spine will learn how to resist external forces to hold on to its neutral position. Your core will be in complete control of your spine. This ability will curtail a rider's unwanted extraneous movements on horseback.

Step One: Kneel with a stability ball in front of you. Wearing your riding helmet will slightly alter your center of gravity to increase the challenge.

Step Two: Place your forearms on the ball.

Step Three: Step your feet back into a plank position. Make sure your ribs stay anchored and keep your spine's neutral alignment.

Step Four: In a controlled fashion, slowly circle your forearms clockwise. The ball should follow your movements (fig. 25.7). Imagine you are stirring up a secret formula for successful riding!

Step Five: Rest by coming to your knees for a few seconds, and then repeat, this time circling your arms counterclockwise. Stop the circling pattern when you match the time (or number of circles) that you did in the clockwise pattern, and rest for a minute.

Step Six: Use your forearms to move the ball and make five horizontal lines, five vertical lines, and five diagonal lines ("X").

Step Seven: Rest for a minute and recruit a helper. Begin to Stir the Pot (Step Four) again. Ask your helper to randomly call out, "Halt!" When you hear that, stop abruptly. This variation is fabulous for developing your reflexes and deceleration stabilizers.

25.7 Stir the Pot

CORE STABILITY EXERCISE 10:
Harnessed Obstacle Walk

You are about to negotiate an obstacle course while a helper pulls and tugs on you using a homemade harness, trying to throw you slightly off balance. Your challenge is to stay centered and on your course. The Harnessed Obstacle Walk is a surefire way to charge up your spinal stabilizers as you move. This exercise will teach you how to hold your position in the saddle while battling the physical forces acting upon you and your horse. You need to wear your riding helmet for this exercise. To make a homemade harness, try using a tube band with handles. You can slip a pool noodle over the band for extra comfort.

Step One: Set up an obstacle course using common barn objects and jumps. Slip your homemade harness around your waist and put on your helmet.

Step Two: Practice walking while staying in vertical alignment. Do not lean in any direction.

Step Three: Now, negotiate the obstacle course as your helper tugs on you in all directions. Stay on your path (fig. 25.8).

CORE STABILITY EXERCISE 11:
Long-Lining for People

This is a great way to challenge yourself and get a sense of what horses might feel like when they are on long lines. Your deep core stabilizers will "plug in" as needed for this unique exercise—and this is exactly what you need them to do when you ride. You will develop muscles that will help keep your seat steadily following your horse, diminishing extraneous wiggles. You need a long length (25 feet or more) of a strong tube band, preferably with handles. Get a helper and wear

25.8 Harnessed Obstacle Walk

your helmet. A noodle around the band at your waist can be used for comfort.

Step One: Tie some tube band handles onto the ends of a long length (25 feet or more) of a strong tube band.

Step Two: Find a slope to work on, preferably one with some irregularities to the footing. Make sure the surface is safe and free of woodchuck holes, sink holes, or other hazards. Put on your helmet.

Step Three: Ask your helper to apply resistance to the band as you stay vertical and walk (fig. 25.9). Do not lean in any direction.

Step Four: Travel up and down hills, as well as across their slopes, as you hold your vertical position and move from your center. Try some "leg-yielding" or "half-pass"!

25.9 Long-Lining for People

25.10 Wiper Hoops

CORE STABILITY EXERCISE 12:
Wiper Hoops

The Wiper Hoops exercise will train your *anti-rotational stabilizers* at the same time it develops your *deceleration muscles*. This exercise mimics the forces acting on your body during transitions on horseback, and teaches it how to transfer and stabilize them. You will need a mini-hoop or Pilates ring to connect your arms and legs with your core, teaching them how to work together to help stabilize your spine.

Step One: Lie on your back, holding an arm hoop or Pilates ring with both hands.

238 | STABLE CORE TRAINING

Step Two: Put both feet in the ring. Keep your legs straight (fig. 25.10).

Step Three: Swing your legs from side to side, abruptly halting just before you feel like gravity is going to pull them to the floor. Using only your core, upright yourself again. No head, arm, or leg involvement is desired here—*it's all about your core*!

Step Four: Add a deceleration challenge by asking a friend to periodically and randomly call, "Halt." Try to halt your legs abruptly, and wait for five seconds before resuming the windshield wiper (side-to-side) action.

Step Five: Add a unilateral component to this exercise by using only one arm on the hoop. Keep the other arm stretched up high over your chest. Do not plant it down for stability.

CORE STABILITY EXERCISE 13:
Perturbances

To practice Perturbances, you'll need a friend who is not afraid to push you around! Wear your riding helmet for this exercise.

Step One: Stand on a few small balance disks or some hay to provide an unstable surface. (fig. 25.11).

25.11 Perturbances

Step Two: Ask your friend to gently throw you off balance by poking you. By responding to perturbances in all directions, you will train your stability muscles to work on demand. This will help you to (hopefully) be able to stay on your horse more solidly for his occasional shy or buck.

CORE STABILITY EXERCISE 14:
Unilateral Leg Raises

Whether riding or standing, your pelvis needs to be supple sometimes and stable at other times. In Unilateral Leg Raises, your pelvis is recruited for stability, an area of training that is often neglected. This is a great way to improve overall

Step Four: Lift one leg 3 to 6 inches off the floor and hold it there for about seven seconds (fig. 25.12).

Step Five: Lower the leg back down, and rest for about three seconds.

Step Six: Repeat with the other leg.

Step Seven: Stay in vertical alignment while you continue to alternate legs to fatigue.

CORE STABILITY EXERCISE 15:
Mounted Imbalances

25.12 Unilateral Leg Raises

dynamic strength and good body control when mounted. Your seat will learn to follow more and drift less.

Step One: Put on a helmet and sit on the edge of a chair with your pelvis held in a slight "ducky tail."

Step Two: Lift both arms overhead but keep the rib cage down and anchored. It's important to not raise the ribs for this exercise.

Step Three: Straighten both legs in front of you, keeping your feet flexed.

I love this mounted exercise for the way it "wakes up" each side of the body and helps balance them out. Make sure you feel solid with this exercise at the walk before trying it at other gaits. One option for this exercise requires a 4-pound ankle weight that will fit around your riding boot (fig. 25.13), but you should begin practicing this unilateral exercise by only dropping one stirrup. If that goes well, take back both stirrups and try using just one ankle weight before moving on.

Step One: Practice riding with just one stirrup at the walk.

Step Two: If that goes well, try it at other gaits.

25.13 Mounted Imbalances

Step Three: Take back both stirrups and add an ankle weight to one leg. Try this on both the left and right sides, for equal amounts of time. Ride with your leg in your "normal" riding position, as if you have your stirrup and there isn't a weight involved.

Step Four: If you feel safe and secure, try it at other gaits.

Step Five: : Once the options in Step Three feel easy, try dropping one stirrup at the walk and adding an ankle weight to that *same leg*. Do this with both legs for equal amounts of time.

Step Six: If it is safe for you, try this at a variety of gaits.

Step Seven: Finally, drop one stirrup and add an ankle weight to the *opposite leg*. Practice this at the walk and on both sides of the body for equal amounts of time.

Step Eight: Once this becomes easy and secure at the walk, you can try other gaits.

CORE STABILITY EXERCISE 16:
Stirrup Stand

Stirrup Stand is a time-honored exercise that I love as much now as when I taught it over 50 years ago. It helps develop balance and body control in the saddle, and teaches your body parts to work more independently. Standing in your stirrups helps you feel your center of gravity and keep it over your base of support, enhancing your stability and ability to meet the physical forces you encounter while riding.

Step One: At the walk, stand up in both stirrups. Do not hinge forward at the hips. Keep your seat over your feet.

Step Two: Alternate sitting five strides with standing five strides. As you get stronger and more stable, try doing every four strides, every three strides, and then every other stride.

Step Three: If this exercise gets easy at the walk, and you feel stable and safe, try it at the trot and canter.

CORE STABILITY EXERCISE 17:
Swinging Gates

Swinging Gates will fire up the higher glutes, which support your back. These are the glutes that enhance your riding and help counteract a hip/pelvis side drift (fig. 25.14). Plus, this exercise teaches each side of the pelvis when and how to stop ("put the brakes on").

Step One: Halt and drop both stirrups. Raise one knee high, letting the lower leg hang toward the ground. Be sure to stay on the vertical—no leaning in any direction.

25.14 Swinging Gates

Step Two: Slowly swing the lifted leg outward to the edge of your natural range of external motion. Hold it there for seven seconds.

Step Three: Slowly bring your leg to the front and return it to your horse's side. Do just one rep.

Step Four: Repeat this exercise for the other leg. Continue alternating sides to fatigue.

chapter takeaway

Muscles that stabilize the core are those that prevent unwanted, risky movements and promote centering. Core stabilization is beneficial to a rider's balance and safety as well as to her ability to give crisp aids. It also deepens her connection to her horse. Exercises to develop core stability muscles are most effective when done from a relaxed, aligned base. It is helpful for a rider to imagine her body as a dressage arena. The center point, "X," is approximately just in front of the second sacral bone (S-2).

CHAPTER TWENTY-SIX

SLAM LESSONS (SEAT LESSONS AND MORE)

WHY SLAM?

I am a firm believer in ground training, but in my experience, the ability of my clients to use these skills and strategies while riding independently doesn't happen rapidly. Instead, new awareness and skills seep into ridden technique slowly, and even longe lessons don't bridge the gap. Many riders are apt to hit a wall of frustration under these circumstances. I began seeking a way that would speed up my students' abilities to integrate newly found muscles, postures, and movement patterns into their independent riding. And eureka—SLAM (Seat Lessons And More) was born! SLAM fit the bill nicely, and progress was rapid. Let's take a closer look.

I found I could teach my riders to feel both their own and their horse's movements best by using proprioceptive props coupled with guided visualizations and imagery. These tools saved riders countless hours of floundering in the saddle, and boosted their awareness and ability to create the desired quality of positive tension. SLAM lessons were the missing link I needed to quickly transfer skills and boost performance.

The props I use include Franklin Method Balls, hot water bottles, plastic disks, sandpaper, ankle weights, bands, noodles, bean bags, dollar store items, and more. Many of these articles have already been mentioned or pictured in this book. You can also be as creative as you like and add to the list of props that develop proprioception as well as a feel for how much or how little to activate muscles and myofascial chains. Know that the objects are meant to only be *temporary* helpers (see sidebar, p. 244).

What follows are some specific ways to go about addressing ordinary challenges and issues using SLAM props.

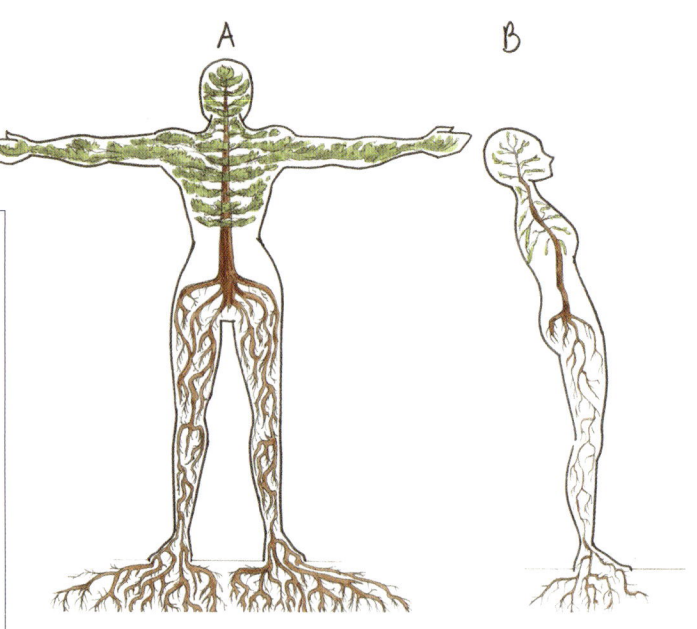

26.1 At the start of a ride, imagine you are a tree with bendable, reaching branches, a solid central channel in your trunk, and roots that ground you to the crust of the earth (Person A). Now imagine yourself as Person B, with the rib cage unanchored and upper body falling behind the vertical, interrupting grounding and the flow of energy.

How to Fade Out a Prop

When you introduce a prop, always remember it's a device intended to temporarily help you activate a muscle, a feeling, or an awareness, and is not to become a support. Enabling the rider to feel and become independent of a prop is crucial, so the goal is to fade out its use before the prop becomes a crutch. Here's an example of how to do that:

SLAM prop: Ankle weights.
First lesson: 45-minute lesson, alternating between using ankle weights for 10 to 15 minutes, then taking them off for 10 to 15 minutes.

Second lesson: Use ankle weights for only 5 to 10 minutes at the start of the lesson.

Third lesson: Use ankle weights for a few minutes, only when and if needed.

A prop should generate some kind of response within the first 5 to 10 minutes. If the prop doesn't seem to be helping in that first lesson, it's ineffective. Abandon it and try something else.

SLAM EXERCISE 1:
You Are a Tree

I like to start out a SLAM lesson by having the rider imagine the inside of her body is filled with a tree. I might even bring in a small tree limb, holding it in front of my body to help with the rider's sensation. I also show the rider a picture or drawing (fig. 26.1). This image helps a rider get in touch with where her "trunk" is and where to feel her "roots." It also helps her to develop an expansive feeling in her upper torso. This imagery is both grounding and centering.

SLAM EXERCISE 2:
Swinging Bridge Imagery

Toward the beginning of a SLAM lesson, I might ask the rider to engage in imagery that I feel could benefit her ride time. For instance, I might ask a rider who is working on following with fluid hips to imagine she is walking across a swinging (suspension) bridge. This image typically promotes suppleness and relaxation in the hips, as well as the knees, ankles, and spine.

SLAM EXERCISE 3:
Belly Button Singing

Most riders agree to sing if I sing with them! Singing helps a rider develop a sense of deep breathing and proper use of the core. I instruct the rider to place one hand on her belly button and breathe in through her nose. On the exhale, we both sing, *"Do-Re-Mi-Fa-So-La-Ti-Do!"* As we sing, I advise the rider to check for the vertical rise of her belly button by placing one hand on it as she holds the reins with her other hand. This action helps put her in touch with her diaphragm, pelvic floor muscles, and the rest of her deep core myofascia. (Horses typically love this exercise!)

SLAM EXERCISE 4:
Metronome Movements

I love using metronomes in SLAM lessons because rhythm is a language both horses and humans instinctively relate to. In Metronome Movements, I set a beat on a metronome that pertains to the rhythm of the gait I am asking a rider to transition to in order to help develop coordination in the rider and improve the timing of her aids. I have used them effectively to help riders get a feel for a horse's swinging back. I might also use them for a rider learning to feel which of the horse's legs is working, as well as when it pushes off, reaches, and lands.

SLAM EXERCISE 5:
Sandpaper Seat

A strip of sandpaper works like a charm to "wake up" sleepy seat bones, hips, or legs. It also helps to prevent a sideways hip/pelvis drift. For example, if someone's hip drifts to the right, the "brakes" in her right hip are sleeping. But when I put a strip of sandpaper under her right thigh and one under her right seat bone, the brakes "wake up," and the right hip stays in place instead of drifting. I carry a roll of coarse sandpaper in my car and cut off strips as needed.

SLAM EXERCISE NO. 6:
Creative Whips

I give credit for the Creative Whips SLAM exercise to Dr. Amy Plavin, DVM. She created this exercise on a practice ride when she had no props available, and wanted to remind herself of the feel of a neutral pelvis (fig. 26.2). The whips give a tiny bit of height to the back of the pelvis, thus encouraging a slight "ducky tail." It works very well!

SLAM EXERCISE 7:
Hot Water Waist Pack

A waist pack can be a wonderful prop for those riders who are working on their rib cage anchors (see p. 139). The pack gives additional weight to the bottom of the rib cage. The rider can

26.2 In the photo, you may notice Dr. Plavin is tapping the side of her face between her right temple and right ear. Tapping this area wakes up your creativity and brings attention to the creative side of your brain. (I offer this tip to those of you who want to create your own SLAM exercises.)

26.3 Believe it or not, there's a hot water bottle inside a pocket of this koala bear waist pack!

feel the type of action and placement needed to bring her ribs downward and rearward (fig. 26.3). The weight of the pack helps to bring her into improved alignment and better spinal stabilization.

SLAM EXERCISE 8:
Mounted Neck Lengthening

Placing one hand behind the neck and pressing rearward as well as upward with the head and neck will lift the "human withers" and achieve the desired alignment (fig. 26.4). A rider should keep her face parallel to an imaginary wall in front of her. No chin poking!

26.4 The rider in this photo is working on correct head alignment, achieved by lengthening through the back of the neck.

SLAM EXERCISE 9:
Hand Ball Helper

I place a Franklin Method Ball between a rider's hands to steady them and to help the rider learn to hold them at a desirable width (fig. 26.5). I have the rider start at the halt and progress through the gaits.

26.5 Franklin Method Balls offer varying types and degrees of proprioceptive awareness, from smooth to spiky. I have the rider try out several pairs before we select the one that enables her to feel the proper hand position the best.

26.6 To get her head, rib cage, and pelvis aligned with each other, a rider can use a dowel as a prop. Here she has placed the back of her pelvis, the area between the shoulder blades, and the back of her head on the dowel.

SLAM EXERCISE 10:
Plumb Line Mounted

When first trying this SLAM exercise, often a student's myofascia isn't lengthened enough for her head to touch the dowel. It should not be forced. The rider must allow the upper torso, neck, and head muscles to lengthen at their own pace. I remind the rider to imagine a wall is in front of her face. The aim is to keep her face parallel to the wall while achieving contact at three points along the dowel (fig. 26.6).

26.7 Riders bring more of their core into their riding with Flying Hugs.

26.8 A Here you see Cassie's torso and hip "drifts."

SLAM EXERCISE 11:
Flying Hugs

Bend from your hips, give your horse a big hug around the neck, and then put your arms out to the sides, just like you did with the Stability Hug on p. 185 (fig. 26.7). Use your deep core to return to your riding position, making sure you don't cling to your horse with your legs and keeping your body well centered and aligned. This SLAM exercise will help you become less "grippy" when you are careful to complete it with no narrowing or pinching of your legs.

SLAM EXERCISE 12:
Fixing the Drifts

Cassie is a trainer who had postural challenges due to significant past injuries. When I started to work with her, she had a significant right hip drift and left upper torso lean (fig. 26.8 A). Guiding her into position with my words or my hands offered

26.8 B & C The props I used to fix Cassie's torso and hip "drifts" (B), and her resulting better balance (C).

only temporary help (fig. 26.8 A). I asked Cassie to insert a textured Franklin Method Ball between the saddle and her right thigh to "wake up" the "brake muscles" of her right hip. I also advised her to place another ball under her left armpit to activate the brake muscles of her left upper torso.

With the props in place, she rode in both directions at all gaits (fig. 26.8 B). With remarkable speed, Cassie came into beautiful, now permanent, alignment (fig. 26.8 C). When I asked her to assume her former position (see fig. 26.8 A), she was stunned at how "off" it felt!

chapter takeaway It's often difficult to transfer skills learned on the ground into mounted work. Use of proprioceptive props, coupled with imagery, helps riders integrate those skills into independent riding. It's all about feel!

PART 3

CHAPTER TWENTY-SEVEN
INVEST FURTHER

STANDARD EQUIPMENT

Whenever you match two asymmetrical beings and attempt to train both of them to be more symmetrical, you are going to have a challenge. It's not enough to sit on a horse a few times a week, or even daily. Stability-focused unmounted work, coupled with dedicated, goal-directed SLAM lessons, has proven to boost rider performance. And improvements in the rider result in gains in horse performance.

Certain basic pieces of equipment can help you achieve your rider fitness goals (see sidebar, p. 252). Collecting this equipment is a good starting point for an "equestrian gym" of your own. You may even already have some of these items (fig. 27.1).

For those of you who have used standard equipment for years and want to spark up your routine or explore how you can benefit further, you can add some pieces of equipment I have successfully used to help riders get to the next level and beyond. But my favorite thing to do is to pair pieces of standard equipment with each other

27.1 This is an array of standard equipment to help you achieve your equestrian fitness goals. (See the Equestrian Gym sidebar on the next page for a list of the items shown here.)

to create unique exercises. The body does not train well with the same-old, same-old system. It "wakes up" with new challenges and variety, which then supercharges you with vibrant energy!

Equestrian Gym: Standard and Additional Equipment

Here is a list of equipment I consider standard:

- Mat
- Eye patches
- Small bouncy balls
- Tennis balls
- Lacrosse balls
- Foam roller
- Hand-held roller
- Tube band roll (single length you can cut)
- Tube band handles
- Resistance bands (with a variety of tension)
- Dumbbells
- Kettle balls
- Metronome
- Stability ball
- Medicine ball (hard)
- Sand filled core ball (soft)
- Wash cloths/towels (to use as shims)
- Kneeling pad
- Tilt board
- Ankle weights (2, 4, and 5 pounds)
- Wrist weights (1 to 2 pounds)
- Push up bars
- Half-moon foam (two 12-inch pieces)
- Duct tape roll

Additional equipment to enhance performance:

- Battle ropes
- TRX®
- Slackline
- Pull-up bar
- Stilts
- Wobble board
- Rebounder (Bellicon® suggested)
- BOSU® Balance Trainer or equivalent
- Arm rings (also suitable for legs)
- Balance pods
- A 2 by 6 inch board about 6 feet in length
- Sawhorses (two)
- Tornado ball
- Slam ball
- Unilateral barbell (homemade)

27.2 Ball Jacks

27.3 Pull-Ups

INVEST EXERCISE 1:
Ball Jacks

Step One: Set a clip-on metronome to your horse's trot rhythm.

Step Two: Do "jumping jacks" while sitting on a stability ball (fig. 27.2). Wearing wrist weights while lifting your arms overhead boosts your heart rate!

INVEST EXERCISE 2:
Pull-Ups

Step One: We've already talked about how hanging is a fabulous exercise for riders (see p. 235). Daily living does not give us much practice at overhead activities, but they are posture enhancers and our riding benefits from them. If you don't have a pull-up bar, you can use a sturdy tree branch or local playground.

Step Two: Try reaching, pulling up, and swinging (fig. 27.3).

27.4 Pendulum Swings

INVEST EXERCISE 3:
Pendulum Swings

Try a little deceleration training using a TRX® suspension strap. This exercise will sharpen up your postural muscles and make you feel solid in the saddle by boosting your body control and ability to move with your horse.

Step One: Start by putting your feet in the loops, and support your body in a front plank position.

Step Two: Begin to rapidly swing both of your legs from side to side (fig. 27.4).

Step Three: Ask a helper to randomly call, "Halt!" When you hear this, stop the motion as quickly as possible.

27.5 Sawhorse Ball Tosses

Step Four: You can also try a Pendulum Swing face-up in an upward facing plank position, with your heels secured in the loops. Raise your hips before you start to swing your legs. *Wheee!*

INVEST EXERCISE 4:
Sawhorse Ball Tosses

Step One: Your stabilizers will do cartwheels over this effective exercise! Mount up on your favorite sawhorse. A piece of foam or half-foam works well as a saddle. Wear your helmet, of course.

Step Two: Toss a 6- to 8-pound medicine ball up in the air, catch it, and begin to toss it toward the left and right (fig. 27.5).

Step Three: When that gets easy, ask a friend to toss it back and forth to you. The more unpredictable the trajectory of the medicine ball, the better it is for developing stabilization.

INVEST EXERCISE 5:
Balance Board

Choose a safe surface such as a lawn or a crash pad for this exercise. The perturbances work wonders to teach the body's core when to automatically kick in for stabilization.

Step One: Hang a smooth board, approximately 2 by 6 inches wide and 6 feet in length, between two sawhorses of the same height.

Step Two: Secure a folded towel or piece of half-foam for a mock saddle on the board, and sit on it (wearing your helmet).

Step Three: Put a "harness" (a tube band with handles and a noodle for comfort) around your waist and establish an aligned position.

27.6 Balance Board

Step Four: Enlist the help of a friend to hold the harness and move around, giving you gentle tugs in all directions as you maintain your relaxed balance (fig. 27.6).

Step Five: When you have mastered this with your eyes open, try it with your eyes closed.

INVEST EXERCISE 6:
Long Line Stop and Go

Step One: Try this human long-lining exercise for front line-back line balance and stability. It will help you to negotiate hills, and quick starts and abrupt stops, when you ride. Keep your helmet on to improve your center-of-gravity awareness.

Step Two: Ask a helper to hold the "reins" and call out "walk," "trot," "halt," and so on. The idea is to negotiate varied footing while executing the commands as quickly as possible (fig. 27.7).

27.7 Long Line Stop and Go

27.8 Overhead Battle Ropes

INVEST EXERCISE 7:
Overhead Battle Ropes

Battle ropes (thick heavy ropes designed for enhancing fitness) in a traditional squat position are great for your core. But the overhead orientation of this battle rope exercise makes it fabulous for equestrians. It is especially good at improving the coordinated workings of several myofascial chains.

Step One: Start by lying down on your back, holding the ends of the rope.

Step Two: With palms up, position your body in the shape of an "I," that is, in one long line.

Step Three: Ask a helper to stand on the halfway point of the rope as you snake and swing the left and right ropes (fig. 27.8).

INVEST EXERCISE 8:
Large Half-Ball Balance

Step One: While wearing a helmet (for maximum benefit), step up onto a large half-ball, and begin tossing a soft but heavy core ball up and down, and from side to side (fig. 27.9).

Step Two: Next, hold the ball with both hands and make big clockwise circles with it.

Step Three: Pause, then make counterclockwise circles.

Step Four: Finally, set the core ball down, and stand on the half-ball for two minutes. It sounds easy, but the half-ball has a mind of its own! Your job is to follow rather than influence it.

Step Five: When the two minutes is up, do the same exercise for one minute on one leg as you abduct the other leg (move it outward).

Step Six: Then balance for one minute on the other leg.

27.9 Large Half-Ball Balance

27.10 Tilt Board Hoops

Step Three: When this exercise becomes easy, try swinging one arm hoop in the forward direction as the other arm hoop swings backward (fig. 27.10).

Step Four: Now try deliberately tapping the tilt board on the ground rapidly as you swing the hoops. You can orient the board so you tap it to the ground in a front-back direction as well as a left-right direction. Try it both ways!

INVEST EXERCISE 9:
Tilt Board Hoops

Step One: Tilt Board Hoops is another multi-tasking exercise that will boost your neuromuscular coordination, whether you are in or out of the saddle. The goal is to balance on the tilt board as you circle both arm hoops. Try this exercise with the tilt board oriented from side to side first.

Step Two: Then try it with the board oriented front to back.

INVEST EXERCISE 10:
People Jumping

Step One: The act of negotiating an obstacle on your own two feet—whether it is a horse jump, a ditch, or a rock—sharpens your reflexes, shortens

27.11 People Jumping

your reaction time, and improves your coordination (fig. 27.11). All these tools help you give well-timed, clear aids to your horse. Plus, jumping is a movement adults often neglect to put in their workout routines.

Step Two: Repeat until you can land softly. Then you will know you used your core for the jump—*yeah!*

INVEST EXERCISE 11:
Unilateral Barbells

Step One: A Unilateral Barbell is the perfect stability bar trainer. It is easily made by attaching a 10-pound ankle weight to the end of a dowel with duct tape.

Step Two: Walk with the bar, and notice how the heavier side prompts your *strength muscles* to work while the lighter side recruits your *stability muscles* (fig. 27.12).

Step Three: Try walking with the Unilateral Barbell for equal amounts of time on both sides.

Step Four: Vary your direction from forward to backward to sideways to "leg-yielding." Include some hills and uneven terrain.

27.12 Unilateral Barbells

27.13 Jumping Jills

27.14 Water Wheel Bounces

INVEST EXERCISE 12:
Jumping Jills

I love the health benefits that *rebounders* give. Rebounders look like miniature trampolines and move body fluids (including the lymph) around so well that I use mine daily.

Step One: In this exercise, you do Jumping Jills, a movement opposite that of a Jumping Jack. When your legs jump outward, your arms are down at your sides. When your legs jump in, your arms are up in the air. This messes with your brain a little, but the coordination benefits are worth the struggle—and it's a fun way to boost your heart rate (fig. 27.13)!

INVEST EXERCISE 13:
Water Wheel Bounces

Step One: A rebounder is a great tool for feeling how to generate and follow springiness on a horse. Now, instead of jumping or pushing down vigorously on the mat of the rebounder, you are going to start by standing still in the center.

Step Two: Get those water wheel hips moving in a forward direction, with left and right hips alternating, as if pedaling a bicycle (you felt this action during the Buttwalking exercises given earlier in this book—see p. 134).

Step Three: When you achieve a good feeling for moving the rebounder through your hip circling action, try it from a kneeling position (fig. 27.14). You will learn that you cannot do this exercise properly without 1) the right amount of positive tension, and 2) proper use of your core.

INVEST EXERCISE 14:
Figures on Stilts

Step One: Stilts are great for learning to put your center of gravity over your base of support. It significantly helps improve your balance, both on and off your horse.

Step Two: Once you have your balance, walk through a dressage test or jumping course pattern on stilts. The skills you gain on stilts transfer well to the saddle. Enjoy the elevated view as you try a shoulder-in (fig. 27.15).

27.15 Figures on Stilts

INVEST EXERCISE 15:
Pogo Core Bounces

Step One: Take a victory gallop on a pogo stick!

Step Two: Use your core to change the length of your stride—from short, bouncy, and bounding, to long, low, and leaping (fig. 27.16). Of course, you will rise to the occasion!

27.16 Pogo Core Bounces

chapter takeaway ✓

Several times a day, take time to center and ground yourself. This will become an established habit that promotes good posture and movement patterns. Additionally, use proprioceptive props coupled with imagery, to foster good alignment. If you move and hold yourself well, you will keep the fluids of youthfulness flowing. Live and ride with passion!

APPENDIX

EQUESTRIAN TRAINING PYRAMID

I developed the Equestrian Training Pyramid to reflect the areas where riders need supportive training. Each block is not an indication of a step that has to be mastered before advancing to the next step. Rather, it is a display of the interconnectivity of various aspects of the rider's physical performance. Consider that a rider needs to constantly change which body parts are moving fluidly and which are stabilizing by holding still. You simply can't know, establish, or feel the lack of movement (stability) in various body parts until you have experienced correct movement of those parts.

The Equestrian Training Pyramid can and should be used unmounted as well as mounted. Only then can a rider fill in the gaps that are limiting her elite performance.

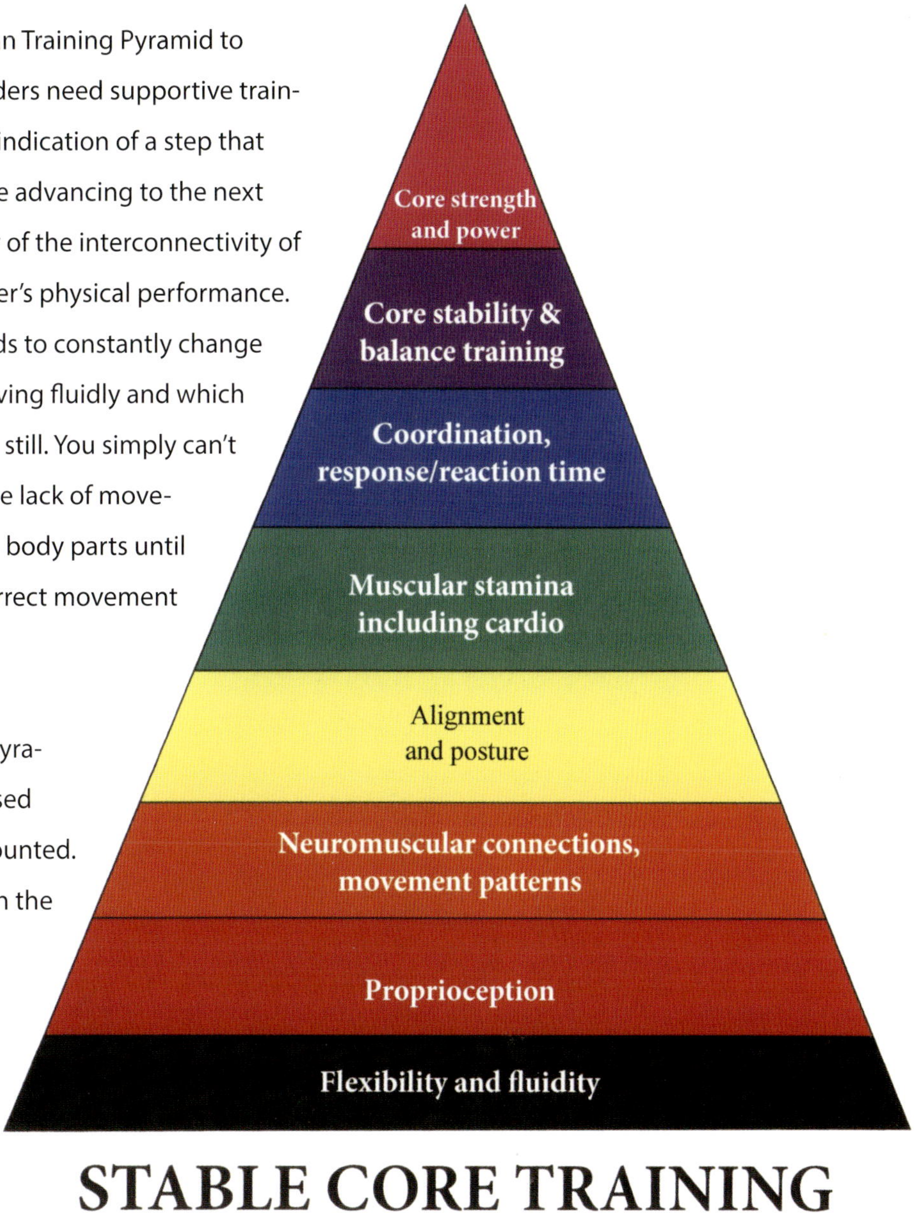

Core strength and power
Core stability & balance training
Coordination, response/reaction time
Muscular stamina including cardio
Alignment and posture
Neuromuscular connections, movement patterns
Proprioception
Flexibility and fluidity
STABLE CORE TRAINING

BIBLIOGRAPHY AND RECOMMENDED READING

Ballou, Jec Aristotle, *55 Corrective Exercises for Horses* (Trafalgar Square Books, 2018).

Baumert, Beth, *When Two Spines Align: Dressage Dynamics* (Trafalgar Square Books, 2014).

Bowman, Katy, *Move Your DNA* (Propriometrics Press, 2020).

Bowman, Katy, *Simple Steps to Foot Pain Relief* (BenBella Books, Inc., 2016).

Brittenham, Greg and Taylor, Daniel, *Conditioning to the Core* (Human Kinetics, 2014).

Broussal-Derval, Aurelien and Ganneau, Stephane, *The Modern Art and Science of Mobility* (Human Kinetics, 2020).

Calais-Germain, Blandine, *Anatomy of Breathing* (Eastland Press, Incl, 2006).

Calais-Germain, Blandine, *Anatomy of Movement* (Eastland Press, Inc., 2005).

Calais-Germain, Blandine, *The Female Pelvis Anatomy and Exercises* (Eastland Press, Inc., 2003).

Campbell, Don, *The Mozart Effect* (HarperCollins Publishers, 1997).

Cohen, Bonnie Bainbridge, *Sensing, Feeling, and Action* (Contact Editions, 2012).

Ellgen, Pamela, *Psoas Strength and Flexibility* (Ulysses Press, 2015).

Feldenkrais, Moshe, *Awareness Through Movement* (Harper One, 1977).

Franklin, Eric, *Breathing for Peak Performance* (Human Kinetics, 2019).

Franklin, Eric, *Dynamic Alignment Through Imagery* (Human Kinetics, 2012).

Franklin, Eric, *Fascia Release and Balance* (Human Kinetics, 2014).

Franklin, Eric, *Happy Feet* (OPTP, 2014).

Franklin, Eric, *Pelvic Power* (Princeton Book Company, 2003).

Franklin, Eric, *Relax Your Neck, Liberate Your Shoulders* (Princeton Book Company, 2002).

Frederick, Ann and Frederick, Chris, *Stretch to Win* (Human Kinetics, 2017).

Gibbons, John, *The Vital Glutes* (North Atlantic Books, 2014).

Gach, Michael Reed, *Acupressure's Potent Points* (Bantam Books, 1990).

Gokhale, Esther, *8 Steps to a Pain-Free Back* (Pendo Press, 2008).

Hanna, Thomas, *Somatics* (DaCapo Press, 1988).

Hitzmann, Sue, *The Melt Method* (Harper One, 2013).

Hogan, Scott, *Built From Broken* (Saltwrap, 2021).

Johnson, Don Hanlon, *Bone, Breath & Gesture* (North Atlantic Books, 1995).

Kofler, Leo, *The Art of Breathing As the Basis of Tone-Production* (Forgotten Books, 2012).

Liebman, Hollis Lance, *Anatomy of Core Stability* (Firefly Books, 2013).

McCluggage, Denise, *The Centered Skier* (Tempest Books, 1997).

McGill, Dr. Stuart, *Back Mechanic* (Backfitpro, Inc., 2015).

McGill, Dr. Stuart, *Ultimate Back Fitness and Performance* (Backfitpro, Inc., 2017).

McKusick, Eileen Day, *Tuning the Human Biofield* (Healing Arts Press, 2014).

Miller, Gill Wright & Ethridge, Pat & Morgan, Kate Tarlow (Eds.) *Exploring Body-Mind Centering: An Anthology of Experience and Method* (North Atlantic Books, 2011).

Morales, Jay Emmanuel, *The Healing Forces of Harmonic Sounds and Vibrations* (JEM Productions, 2017)

Myers, Thomas W., *Anatomy Trains* (Elsevier, Ltd., 2014).

Porter, Kathleen, *Natural Posture for Pain-Free Living* (Healing Arts Press, 2006).

Promislow, Sharon, *Making the Brain Body Connection* (Enhanced Learning & Integration, Inc., 2005).

Richey, Brian, *Back Exercise* (Human Kinetics, 2021).

Schleip, Robert, *Fascial Fitness* (Lotus Publishing, 2017).

Schneider, Meir, *Vision for Life* (North Atlantic Books, 2012).

Staugaard-Jones, JoAnn, *The Vital Psoas Muscle* (North Atlantic Books, 2012).

Steinkraus, William, *Reflections on Riding and Jumping* (Trafalgar Square Books, 1997).

Swift, Sally, *Centered Riding* (Trafalgar Square Books, 1985).

Swift, Sally, *Centered Riding 2* (Trafalgar Square Books, 2002).

Todd, Mabel Elsworth, *The Thinking Body* (The Gestalt Journal Press, 2008).

Wanless, Mary, *The New Anatomy of Rider Connection* (Trafalgar Square Books, 2017).

Warren, Sarah, *The Pain Relief Secret* (TCK Publishing, 2019).

Wylde, Suzanne, *Moving Stretch* (North Atlantic Books, 2017).

Xenophon, *The Art of Horsemanship* (Dover Publications, 2006).

ACKNOWLEDGMENTS

First and foremost, my heartfelt thanks to the hundreds of horses and thousands of riders who I have had the pleasure of knowing and teaching. They have led me to the discoveries of this book. And to "Sis," a neighbor's horse, to whom I first fed an apple as a toddler. I can still feel your whiskers tickle my tiny hands.

The writing of this book was profoundly influenced by Sally Swift, Mable Todd, Eric Franklin, Thomas Myers, Katy Bowman, Kathleen Porter, and Bonnie Bainbridge Cohen. I am indebted to them for the solid foundation they provided.

The blueprints of this book were born in the barn of Miss Finley Peterson, whose youthful joy and spirit are sprinkled throughout these pages. I am equally indebted to her parents Eric Peterson and Patty Kuzmickas.

I am extremely grateful to the following for providing training grounds and amazing support on numerous occasions: Heidi Hauri-Gill, Bob Gill, Gayle Davis, Bekki Read, and Jayson Benoit. I also appreciate permission to use the grounds from the following: Jennie and Dave Lepore, Sue and Robert Miller, Lois and Lee Resseguie, and Ruth Hogan-Poulsen.

A grateful bow goes to Pam and Doug Tengdin for their assistance and support. Another bow goes to Jennie Lepore for keeping me on my toes!

My gratitude goes to Ann Raynolds, Gail Edgerly, Lynne Naughton, and Barbara Wilson for wrapping me in support during this book writing process!

Amy "Coy" Brooks, I thank you for rubberstamping the farthest reaches of my creativity—no matter how weird it got!

I extend my full thanks to my helpers…to Satu, my gifted young illustrator, whose future knows no bounds…and to Jayson, my skilled photographer with exemplary patience and flexibility.

I send hugs to all my models (both humans and horses), who were always ready and raring to go at a moment's notice. Special thanks are due to "Tricreek Loch Corrib" of Round Robin Farm in Tunbridge, Vermont. He was a last-minute substitute who stepped up to the plate admirably for many of this book's photos.

My heartfelt appreciation goes to the following for sharing their thoughts on the team concept in chapter 20: veterinarian Dr. Amy Plavin, DVM; farrier Robert Oaks; assistant farrier Austin Blake; Grand Prix dressage rider and trainer Joy Congdon; and barn manager of Round Robin Farm in Tunbridge, Vermont, Pat Read.

I am deeply indebted to Martha Cook and Rebecca Didier of Trafalgar Square Books. They saw me teach, envisioned this book, and led me by the hand on a journey of publishing that was beyond my wildest dreams. Thank you to Caroline Robbins, Publisher at Trafalgar Square, who brought us *Centered Riding* in 1985, and then agreed to publish my book, 40 years later. And thank you to Christina Keim, Lizzie Gray, Lauryl Eddlemon, and Michelle Guiliano for their efforts to ensure quality editing, proofreading, book design, and indexing at TSB.

Models for *Stable Core Training:* Bodhi Benoit, Austin Blake, Amy Brooks, Emily Brown, Morgan Brown, Joy Congdon, Jessica Covey, Lexaphino Angelis Evans, Giovanna (Jennie) Lepore, Cassie Medynski, Susan Miller, Molly O'Hara, Robert Oaks, Angela Orlando, Finley Peterson, Amy Plavin, Bekki Read, Pat Read, Lois Resseguie, and Allyson Tessier.

ABOUT THE ARTIST

Satu R. Young was 16 when she was asked to illustrate *Stable Core Training*. She jumped at the opportunity to pursue her two favorite things: horses and art. This project seamlessly fit into her homeschooling curriculum. She lives in the Green Mountains of Vermont with her family, two cats, a bunny, and a horse named Patch.

INDEX

Activated Riding (exercise), 117
Activation. *See* Muscle activation; Muscle activation exercises
Active rest, 117
Acupressure
    for fluidity, 92–93, 188
    for grounding, 20
    for organs, 202
    for tension release, 125
Adductor Lifts (exercise), 111
Adductors, 108, 109, 111
Alexander, Gerda, 202–203
Alignment. *See also* Postural patterns and self-carriage
    explored, 12–15
    of head, 149–151
    positive tension and, 23–24, 31
    self-correction of, 192–194
    vertical alignment, 16–18
Anatomy Trains (Myers), 94
Ankles. *See* Feet, ankles, and legs
Arena Skipping (exercise), 211–212
Arm Lines, 99
Arms. *See* Shoulders, arms, and hands
Assistance of the Tongue (exercise), 36
Asymmetry awareness, 200–201
Axis Turn (exercise), 9

Baby Bounce Squats (exercise), 136
Backpack Breathing (exercise), 39–40
Back to Blades (exercise), 85–86
Balance Board (exercise), 255
Balance Board Ball (exercise), 11

Ball Balancing Walk (exercise), 234
Ballistic, bouncy stretches, 101, 104–105
Ball Jacks (exercise), 253
Barbell Head Balances (exercise), 153
Barefoot Grounding (exercise), 22
Barrel Roll (exercise), 125
Base of Skull Point (exercise), 125
Base of support, 12–14
Basketball Bounces (exercise), 91
Battle ropes, 256–257
Belly Button Singing (exercise), 245
Belly Button Vertical Breathing (exercise), 212
Belly Release (exercise), 205
Beneficial sounds. *See* Sounds
Benoit, Bodhi, 198
Blake, Austin, 196
Bobbleheads (exercise), 151
Body pulses, 44
Bones, Breath, and Gesture (Alexander), 202–203
Boot Flicks and Pulls (exercise), 226
Bounce Away (exercise), 91
Bouncy, ballistic stretches, 101, 104–105
Bouncy Ball Glow (exercise), 60
Bouncy Ball Warm-Up (exercise), 213
"Bouncy" energy, 94–95
Bow to Squat (exercise), 71–72
Bracing, 179, 222–223
Breastbone lift, 142
Breathing
    chapter takeaway, 41

    fascia and, 95
    organs and, 201, 203
    pelvic floor muscles and, 132–133
    as rider's fuel pump, 33–35
    self-correction and, 193
    in synchrony with horses, 206–209
    whole body breathing, 32–33, 41
Breathing exercises, 35–41, 212–214
    Assistance of the Tongue, 36
    Backpack Breathing, 39–40
    Belly Button Singing, 245
    Belly Button Vertical Breathing, 212
    Checking for Verticality, 35
    Do Re Me, 36
    Hands-Free Balloon Breathing, 39
    Heart Breathing, 213–214
    Lying Diaphragm Stretches, 38
    Play an Instrument, 225
    Playing Instruments, 41
    Posture Breathing, 82
    Stability Breath Practice, 232–233
    Standing Diaphragm Stretch, 37
    for tension release, 121
Bubbling Spring Acupressure (exercise), 92, 188
Buttwalking (exercise), 134, 176–177

Calf Lengthening (exercise), 174
Calmness, beneficial sounds for, 208
"C"-curve (side bend), 23, 78–80, 98–100, 144–145
Cellular breathing, 33, 41
Centered Riding books, 92, 160

The Centered Skier (McCluggage), 229
Centering, 7–9, 208
Centering exercises
    Axis Turn, 9
    Balance Board Ball, 11
    Half-Ball Head Balance, 10–11
    Move from Your COG, 10
Center of gravity, 12–14
Chakras (energy centers), 206
Checking for Verticality (exercise), 35
Chicken Wing (exercise), 143
Cohen, Bonnie Bainbridge, 75, 100
Congdon, Joy, 197
Constructive rest pose, 118
Cool-downs
    background and overview, 210–211
    chapter takeaway, 220
    exercises, 211–220
Coordination. *See* Movement patterns and mobility
Core activation exercises, 225–227
Core activation exploration, 221–224, 227. *See also* Deep core stabilization
Core Walk (exercise), 225
Crawling, 19, 22, 65, 134–135
Crawling (exercise), 22
Crawling on Forearms (exercise), 134–135
Creative Whips (exercise), 246

Deep breathing, 33
Deep Core Sounds (exercise), 226
Deep core stability exercises, 228–242
    Ball Balancing Walk, 234
    components of, 228–230
    Dress-Ups, 231
    Hanging Froggy Lifts, 235
    Harnessed Obstacle Walk, 237
    invest further exercises, 253–262
    Long-Lining for People, 237–238
    Medicine Ball Tosses, 234–235
    Mounted Imbalances, 240–241
    One-Arm Shopping, 232
    Perturbances, 239
    SLAM (Seat Lessons and More), 243–250
    Stability Breath Practice, 232–233
    standard equipment, 251–252
    Stirrup Stand, 242
    Stir the Pot, 236
    Swinging Gates, 241
    Unilateral Leg Raises, 239–240
    Unilateral Step-Ups, 232
    Warm-Up Logs, 231
    Wiper Hoops, 238–239
Deep core stabilization, 199–262
    background and overview, 2–3, 199
    beneficial sounds, 206–209
    core activation exercises, 225–227
    exploration, 221–224, 227, 242
    invest further, 251–262. *See also* Invest further
    ride from your guts, 200–205
    warming up and cooling down, 210–220
Deep Front Line, 99
Developing feel, 43. *See also* Proprioception and feel development; SLAM lessons
Diagonal Connections (exercise), 29–31
Diaphragm, 33–35, 132, 206
Diaphragm exercises, 35–38, 139–141
Distance Proprioception (exercise), 49
Do Re Me (exercise), 36
Dress-Ups (exercise), 231

"Ducky tail," 18, 126, 128
Duct Tape Roll Up (exercise), 151–152

Elbows, 160. *See also* Shoulders, arms, and hands
Elegant Mansion Acupressure (exercise), 92–93
Energy centers (chakras), 206
Exploring Body-Mind Centering (Cohen), 75
Eye Crossovers (exercise), 58
Eyes. *See* Vison and visualizing
Eyes Shut Touching (exercise), 46

Fascial connections, 94–106
    background and overview, 94–98
    core activation exercises, 225–227
    core activation exploration, 221–224, 227
    exercises, 102–106
    riding position and, 98–101
    self-assessment of, 96–97
Fascial rollers, 98, 101, 106
Feel, 43. *See also* Proprioception and feel development; SLAM lessons
Feel Your Seat Bones (exercise), 47
Feet, ankles, and legs, 166–171
    ankles, 170
    chapter takeaway, 174
    exercises, 171–174
    feet, 166–170
    leg position, 170–171
    posting, 171
Figure Eight Hip Circles (exercise), 216–217
Figures on Stilts (exercise), 261
Fixing the Drifts (exercise), 249–250
Flag Walk (exercise), 51–52

Flexibility, 66–67
Fluidity
    beneficial sounds, 208
    exercises, 91–93
    inner nourishment and, 188
    of movement, 66
    secrets of, 88–90, 93
Flying Hugs (exercise), 249
Foam rollers, 98, 101, 106
Football Shoulder Drops (exercise), 72–73
Foot Twists (exercise), 172–173
Forward gaze, 57
Foundation of riding well, 5–86
    alignment, 12–18
    background and overview, 1–2, 5
    breathing as a fuel pump, 32–41. *See also* Breathing; Breathing exercises
    centering, 7–9
    centering exercises, 9–11
    developing feel, 42–52. *See also* Proprioception and feel development
    grounded explored, 19–20
    grounding exercises, 21–22
    grounding in the saddle, 20–21
    movement, 64–73. *See also* Movement patterns and mobility
    positive tension, 23–31
    postural patterns, 74–86. *See also* Postural patterns and self-carriage
    vison and visualizing, 53–63
Fountain of youth and vitality, 88–89
Franklin, Eric, 43
Franklin Method™, 43
Full (whole) body breathing, 32–33, 41
Full activation of muscles, 108

Full Body Shakes (exercise), 212
Functional Lines, 99

Gestalt (right-brained) thinking, 54
Gluteal muscles
    everyday activities and, 64
    hips/spine exercise for, 183
    imagery for activating, 66
    mobility exercises for, 67–72
    muscle activation exercises for, 113, 114–117
    myths and facts about, 109–110
    postural patterns, 78–80
Glute Poke and Punch (exercise), 113
Goldilocks Zone (exercise), 27–28
Good posture. *See* Postural patterns and self-carriage
Grounding, 19–22
    background and overview, 19–20
    beneficial sounds, 208
    chapter takeaway, 22
    exercises, 21–22, 121, 214
    in the saddle, 20–21
    self-correction and, 193
    for tension release, 121
Grounding Stance and Walk (exercise), 214
Growing Roots (exercise), 22
Guts, riding from. *See* Visceral approach to core stabilization

Half-Ball Head Balance (exercise), 10–11
Hamstrings
    mobility exercises for, 70–72
    muscle activation exercises for, 114–117
    myofascial exercises for, 103–104

    myths and facts about, 109
    postural patterns, 77, 78
Hand Ball Helper (exercise), 247
Hands. *See* Shoulders, arms, and hands
Hands-Free Balloon Breathing (exercise), 39
Hanging Froggy Lifts (exercise), 235
Harnessed Obstacle Walk (exercise), 237
Head. *See* Neck and head; Neck/head exercises
Head Band Squat (exercise), 214–215
Head Hangers (exercise), 155–156
Head Planks (exercise), 152–153
Head Wiggles (exercise), 215–216
Heart Breathing, 213–214
Heel Skating (exercise), 183
Heel Walk (exercise), 172
Hip Extension Release (exercise), 182
Hip flexors, 71, 109, 182
Hip Hinges (exercise), 67–69
Hip rotators, 216
Hips and spine, 175–180, 185
    exercises, 134–135, 175–177, 180–185, 216–218
    fluidity of hips, 175–177
    hip rotators, 176, 216
Honking, 142
Hoof Picks (exercise), 127
Hot Water Bottle Balancing (exercise), 46–47
Hot Water Waist Pack (exercise), 246–247
Human Lead Rope (exercise), 82–83
Hypermobility, 66–67

Imagery, 55–56, 57. *See also* Vison and visualizing
Independent Body Parts (exercise), 114

Inner nourishment, 188–189
Internal trainer, 202–203
Intuition, beneficial sounds for, 209
Invest further
  chapter takeaway, 262
  exercises, 253–262
  standard equipment, 42–43, 244, 251–252
Isometric hold, 107–108
Isometric pull, 24. *See also* Positive tension; Positive tension exercises

Jaw placement, 155
Jaw relaxation, 150
Jumping Jills (exercise), 260

Kegel exercises, 133
Kitchen Counter Stretch (exercise), 162
Knowing vs. feeling, 43

Large Half-Ball Balance (exercise), 257
Lateral Lines, 99
Left Side Activation (exercise), 112–113
Legs. *See* Feet, ankles, and legs
Lengthening versus stretching, 100–101
Lizard Crawl (exercise), 135
Logical (left-brained) thinking, 54
Log rolling (rolling on the floor), 201, 231
Long Line Stop and Go (exercise), 256
Long-Lining for People (exercise), 237–238
Low Back Disorders (McGill), 107
Lying Diaphragm Stretches (exercise), 38
Lymph system, 88–89

Marble Heads (exercise), 154
Massaging with fascial rollers, 98, 101, 106
McCluggage, Denise, 229
McGill, Stuart, 107
Medicine Ball Tosses (exercise), 234–235
Meditation Walk the Course (exercise), 124
Metronome Movements (exercise), 245
Mindfulness, for tension release, 122
Mini trampolines, 260–261
Mounted Arm Sliders (exercise), 145
Mounted "C"-Curve Iron Out (exercise), 144–145
Mounted Hand Proprioception (exercise), 48
Mounted Imbalances (exercise), 240–241
Mounted Neck Lengthening (exercise), 247
Mounted Rib Cage 360s (exercise), 145–146
Mourning doves, 208
Move from Your COG (exercise), 10
Movement patterns and mobility, 64–73
  chapter takeaway, 73
  exercises, 67–73
  fluidity of movement, 66
  mobility, 66–67
  movement explored, 64–65
  neuromuscular functioning, 65
  pelvic balance and, 127
Muscle activation, 108–109, 110, 118
Muscle activation exercises, 111–117
  Activated Riding, 117
  Adductor Lifts, 111
  Glute Activation Walk, 114–117
  Glute Poke and Punch, 113
  Independent Body Parts, 114
  Left Side Activation, 112–113
  Triceps Shake and Wiggle, 113
Muscle myths and facts, 107–110
Muscle rest and recovery, 117–118
Muscle tone, 23–25, 31. *See also* Movement patterns and mobility; Muscle activation; Muscle activation exercises; Positive tension exercises
Musical freestyles, 209
Myers, Thomas W., 94
Myofascial, defined, 94. *See also* Fascial connections

Near-to-Far Focus Flutters (exercise), 59–60
Neck and head, 147–156
  chapter takeaway, 156
  exercises, 151–156, 214–216
  head alignment, 149–151
  jaw placement, 155
  jaw relaxation, 150
  neck connects, 147–148
  tongue placement, 155
Negative tension, 33, 122
Neuromuscular functioning, 65
Neutral pelvis, 18, 126–128, 138
Neutral spine, 178
Nose Plant Squats (exercise), 70
Nourishment
  inner, 188–189
  outer, 186–187

Oaks, Robert, 196
Ogilvie, William Henry, 207
One-Arm Shopping (exercise), 232
One Stirrup Work (exercise), 183–184

Organs. *See* Visceral approach to core stabilization

Outer nourishment, 186–187, 189. *See also specific exercises*

Overhead Battle Ropes (exercise), 256–257

Overhead Rope Pull (exercise), 161–162

Overhead Wall Bird Dogs (exercise), 219

Overhead Wall Press (exercise), 83–84

Palming the Eyes (exercise), 58

Pandiculars (exercise), 102

Pandicular stretches, 95, 98, 101, 102–104

Peace, beneficial sounds for, 208

Pelvic Connections (exercise), 138

Pelvic floor muscles (PFM), 126, 131–133, 205

Pelvic floor muscle exercises, 133–138, 218–219

Pelvic tilt and arch, 18, 126–128, 138

Pelvis (neutral) exercise, 127

Pelvis position and balance, 127–131, 169, 171

Pendulum Swings (exercise), 254

People Jumping (exercise), 258–259

Personal flow, 89

Perturbances (exercise), 239

Photo Imagery (exercise), 45

Plavin, Amy, 194–195, 246

Play an Instrument (exercise), 225

Playful Movement (exercise), 122–123

Playing Instruments (exercise), 41

Plumb Line Mounted (exercise), 248

Pogo Core Bounces (exercise), 262

The Pokes (exercise), 81–82

Pony tail vision, 53–55

Pop-Up Stance (exercise), 136–137

Pop-Up Walks (exercise), 218–219

Positive Affirmations (exercise), 220

Positive tension, 23–25, 31, 122, 179, 209

Positive tension exercises, 26–31

Posting, 171, 174

Postural patterns and self-carriage, 74–86. *See also* Alignment

    beneficial sounds for, 208

    breathing for, 33–35

    chapter takeaway, 86

    core activation exploration, 221–224, 227

    feet, ankles, and legs, 169, 170

    good posture characteristics, 74–76

    posting and self-carriage, 171, 174

    rib cage and, 139–141

    riding posture tips, 76–80

    self-carriage, defined, 25, 81

    self-carriage exercises, 81–86

    self-correction of self-carriage, 193

    vision and, 54, 56, 63

Posture Breathing (exercise), 82

Power Buttwalking (exercise), 134, 176–177

Proprioception and feel development, 42–52

    art of feeling, 43–45

    body pulses, 44

    chapter takeaway, 52

    exercises, 45–52

    props for, 42–43

    SLAM lessons, 243–250

Props, 42–43, 244, 251–252. *See also specific exercises*

Psoas, 77

Pull-Ups (exercise), 253

Pulses, 44

Read, Bekki, 116, 198

Read, Pat, 198

Rebounders, 260–261

Reflections on Riding and Jumping (Steinkraus), 180

Reich, Mary Ann, 197

Resistance stretches, 95, 98

Resseguie, Lois, 196

Rest and recovery, of muscles, 117–118

Rib cage, 139–146

    chapter takeaway, 146

    exercises, 143–146

    rib anchor explored, 139–141

    sternum lift, 142

Rib Cage Pulls (exercise), 144

Rib Cage Trainers (exercise), 143

"Ride a wave," 90–91

Rider Biomechanics (Wanless), 98

Ride Your Noodle (exercise), 180

Riding from your guts. *See* Visceral approach to core stabilization

Riding position

    background and overview, 2, 87

    fascia and, 94–106. *See also* Fascial connections

    feet, ankles, and legs, 166–171, 174

    feet/ankles/legs exercises, 171–174

    fluidity secrets, 88–90, 93. *See also* Fluidity

    hips and spine, 175–180, 185

    hips/spine exercises, 134–135, 175–177, 180–185, 216–218

    muscle activation, 108–109, 110, 118

    muscle activation exercises, 111–117

    muscle myths and facts, 107–110

muscle rest and recovery, 117–118
neck and head, 147–151
neck/head exercises, 151–156
nourishment and, 186–189
pelvic floor muscles, 126, 131–133
pelvic floor muscle exercises, 133–138, 205, 218–219
pelvic tilt and arch, 18, 126–128, 138
pelvis (neutral) exercise, 127
pelvis position and balance, 127–131, 169, 171
posture tips, 76–80. See also Postural patterns and self-carriage
rib cage, 139–146
shoulders, arms, and hands, 157–160
shoulders/arms/hands exercises, 161–165, 165
teaching, 190–198
tension and, 119–122, 125
tension release exercises, 122–125
Riding well. See Foundation of riding well
Right-brained (gestalt) thinking, 54
Ring Geometry Proprioception (exercise), 50–51
Roll 'Em (exercise), 93
Rolling on the floor (log rolling), 201, 231
Rolling Out (exercise), 106
Rotator cuff, 157

Sacrum Sink (exercise), 21
Sandpaper Boards (exercise), 26–27
Sandpaper Seat (exercise), 245
Sawhorse Ball Tosses (exercise), 254–255
Sawhorse exercises, 11, 254–255
Scap Pushes (exercise), 162–164
Scoop the Goop (exercise), 225
Scorpion Seat (exercise), 181

Seat Lessons and More. See SLAM lessons
Self-acceptance, 189
Self-carriage. See Postural patterns and self-carriage
Self-compassion, 193
Self-correction, 191–194
Sensing, Feeling, and Action (Cohen), 100
Shaking muscles, 108
Shaking Out Unwanted Energy (exercise), 21
Sharp Eyes (exercise), 60–62
Shifting Eyes Balance Poses (exercise), 58–59
Shoulders, arms, and hands, 157–165
  chapter takeaway, 165
  exercises, 161–165
  jobs for arms and hands, 158–160
  shoulder complex, 157–159
Side bend ("C"-curve), 23, 78–80, 98–100, 144–145
Side Slides (exercise), 173
Side Superhero (exercise), 86
Side-Tap Walk (Bouncy Type exercise), 104
Side Wall Circles (exercise), 217–218
Single Leg Hip Hinge (exercise), 68–69
Single Leg Wall Push (exercise), 84–85
Sinking brain, 19–20
SLAM (Seat Lessons and More) lessons, 243–250
  background and overview, 2–3, 243–244
  Belly Button Singing, 245
  chapter takeaway, 250
  Creative Whips, 246
  Fixing the Drifts, 249–250
  Flying Hugs, 249
  Hand Ball Helper, 247

Hot Water Waist Pack, 246–247
  Metronome Movements, 245
  Mounted Neck Lengthening, 247
  Plumb Line Mounted, 248
  prop fade-outs, 244
  Sandpaper Seat, 245
  Swinging Bridge Imagery, 245
  You Are a Tree, 244
Slither and Shake (exercise), 91
Slomos (exercise), 171, 174
Soft Eyes (exercise), 62–63
Sounds, 206–209, 223, 226
Sounds for the Pelvis (exercise), 137
Spine stabilization, 107, 108, 127, 177–180
Spiral Line, 99
Stability Breath Practice (exercise), 232–233
Stability Hug (exercise), 185
Stabilization. See Positive tension; Positive tension exercises
Stable Core Training
  background and overview, 1, 3
  finding your position, 2. See also Riding position
  riding well, 1–2. See also Foundation of riding well
  stabilizing your deep core, 2–3. See also Deep core stabilization
Standard Hip Hinge (exercise), 67–68
Standard stretching, 100–101. See also Stretching
Standing Diaphragm Stretch (exercise), 37
Standing Straddle Bend (Pandicular Type exercise), 103–104
Steinkraus, William, 180
Sternum lift, 142
Stilts, 261

Stirrup Stand (exercise), 241
Stir the Pot (exercise), 236
Stress and tension, 119–120, 125. *See also* Tension; Tension release exercises
Stretching
    hypermobility and, 66–67
    lengthening versus, 100–101
Superficial Back Line, 99
Swift, Sally, 92, 160
Swinging Bridge Imagery (exercise), 245
Swinging Gates (exercise), 242

Taffy Eyes, 56
Tai Chi, 66
Target Practice (exercise), 67
"T" Arm Cavalletti/ Jumping (exercise), 184
Teaching humans and horses, 190–198
    art of self-correction, 191–194
    rider's team, 194–198
    sense, feel, and discover, 190–191, 249–250. *See also* Proprioception and feel development
Tension
    chapter takeaway, 125
    letting go techniques, 120–122
    self-correction of, 193
    stress, 119–120
Tension release exercises, 122–125
The Pokes (exercise), 81–82
The Thinking Body (Todd), 117–118
Thin Straw (exercise), 124

Throat Warm-Ups (exercise), 213–214
Tighten and Shake (exercise), 124–125
Tilt Board Hoops (exercise), 258
Todd, Mabel Elsworth, 117–118
Toe Spreading (exercise), 172
Tongue, 36, 155, 225
Trace a Horseshoe (exercise), 164
Trainers. *See* Teaching humans and horses
Trapezius, 108–109
Triceps, 113, 160
Triceps Shake and Wiggle (exercise), 113
Trigger points, 98
Trunk Circles (exercise), 216
TRX® suspension strap, 254
Turning Head Hovers (exercise), 152

Unilateral Barbells (exercise), 259
Unilateral Leg Raises (exercise), 239–240
Unilateral Step-Ups (exercise), 232

Vertical alignment, 16–18
Vertical breathing, 35
Veterinarians, 194–195
Vibrational energy, 206–209
Visceral approach to core stabilization
    acupressure for organs, 202
    asymmetries, 98–100
    background and overview, 200–202
    Belly Release, 202–205
    beneficial sounds for organs, 209
    chapter takeaway, 205

    ride with passion, 202–204
Vision and visualizing, 53–63
    of courses or dressage tests, 124
    exercises, 56, 58–63
    imagery exploration, 55–56, 57
    pony tail vision, 54
    rider's vision, 53–55
    for SLAM lessons, 245
    Taffy Eyes, 56

Waking-up muscles. *See* Muscle activation; Muscle activation exercises
Wall Push (exercise), 226
Wall Springs (Bouncy Type exercise), 105
Wanless, Mary, 98
Warm-Up Logs (exercise), 231
Warm-ups
    background and overview, 210–211
    chapter takeaway, 220
    exercises, 211–220
Water-skiing position, 7, 222
Water Wheel Bounces (exercise), 260–261
Whinnying, 207, 223
Whole body breathing, 32–33, 41
Whole Body Scramble (exercise), 227
Wiper Hoops (exercise), 238–239

You Are a Tree (exercise), 244
Youth and vitality, fountain of, 88–89
Yo-Yo 'n Hoop (exercise), 164–165

"Zip" your core, 224